A Businessman's Guide to the Wholesale Markets of Guangzhou

Christian D. Taulkinghorn

2012 Christian D. Taulkinghorn

The primary aim of this book is to share knowledge. It is completely free from copyright restrictions.

If you purchased this book: Thank you for supporting my work! Your purchase motivates me to continue producing new material. Every sale is important to me, both financially and personally. Please feel free to share this book with all of your friends.

If you did not buy this book: I hope that you enjoyed reading this work. I understand that limited distribution networks mean that this book is not available for sale in many parts of the world, or even to those without credit cards. I also understand that for many people, file sharing networks are the only way to access ebooks like this. If you enjoyed this book then please help spread the word by voting it up and leaving positive reviews on the tracker site where you found it. Please support private trackers with donations whenever possible.

ISBN: **1516899997**
ISBN-13: 978-1516899999

CONTENTS

Section Two – Markets

ACKNOWLEDGMENTS

My sincerest thanks to Mr Hobbs for his extended hospitality and to Miss Mao for her enthusiasm and encouragement.

1 GUANGZHOU - THE WORLD'S NUMBER ONE SHOPPING DESTINATION

Guangzhou is the beating heart of a province that has long been described as the "Workshop of the World." In the 21st century our homes and offices are filled with items that are 'Made In China.' Guangzhou, in the Pearl River Delta, is by far the largest source of these goods. This province is the world's largest producer of everything from oil paintings to computer parts. Almost anything that can be manufactured is now made in a factory in this region. This is home to the world's largest chewing gum factory, the largest toothpaste producer, the largest air-conditioner compressor plant and the largest circuit board production base. 85% of the world's artificial Christmas trees and 95% of the world's microwave ovens are made here. Stainless steel production surpasses anywhere else on the planet and the region has recently become the largest exporter of cars in China. If you are looking to buy products at a small fraction of prices that are charged in the rest of the world, then this is the number one location on the planet. Merchants flock here from every country on Earth with very good reason. Guangzhou is so huge that it is almost beyond description. Truly an Asian mega-city. You can drive for over an hour and still be hemmed in by high-rises. Beijing has managed to retain some space between buildings but parts of Guangzhou have become the very densest of concrete jungles. Away from the soaring citadels of commerce, the city has preserved large parts of its architectural heritage quite successfully. Much of the Liwan district looks more like Suzie Wong's neighbourhood than modern day Wanchai ever can. Colonial splendour is still in evidence on Shamian Island and in Dongshan district. Despite the shiny new CBDs, much of Guangzhou still has a very human scale to it. The cost of living remains much lower than Shanghai, Shenzhen and Hong Kong. Thanks to its history of international trade, there are more English speakers here than any other Chinese city.

Guangzhou is 160 kilometres north of Hong Kong, and is China's fourth largest city after Shanghai, Beijing and Tianjin. The 2010 census put the population at 12.78 million but some experts estimate that in reality, it is more like 20 or even 25 million. It has been a major trading centre and gateway to the outside world for many centuries. As early as the 7th century Guangzhou had 200,000 foreign residents, including Arabs, Persians, Indians, Africans and Turks.

Despite its popularity among business people, Guangzhou is almost ignored by most of the major guidebooks. These tend to include only a few cheesy sights, and some notorious restaurants that specialize in snakes or other weird meat dishes. The result is that many travellers see Guangzhou simply as a stopover on the way to somewhere else. At the other end of the corporate scale, international buyers fly in for a few days, are ferried around by factory owners who guard them like golden geese As a result they see little beyond their five-star hotel suites. This book is written for everybody in between those two extremes.

While there is some limited information on the internet concerning Guangzhou wholesale markets, most of it is unreliable, disorganised and of poor quality. Descriptions of particular markets are translated directly from Chinese into a Chinglish that is almost unintelligible to most readers. Until now, there have always been far more people seeking answers to inquiries than those providing concrete useful information. It is for this reason that I have decided to write this book, and it is the very first time that all of this scattered information has been bought together into one volume. While I have written extensively about the city on previous occasions for magazines and international travel guides, these were by necessity, so compact that it was impossible to fully explore this vibrant trading hub in the way that it deserves. This entirely new volume aims to finally do justice to the world's greatest shopping city.

2 WHAT TO BRING

Most things can be acquired cheaply and easily upon arrival in Guangzhou, and while there used to be a long list of items that were notoriously difficult to find on the Mainland, this is thankfully, no longer the case. Some items remain uncommon or expensive. I usually stock up with cheap deodorant, which is an example of something that is still relatively pricey in China. The rest of my space, I try to give over to gifts that simply cannot be found anywhere on the Mainland. A few well chosen gifts are always handy for those who might help me out while I am on the road. These will probably be different for you but I am sure that you will be able to find speciality items in your part of the world that you can bring with you to put a smile of people's faces. At the moment, I am carrying tea from Sabah and the Cameron Highlands in Malaysia, as well as the famous Old Town brand of hazelnut coffee from Alor Setar in Kedah. Both of these are always very much appreciated.

I always carry a few novelty bills in my wallet to break the ice with sellers and servers. Offering to pay with a million dollars or even a billion dollars quickly defuses any tension that a local might have, if they are nervous in dealing with a foreigner

The contents of a first aid kit is a very personal selection but I always try to carry a few Compeed blister plasters, a stretchy compression bandage and plenty of headache tablets. I find that tea tree oil works best for me in treating bites, cuts and scratches. I also carry a small jar of clove oil, as there is nothing worse that being stuck on the road with toothache when there is not a decent dentist for miles. In the bad old days, I was forced to visit a small village orthodontist where he had jury rigged a cycle-chain with pedals to a dining room chair. If any drilling work was required, the patient was expected to pedal and provide the power. On another occasion, I was stuck in a dental hospital that only carried domestically produced anaesthetic, which was completely useless. Rather than going through a couple of hours of oral torture, I opted to go to a different clinic where they still had some imported anaesthetic from Germany. The best option is simply to avoid any dental problems if at all possible. I try to have a regular annual check in Thailand, where the dentists are some of the best in the world, and also some of the cheapest.

In the hot and humid coastal cities, I end up sweating like a choirboy in the vestry, and so I always carry a bunch of electrolyte sachets, so that I can replace all the salts that I lose while I am out exploring. These are very uncommon in China and so I always stock up in Bangkok. Many people find that the heat and humidity causes unpleasant rashes to develop in the most uncomfortable places. The climate in many parts of China (especially in the Pearl River Delta) is wet and humid, which can lead to some very nasty rashes and skin infections. One particularly unpleasant manifestation is crotch rot, so make sure that you pack an effective fungicidal cream such as Tonaf or B-Ketoconazole.

Cities in the Pearl River Delta such as Guangzhou and Shenzhen are hotbeds of mutant virus strains. This geographical area is the original source of new flu strains such as SARS and bird flu. Considering the climate, the geography and conditions into which some 300 million souls are tightly packed, this is of course hardly surprising. Every time I arrive in Guangzhou I am struck down with a nasty dose of flu, usually within a week of being there. Whether it is being squeezed up against all the sneezers, open mouthed yawners, hawkers and spitters on the subway, or whether it is transmitted though the thick, clogging pollution, I am not sure, but it is a predictable and repetitive occurrence that afflicts most international visitors. In addition, Guangzhou is currently suffering from a dengue fever outbreak, not to mention the fact that many of the residents of Chocolateville are from East African countries being ravaged by Ebola. I can think of quite a few longer term residents who are so depressed by their job situation, work prospects and living conditions that they seem to have a year-round cold as a result. In order to avoid this, I have discovered that Bifidobacterium animalis lactis Bi-07 and Lactobacillus acidophilus NCFM can help reduce the duration and severity of the common cold and flu by enhancing the body's production of antibodies. It certainly helped me avoid the usual sniffles and flu bugs on my latest trip. In addition, it is important to keep these probiotics as strong and healthy as possible. The bacteria in your colon for example thrive on non-digestible fibre, also known as prebiotics and they can be fed with two to four servings of garlic, whole grains, artichokes, bananas or honey. Some probiotic supplements come with prebiotics in them often referred to as inulin. Bacteria in the gut love fibre, breaking it down, and leaving behind nourishing acids, so it is a win-win process. Saccharomyces boulardii weeks before your trip, may also help prevent traveller's diarrhoea, which usually comes from ingesting food or water that has been contaminated with bacteria.

Do note that China has different power sockets to other countries, so you will need to prepare for that accordingly. Chargers, earphones, data cables tend to get entangled in themselves but if you pack them in a spare glasses case, they will always be neat and easy to use! Remember that newer model hotel room TVs can charge up any device with a USB slot.

Be careful which brands you choose for vitamins and supplements. The first time that I landed in Shanghai back in the nineties, I had a great deal of difficulty explaining the big tub of multi-vitamins that was stashed away in the bottom of my case. When the customs officer at Hongqiao Airport saw the English brand name, 'Superdrug' emblazoned in big letters on the plastic container, his eyes lit up as though he had just hit the jackpot. It certainly did not help that I also had a joke tin of nuts, that I occasionally used as a prize during corporate coaching sessions. When they insisted on opening it and a six foot snake leapt out, they were far from amused. At the time, I was sure that my first night in China was going to be spent in a police cell.

3 WHERE TO STAY

Despite the fact that nationwide there are two new luxury hotels being built every single day in China, as well as an estimated 100 million vacant apartments, accommodation in Guangzhou can still be crowded and expensive. Many visitors are particularly offended by the price gouging that takes place during the Trade Fair when hotels triple their prices.

Budget

It is very difficult to find any kind of room for less than 200 RMB in Guangzhou. There are small business hotels catering to locals for less than this but nearly all of them will ask for a hukou (local ID card) and it is doubtful that any of the staff will speak English. Still, if you plan for 200 - 300 RMB, you can still find clean, satisfactory rooms. If you are in town for business, try to choose somewhere that is located near to a subway line. Guangzhou does have a good bus network but it can be a little intimidating for first time visitors. My personal recommendation is the area around the old library, known as Nong Jiang Suo or the Peasant Movement Institute. This is a typical red-tourism attraction where Chairman Mao taught the masses the art of guerilla warfare. It is an original part of city where the older generation still makes up a large part of the population, but is very central and therefore convenient.

Services such as Couchsurfing have not really caught on in Guangzhou as they have in other places, so it is not really worth the effort looking for this kind of accommodation in China.

The Garden Inn 广州岭南佳园中山四路店
There are a number of local hotel chains like this one

and all of them represent good value. With a metro station just meters from the front door, this is my first choice whenever I am lucky enough to return to Guangzhou. Rooms are simple but clean and the price is almost unbeatable. I would not recommend them for couples however, as the bathrooms do not have doors. In addition, the beds are quite hard, just as the locals prefer them. Occasionally there is an English speaker at reception, but as the clientèle is 99.9 percent Chinese, do not expect a twenty-four hour interpreter on the front desk. I like the very central location plus the fact that there is a train ticket sales office just down the street, as well as lots of interesting local food options in what is still a very traditionally Cantonese area of the city.

Address: 388, Dezheng Middle Road 越秀区德政中路388号

7 Days Inn 7天广州仓边路店

Just off Changbian Road, barely five minutes from the Nong Jiang Suo Subway Station. Spartan but inexpensive rooms that are popular among young Chinese business travellers. As yet undiscovered by westerners. The 7 Days Inn on the busy Beijing Road has over 300 English language reviews on Tripadvisor. This branch does not even have one.

Address: 184, Haoxian Road 越秀区豪贤路184号

New East Hotel 广州新东方商务酒店东风东店

Centrally located with three subway stations within ten minutes walking distance. Taojin and Xiaobei are just to the north, but the route down to Nong Jiang Suo station is especially refreshing, in this otherwise overpowering city. Guangzhou Greenway is a rehabilitated creek that has been transformed into a charming stream-side walkway that runs parallel to Yuexiu Bei Lu. The hotel itself is a converted office block with basic but comfortable rooms and is almost surrounded by barracks of the various arms of the military, so security should never be an issue.

Address: 518 Dongfeng East Road 越秀区东风东路518号

Mid Range

Bauhinia Hotel 宝轩酒店

A more recently opened hotel with rooms that are still in good condition. The polite and friendly English speaking staff speak volumes about the Hong Kong owners. The location is very close to one of the largest and most popular wholesale districts in the city, as well as the main Immigration Office.

Address: 151, Jiefang South Road 越秀区解放南路151号

Guoxiang Hotel 国祥大厦

A recent refurbishment has seen the rooms here halved in size with prices doubled, and yet this is still one of the better options nearby the Train Station. Rooms are surprising opulent for the price and the hotel is very popular with Arab and African traders. There are even signs in the room explaining that that the kettle is only for making tea and not soup or other dishes. God alone knows what kind of goat curries some of the previous guests must have been trying to cook up in them. The staff speak reasonable English, although the smiles are a bit fake. Still in China, even a fake smile is better than the usual grimace or scowl.

Address: 66, Zhanqian Road 荔湾区站前路66号
Directions: From Guangzhou Railway Station Subway take exit D1 which emerges on the opposite side of the road, outside the bus station. Turn right and look for the Number One Tunnel which you can follow all the way to the end, and the Guoxiang is about another 100 metres.

Aiqun Hotel 爱群大厦

A classically designed Art-Deco three-star hotel located on the north bank of the Pearl River, which managed to survive the Japanese bombing of the city in WWII, even though it was the tallest building in Guangzhou from 1937 to 1967. The ground floor is the traditional veranda style (骑楼) that was first introduced by the British, and is an excellent example of the local vernacular architecture.

Address: 113, West Yanjiang Road
广州市越秀区沿江西路113号

Luxury

The Garden Hotel 花园酒店

The Garden Hotel is the biggest hotel in China, with 1147 rooms. It is also one of the oldest hotels in the city and is starting to show its age. Most of the the best staff have been poached by newly opened five-stars in other parts of the city. In my view, this is a bit of a dinosaur, and is over-priced and over-rated.

Address: 368, Huanshi Dong Road
越秀区环市东路368号

The Westin 广州海航威斯汀酒店

Room sizes are huge, well designed and have comfortable beds. Views are fantastic, especially the rooms facing the Guangzhou skyline and the Canton Tower light show. Ask for a corner room and you get two floor to ceiling windows. Staff service is good but breakfast is so-so and wifi still requires payment which is ridiculous. Get an SPG Loyalty Card before you stay (free from their website) and you will get complimentary wifi.

Address: Linhe Middle Road 天河区林和中路6号

Ritz Carlton 广州富力丽思卡尔顿酒店

Luxe brands like this really do not need guide books to help them attract customers. This particular property overdoes it on the chintz and bling, with extremely gaudy marble bathrooms, but that will probably appeal to a certain section of the population.

Address: 3, Xing'an Road 天河区珠江新城兴安路3号

The White Swan Hotel 白天鹅宾馆

One of China's first luxury hotels built in 1982, an ugly, labyrinthine eyesore that has all but destroyed the island's colonial atmosphere. Many agencies organizing adoptions use the White Swan; the US embassy used to be located just next door. Every floor is fully stocked with diaper service, parents get a free toy for their kids, and the hotel goes quiet at nap time - no wonder it has been nicknamed the White Stork. Former guests include Queen Elizabeth II and President George H. W. Bush. These days it is looking a little run down, especially compared to the dozens of new five stars that have sprung up around the city in the last ten years. I can remember one trade fair delegate wanting to return here after a long day at the exhibition who could not remember the Chinese name of the hotel and simply flapped his arms wildly at the taxi driver. About an hour later he arrived at the airport way on the far outskirts of the town. In 2007, the North Korean dictator, Kim Jong Il paid a surprise visit to Guangdong, in order to inspect the successes of the Special Economic Zones. For his arrival the White Swan kicked out every single guest at very short notice so that the paranoid, oddball tyrant could have the delicatessen, the discos and the air-conditioned bowling centre all to himself. At the time of writing, the White Swan is closed for extensive remodelling but should be open again by the middle of 2015.

Address: 1, Shamian South Street 荔湾区沙面南街1号

Longer Term Accommodation in Guangzhou

Guangzhou is China's third most densely populated city and yet, it continues to attract expatriates due to the many business opportunities it offers. The main obstacle is that relatively few landlords are willing to rent to foreigners, as it means that they will have to be formally registered and therefore have to pay tax. Another problem is that landlords will often ask for six months rent in advance, which can make this a surprisingly expensive proposition. At the end of the contract, Chinese landlords are often tempted to stiff their tenants, as there is nobody for them to complain to, and they can repeatedly get away with it.

There are a number of different types of accommodation options in Guangzhou, namely apartments, villas, studios and houses. Your choice will mainly depend on your budget and the length of your stay in the region. Most of the new houses you will find in Guangzhou are unfurnished. As regards apartments and studios, these are quite old and the furniture is often in poor condition.

To rent a studio in Guangzhou, you will need an average of 1,800 yuan per month, if you can find one in the first place that is. For a two-bedroom apartment, you will need at least 4,500 yuan per month and around 6,000 to 8,000 yuan per month for a three-bedroom apartment. For villas, rents start at 10,000 yuan a month. Note that maintenance and care-taking fees, as well as electricity and water bills are usually the responsibility of the tenant.

It is difficult to find good value accommodation in Guangzhou on the Internet or by viewing classified ads. A better option but more expensive option is to register with a real estate agency.

Useful links:
Expat Blog – Housing offers in Guangzhou
Roomorama - www.roomorama.com
Air BnB - www.airbnb.com

Gabino Home China - china.gabinohome.com/en

4 WHERE TO EAT

Cantonese people spend three times as much on dining out as the average Shanghainese, and a whopping seven times more than the national average. Despite the international reputation of Cantonese cuisine, much of it is merely status food rather than true gastronomic delights. Often the visible cost of a dish (and the status that it therefore conveys upon the customer), is more important than the actual quality or even the taste. This means that nouveau riche delights such as bird's nest soup (which looks and tastes like snot) or that other great favourite, shark's fin soup are massively popular. Remember that fine dining was seen as bourgeois and reactionary during the Cultural Revolution and its most skilled proponents were summarily executed. Quality cuisine has not therefore had a chance to develop and refine itself as it has in Europe or South East Asia.

While it is Cantonese food that captures the headlines, the local passion for eating has ensured that an eclectic mix of international flavours has established a presence here. Not only does Guangzhou provide the chance to sample many provincial cuisines, an abundance of Asian, Middle Eastern, and even European creativity can now be tasted here. Guangzhou's expat community has changed rapidly in the last few years and this can be seen in the number of international cuisines available. Overpriced generic brands such as the Hard Rock Café were not able to survive here but have been replaced with a wide variety of international flavours, from Nigerian to Scandinavian

As inflation climbs, many eateries are looking for ways to cut costs. Some places have resorted to gutter oil, (recycled cooking oil) while others have gone to the extremes of adding toxic ingredients such as melamine in the dairy products and formaldehyde in the beer. While there is much less transparency in Chinese food than there is in western countries, there is at least plenty of choice. Here are a selection of my own favourites.

Cantonese Cuisine

Bei Yuan Jiujia 北园酒家

The Cantonese seem to be the most raucous of all Chinese diners, and the main restaurant choices for classic Cantonese food such as dim sum, are bedlam. The Bei Yuan dates from the 1920s, although the current two-story building with courtyards is newer, built around a garden and pond. There is dim sum here all day for about 5–10 RMB per steamer and a generous menu of Cantonese classics, with some English translations. Try huadiao zhu ji (chicken cooked in yellow wine—although some might argue this is really a Zhejiang dish), tang cu su rou (sweet-and-sour pork), and jiuhuang rou si (sliced pork with yellow chives). The typically garish carpets, screens, and chandeliers are in odd contrast to a central green space. There are twin entrances—the left is for the traditional Cantonese dishes; the right is for a Chaozhou (Chiu Chow) restaurant, with the roast goose dishes typical of that area of north-east Guangdong.

Address: 202, Xiaobei Road 越秀区小北路202号
Contact: 020 8356-3365

Dongjiang Seafood Restaurant 东江海鲜大酒楼

While Cantonese food can now be found all over the world, the enormous, multi-story, football field sized restaurants remain something that can only be seen in Guangzhou. Many places compete to be the largest (the title is currently held by Fisherman's Wharf, more the size of a theme park than a restaurant, in the suburb of Panyu) but most branches of the Dong Jiang chain are vast enough to impress. This particular location stretches over five floors with room for more than 3000 diners, and even spills out on to the side walk later in the evening. Huge tanks of seafood fill the first floor, with many obscure, strange-looking varieties available at higher prices. Crocodiles with their mouths taped shut crawl along the floor. Beginners may want to start with a plate full of steamed shrimp and another of jumbo scallops, before they proceed onto local exotica such as water beetles and horseshoe crabs. When ordering live seafood, prices are by weight, not per piece. It is relaxing to sit on the balcony and watch the people, and then enjoy a walk along the Pearl River. The river cruise dock is also nearby. Restaurant rush hour is early Sunday evening, when it seems like every family in the city is heading out to eat. If you can even find a seat, the noise will be deafening (when eating, Cantonese seem to use a speaking volume that westerners would only ever use to shout at their children), but it will be an experience that you will be unable to replicate anywhere else on the planet.

Address: 2, Yanjiang Lu, beside Haizhu Square 海珠广场 沿江路2号

Contact: 020 8318-4901

Also at 276, Huanshi Zhong Lu, opposite the children's activity canter

Contact: 020 8322-9188

Tao Tao Ju 陶陶居

Founded in 1880, the signboard above the front door was written by Kang Youwei, a famous Chinese scholar, noted calligrapher, prominent thinker and reformer of the late Qing Dynasty. For more than one hundred years, this has been one of the most popular tea houses in Guangzhou, and has attracted many famous scholars and poets. Even now, noted calligraphers and Chinese painters regularly exhibit their latest works here. There is also the Tao Tao Stone Room, where guests can see a collection of ancient viewing stones. In the dining hall, there is a Xi Guan Ancient Platform, where well-known storytelling performers in Guangzhou are invited to give performances. Tao Tao Ju is not only famous for its dishes, but also for its moon cakes. In addition, they claim to hire people specially to carry the water from Jiu Long Spring (or the Spring of Nine Dragons) up on Baiyun Mountain, which they use exclusively for cooking and making tea. The speciality here is Tao Tao Ginger and Shallot Chicken but other local favourites include pig brain and fish soup, scrambled crab meat with ginger and green onion, West lake chrysanthemum fish and baked chicken in salt and ham with tripe.

Address: 20, Dishi Pu Road, Liwan District
荔湾区第十甫路20
Contact: 020 8139-6111

Other Cantonese Signature Dishes
Dragon, tiger, phoenix and chrysanthemum soup: 菊花龙虎凤
Dragon, tiger and phoenix actually refers to snake, cat and black chicken. The recipe is to cook a soup with the snake pieces, chicken, cat, winter mushrooms and sweet dates.
Roast goose: 潮莲烧鹅
The best roast geese are the smaller black geese from Qingyuan county. The wings, feet and entrails being removed, the body is then besmeared with five fragrant seasonings, swiftly boiled, doused with cold water, coated with sugar cane juice, air-dried and preserved. There are many roast goose shops in Guangzhou, among which the most famous are Yuji in Changdi and Shenjing roast goose on Changzhou island in Huangpu District.
Taiye chicken: 太爷鸡
Named after an ancient mayor from the late Qing dynasty who invented this dish during his retirement. The cooking method is to boil the chicken in a special salt soup and

then smoke it with fried black tea leaves and honey.

Crispy skin chicken: 脆皮鸡

As one of the famous chicken dishes of Guangzhou, it was created by Datong Restaurant in the 1940's. The chicken skin is crisp, the bones are tasty and the meat is tender and delicious.

Winter-melon soup: 冬瓜汤

This soup is popular as a cooling dish in the summer time. The edge of the melon is cut to tooth-like pattern and birds and flowers are carved onto the exterior. Ingredients include turkey, ham, crab, oyster and frog.

Crispy suckling pig: 脆皮烤乳猪

Braised shark's fin with crab meat: 蟹肉干捞翅

Braised imperial bird's nest with crab meat: 胭脂官燕

Braised sliced abalone with sea cucumber: 海参焖鲍片

Sautéed diced pork with cashew nut and vegetable croutons: 腰果肉丁

Sautéed crab meat with seasonal vegetable: 蟹肉时蔬

Steamed chicken with black mushrooms: 北菇蒸鸡

Yannan Fei Tian Tea duck: 雁南飞茶田鸭

Scrambled egg with shrimps: 滑蛋虾仁

Deep-fried seafood with mayonnaise wrapped in rice paper: 沙律海鲜卷

Soups

Shredded abalone and assorted dried seafood in soup: 鲍参翅肚羹

Sweet corn soup with crab meat: 蟹肉珍珠羹

Sweet corn and bean curd soup: 豆腐栗米羹

Seafood soup with sweet and soya sauce: 海鲜酸辣汤

Parsley and preserved egg with fish sliced in soup: 皮蛋鱼片汤

Seafood soup and fish maw with sea food: 紫菜海鲜鱼肚羹

Dim Sum

Guangzhou is famous for its snack foods, or dim sum, and extended sessions of morning and afternoon tea are an integral part of the city's culture. In Cantonese-style tea restaurants, carts are wheeled from table to table, from which diners can choose tapas-portioned dishes.

For a 100% reliable experience, I would recommend two of the larger, well established eateries.

Lei Garden Restaurant 利苑酒家 (宜安广场店)

This is one of the best Cantonese restaurants in Guangzhou but the price reflects the quality. Not only is it famous for its dim sum but its seafood is also outstanding. For the best experience, it is better to take a local with you to take care of ordering and communication. Even so, the staff are polite and professional, as would be expected of a Hong Kong run establishment.

Address: 4th Floor, Yian Plaza, 33, Jianshe Liu Ma Lu 建设六马路宜安广场

Contact: 020 8363-3268

Landmark Canton Hotel 华厦大酒店

Located on the second floor, this is a huge restaurant that is always busy, with hundreds of locals eating here at all times of the day. Do not miss the shrimp dumplings (薄皮鲜虾饺 'har gow' in Cantonese). Reasonable prices, open until very late, and a constant stream of local diners going up the escalator.

Address: 8, Qiaoguang Road, Haizhu Square 越秀区海珠广场侨光路8号

If you are feeling a little more adventurous, here are two more of my favourite dim sum eateries that are a little less easy to locate.

Hao Ying 灏盈早点

No English menu here but there is a dim sum happy hour here from 2pm and 5pm, when all dim sum is 30% off. Try the 'lau sa bao", steamed sweet buns with duck egg yolk filling.

Directions: From the Subway Sandwich Store on Jian Shi Liu Ma Lu near Garden Hotel, walk down to the corner of Dong Feng Dong Road and turn right. Hao Ying is at the foot of the pedestrian footbridge, on the right hand side.

Address: Dong Feng Dong Lu 东风东路

Chau Kee 周记饕之家

Amazing prawn dumplings and char sui bao (bbq pork buns with honey glaze) to die for. Even better, there is a picture menu which means that everything is hot and fresh, instead of being stale from being pushed around on a trolley for ages. Four of us can stuff ourselves here and it still hard to break 100 RMB. They have a picture menu, it is noisy and a bit smoky at times, but everything is screaming fresh and very authentic.

Directions: take Exit D out of the Chen Clan Academy station and walk west about 15 minutes on north side of Zhong Shan Ba Lu. Turn down a side street just past Vanguard and Gome and the bank of China. This is called Zhoumen Lu and runs underneath an apartment building. It is a couple of minutes walk on the right side of the road and upstairs, just past the dentist office and two bakeries.

Address: 26, Zhoumen Lu, Zhongshan Ba Lu 荔湾区中山八路周门街26号自编1-4号

Contact: 020 8172-6774

For those on a minimal budget, here are four more examples of delicious Cantonese eateries that will definitely not break the budget.

Jian Yi Mian Dian 坚记面店

Just past the Sacred Heart Cathedral, tucked in amongst all the dried seafood shops is a little hole-in-the-wall eatery that serves the most delicious meat and mushroom dumpling soup for just 9 RMB. I often park myself at one of the outside tables. in-between exploring the many wholesale markets here, and although always see many foreigners walking past, I have never seen anybody else with the courage to sit down and order.

Address: 322, Yide Lu 一德路322号

Yin Ji Chang Fan Dian 穗银肠粉店

Just 5 minutes' walk from China Plaza, Yin Ji is perhaps the best place on the planet to sample the most delicious 'chang fen', a steamed rice-flour pancake served in soy sauce. Although it is massively popular with locals and busy at all times of the day and night, the only other foreigner that you will ever see here is me. Ask for xian xia ji dan chang (鲜虾鸡蛋肠) and you will get a tasty shrimp and egg dish that is the epitome of Guangzhou food. Ask for some jok (粥) and you tiao (油条) and you will get some congee (thick rice broth with shredded pork skin) and tasty fried bread sticks for dipping. Fantastic fare at ultra-low prices and a secret that few other tourists will ever find.

Address: 94, Dong Chuan Lu 东川路94号

Directions: On the left, just past the Provincial Cardiovascular Hospital opposite the Songsha air-conditioner store.

Dayang Coconut Chicken Shop 大洋椰子鸡汤

Just along Wenming Road from the dessert shops mentioned below, is a coconut chicken soup that is always my first visit whenever I get back to Guangzhou. From a space that is barely a few square meters in size, a constant queue spills out onto the pavement at almost every hour of the night and day. This alone shows the popularity of this local favourite. Chicken steamed in a Hainan coconut (椰子鸡汤) has the most delicate yet sumptuous flavour, which is why the tables are always full and there are so many customers waiting to take their place. Steaming dishes are piled high to the ceiling and if you are lucky your might see a trap door open in the corner of the shop, from where the staff will start bringing up even more trays of this local delicacy. At just eighteen RMB per shell, this really is one of Guangzhou's best bargains. Foreigners are an extreme rarity so do not be surprised if you are treated with a little more respect than usual, and the other diners try to strike up a conversation with you.

Address: 160, Wenming Road 文明路160号

Kung Fu Fast Food 正功夫

    With Chinese authorities growing increasingly nationalistic and the rest of the population following suit, locally branded fast-food chains are making an impromptu resurgence. Rather surprisingly, given what a huge hit Western chains were when they first opened in China, the passion for McDonald's is beginning to wane and some KFCs are even closing down. But fast-food fans need not fear, as the Kung Fu chain is quickly taking up the slack. Kung Fu, which opened its first branch in 1994, now operates 90 restaurants in Guangdong, 300 across the Mainland, and hopes to become the top Chinese fast-food chain in the country within five years. Relying heavily on the Bruce Lee brand, the menu consists of steamed dishes with fresh ingredients and simple seasoning, such as pork ribs with soy bean sauce, chicken with mushroom, beef with pickled vegetable, Taiwan-style minced pork, and eel, all priced between 20 and 30 RMB. The restaurant chain believes that a Cantonese-style steamed meal is a healthier alternative for customers - they are probably right. All dishes are accompanied by a choice of herbal soup such as chicken with ginseng soup, dried bok choy steamed with pig bones soup, or mushroom steamed with duck soup.

Address: 7/F, China Plaza 中华广场 7F
Contact: 020 8386-8999

Cantonese Desserts

For those with a sweet tooth, Guangzhou offers a wide variety of inexpensive and delicious Cantonese dessert shops. There is a very well-known cluster of these on the junction of Dezheng Lu and Wenming Lu, near Nong Jiang Suo subway station. My own favourite among these is the Bai Hua Dessert Store (百花天平 Bai Hua Tian Ping). Founded in 1986, it has become renowned for its wide selection, great taste and reasonable prices. The proof can be seen in the number of customers and frequent daily queues outside.

The most popular dish is double layer milk (双皮奶 - shuang pi nai). Famous locally for over a century, this is simmered milk with a covering made from a mixture of egg and milk. Other favourites include double-boiled birds' nest in coconut milk (椰汁燉官燕), double-boiled toad and red dates in rock sugar syrup (雪蛤炖燉红莲), Chinese dumplings with coconut (椰汁馒头) and sweetened sago cream with seasonal fruit (鲜果西米露). Seasonal hot drinks created by the owner are also popular here. Red bean, wheat and coconut juice sago are three ingredients for a spring drink, while red bean, wheat and taro sago are used in winter drinks.

Address: 210, Wenming Lu (Opposite Sun Yat-sen Library) 文明路210号, 孙中山图书馆对面

Another famous location is the Nanxin Milk Desserts Expert 南信牛奶甜品专家

Popular choices include tofu pudding, (豆腐花) red bean paste (紅豆沙), green bean paste (綠豆沙), guilinggao, (龟苓膏 - herbal turtle jelly), black sesame paste, (芝麻糊), sago, (西米露) milk papaya (木瓜奶汁)

and tang yuan (汤圆 sweet balls). All come highly recommended, as are the fusion desserts such as papaya with sago, (西米布丁) or coconut with milk paste (椰汁奶昔). If you find that the double layer milk (双皮奶 - shuang pi nai) is too sweet, then opt instead for the ginger milk curd (姜撞奶).

Address: 47, Dishi Fu Lu 荔湾区第十甫路47号

Egg tarts 酥皮鸡蛋挞

Egg tarts are a pastry commonly found in Hong Kong and Guangdong. Often baked in a round pastry mould, the egg tart consists of an outer puff pastry crust filled with egg custard, which is a mixture of sugar and egg. Unlike English custard, milk is normally not added to the egg custard, and the tart is sprinkled with ground nutmeg or cinnamon before serving. It is served hot rather than at room temperature. Today, egg tarts come in many varieties, including honey-egg, chocolate tarts, ginger-flavoured egg, and even green-tea-flavoured tarts.

Exotica and Endangered Species

The Cantonese are well known for their fondness of eating wild animals. The First Village of Wild Food restaurant offers flying fox, civet cats, small deer, several species of birds and wild boar. Most of the animals are kept down stairs in cages in very unpleasant conditions. The Sent Down Youth No. 1 Village Wild Flavour Restaurant in Lianbian outside Guangzhou offers herons, snakes, baby deer, flying foxes, and dozens of other species in a dining area decorated with kitschy Mao era posters. Dog meat can still be found in Guangzhou although it is not as popular as it is in the neighbouring provinces of Guangxi and Guizhou. Specimens are usually mistreated mutts with about as much meat as a Syrian refugee and are probably best avoided. If you really want to sample canine cuisine, wait until you get to Korea where the big muscular Chindo's are bred especially for the purpose. Eating dog in China is by like eating one of those skinny cows seen roaming around Mumbai, as compared to a juicy steak of marbled Kobe beef.

Other Chinese Cuisine

Mao's Home 毛家饭店

Mao's Restaurant is one of the most popular restaurants in Guangzhou, serving authentic, strong-flavoured Hunan dishes. Mao's favourite, hong shao rou (braised fatty pork), and ban huo bei yu (smoked fish with dried red chilli) are must try dishes but other recommendations include the stewed bone soup and the fried shrimps.
Address: 2/F, Xianglong Garden, 181, Tianhe Beilu 天河北路175-181号 祥龙花园2楼
Contact: 020 8525-0519

Dong Bei Ren 东北人

One of the most successful chains in the region, Dong Bei Ren offers the opportunity to try northern cuisine in a southern city. I highly recommend that you sample as many different kinds of jiaozi (resembling miniature ravioli) as possible. Other specialities include chicken with stewed mushroom, pork stewed noodles, and lamb dumplings. So many carts will come wheeling past your table that you may not even need to consult a menu. Accompany it with great-value fresh fruit juices or even a sweet red wine that might surprise with its potency. The bright flowery uniforms and décor should make branches easy to spot, but watch out for all the copycats that are springing up.
Address: 2F Lanbaoshi Mansion, Renmin Lu 越秀区人民北路668号蓝宝石大厦2楼
Contact: 020 8135-1711

Additional branches at
Tian He Nan Er Lu 36 天河南二路 36号
Contact: 020 8750-1711
Taojin Bei Lu 淘金北路
Contact: 020 8357-1576
He Qun Yi Ma Lu 65-7 合群一马路 65-7号
Contact: 020 8760-0688

Vegetarian Cuisine

Fo World Sushishe 佛世界素食社
This restaurant is hidden in a small street, and is especially crowded on the 1st and 15th of each lunar month. Part of the profits is given to the neighbouring temple so feel free to go to town on the alcohol-free beer that is imported from Korea
Address: 2-8, Niunaichang St, Tongfu Middle Road 海珠区同福中路牛奶厂街二圣宫前2-8号
Directions: Metro Line 2 The 2nd Workers' Cultural Palace
Contact: 020 8424-3590

Indian Cuisine

Haveli Restaurant & Bar 康乐宫印度餐厅
With its shady garden setting, Haveli has great reputation for its delicious food and cozy atmosphere. I can personally recommend the roast chicken, curry shrimp, curry goat and mango lassis. The Punjabi buffet (88RMB including beer and soft drinks) is massively underrated. Just a few minutes walk from Taojin metro.
Address: 2, Aiguo Road, Overseas Chinese Village 广州市越秀区华侨新村爱国路2号
Contact: 020 8359-4533

Western Cuisine

13 Factories

Probably the best American style cuisine in Guangzhou, specialising in Cajun food. Try the duck gumbo. Even the small size is an ample portion. Spicy and tasty. Grillades and grits is one of my favourite New Orleans dishes. They have it here and it is just delicious. For dessert, check out the Bananas Foster. Other Southern dishes of note include great fried chicken and country fried steak. Everybody loves the cajun fries with dipping sauce and the pulled pork sliders are always a treat. Comfort food done that is very well. It is a small operation with limited staff and a New York owner that spends most of his time in the kitchen. The place has developed a cult following and it is well deserved. A little oasis of America right in the heart of Guangzhou, clam chowder, chicken pot pie, jambalaya, po' boys, pulled pork mini hamburger, spicy shrimp tempura, spicy baked fish with risotto. For dessert, look out for peach cake, chocolate mousse or crème brulee. To wash it all down, Pabst on tap and even chocolate stout. Afterwards, stroll a hundred metres over to the art gallery where there are usually some interesting exhibits. It can be hard to find. Best way is to go south on Ti Yu Xi Lu.. When you see the Family Mart on the right turn right at that Street.

Address: 7, Tianhe Bei Jie, Ti Yu Xi Lu (Behind Chengjian Da Sha, City Development Plaza, and next to the North Gate of Tianhe Da Sha) 天河区体育西路城建大厦后门

People's Cakes & Coffee

A popular café run by two Korean sisters now has three locations citywide, each with a great selection of home-made pastries and tasty sandwiches. The fresh-made fruit juices are particular good. English speaking staff in all stores. A delivery service is also available. At night it turns into a popular drinking spot.

Address: Shop 106-107, 8 Xingsheng Lu, Liede, (3 doors down from Hooley's) 天河区兴盛路8号106-107铺
Contact: 020 3805-1538

European Cuisine

1920 Restaurant and Bar

This very popular place is self-proclaimed as Guangzhou's first German restaurant and serves equally well as a pub. Paulaner Weissbier and Bitburger are on tap for 48 RMB, while draught Heineken (40 RMB) and Tiger (30 RMB) are also offered. A number of other imported German beers are offered by the bottle and there is a good selection of cocktails for 45-50 RMB. The daily happy hour from 5pm-8:30pm takes about 30% off these prices. On the food menu, snacks and sandwiches are 40-60 RMB while main courses range from 68 RMB for schnitzel up to 148 RMB for sirloin steak. There is an outdoor beer garden, though the ambiance suffers from traffic noise on Haizhu Square, while the restaurant's interior is stylish but cosy. The building was built by Germans in 1920 and was once a power station.
Address: 183, Yanjiang Xi Lu 请带我去江西路183号
Contact: 020 8333-6156
Directions: Take Exit D from Haizhu Square subway station and head directly towards the river. 1920 Restaurant and Bar is on the corner.

La Seine 塞纳河饼屋

They put on a spectacular weekend buffet brunch for a mere 98 RMB – all you can eat, including one coffee. The absurdly pretentious service will help you forget that you are paying less than you would for the salad bar at Sizzler back home. La Seine is well worth visiting at other times as well, although the new ownership is gaining mixed reports.
Address: 33, Qingbo Lu (G/F Xinghai Concert Hall),

Ersha Island 二沙岛晴波路33号星海音乐厅首层
Contact: 020 8735-2222 ext. 888

Le Saint-Tropez 法国紫色餐厅

Excellent service and quality food make the relatively high prices worthwhile here. A wide daytime dining menu makes way for one of the most popular bars in the evening when Saint Tropez turns into a favourite expat nightspot.
Address: 13A17, 1, Jianshe Liu Road 建设六马路1号前栋13A17号
Contact: 020 8388-0441

Middle Eastern

Hadhramaut

The area around Xiaobei Lu is filled with Muslim eateries but many of them are overcrowded and overpriced. My personal favourite is the Yemeni restaurant Hadhramaut, just two minutes from Xiaobei Subway Station on line five. Apart from all the usual Arab standards, the Mandi, a traditional Yemeni meat and rice dish from the Hadhramaut region, is outstanding.
Address: 2/F Hong Hui International Trading Mall, Yi Dong Building, Huan Shi Middle Road 怡东大厦, 环市中路, 香港惠国际贸易商城
Contact: 020 2281-2688

African Cuisine

Best-Way African Restaurant

Hidden away in the bowels of a trading centre up on the other side of San Yuan Li, this is an authentic Nigerian restaurant. I am always the only non-African in the place but I am fast developing a taste for the Igbo style cuisine such as the semo and egusi soup, and I simply cannot get enough of the malt drinks. Plus, they always have Fela

Kuti on the sound system which always puts a big smile on my face.

Address: No. 003 1/F Jindu Bldg, 99, Guangyuan West Road (opposite Canaan Market) 金都大厦广元西路99号 (迦南外贸服装城对面)

Contact: 020 6114-7501

Japanese Cuisine

Japan Fusion 中森名菜日本料理

Reputedly the largest Japanese restaurant in Asia, but the equally huge menu reveals a strong inclination toward Cantonese flavours. At lunchtime, the vast expanse of tables, teppanyaki plates, and sashimi bars is flooded to capacity, hardly a surprise considering the choice of excellent-value set lunches available. Great for lunch on the way to or from the station, but watch out in the evening when prices rise sharply.

Address: 2/F 358–378, Metro Plaza, Tian He Bei Lu 天河北路358-378号都市华庭2层

Contact: 020 83884-5109

Korean Cuisine

Qing Wa Ju Korean Restaurant 青瓦居韩国料理

Not only the most authentic Korean food in Guangzhou but also the most reasonable price. Always an imaginative selection of complimentary starter dishes and very reliable version of all the Korean standards. A good clear picture menu and polite, attentive service.

Address: 117, Shuiyin Lu, West Gate of Dongfeng Park 广州市越秀区水荫路117号之114号

Contact: 020 8725 1929

5 WHERE TO RELAX

Guangzhou is first and foremost a gritty business city, and if you are from a consumer-culture background, then the shopping opportunities alone will be fascinating. Of course, there are places beyond the normal tourist spots that are also worth a visit. Here are a handful that did not make into the guidebooks but ones which I think are fascinating anyway. I have heard many people saying how there is nothing to see in Guangzhou, but I have to disagree. There is a lot to see, you just have to know where to go.

I personally would avoid the Zhujiang New Town area in the east of the city. This is the third attempt that local authorities have had at creating a CBD in Guangzhou, probably because they can make so much money on land grabs every time they decide to relocate the centre of the city. The result is wealth-gap ghetto, filled with social-climbing nouveaus and witless expats. The area may have some appeal if you enjoy Shanghai and Dubai. The sights here are typically pretentious. They include the maze-like Guangdong Museum (plenty of offensive Opium Wars propaganda lies here), the enormous Guangzhou New Library (designed to resemble the character 'zhi'(之), where officials obviously think that if you spend enough money on a building then nobody will notice the dearth of materials inside, and the spaceship-like Guangzhou Opera House, yet another pointless exercise, when so many international acts are barred from the country. These modernist fantasies line a leafy but otherwise sterile green axis known as Huacheng Square, designed by Heller Manus Architects from San Francisco.

Redtory 红专厂

Similar to Tianzifang of Shanghai or 789 of Beijing, this was until recently an area of abandoned factory buildings that have been revitalized and transformed into a vibrant artistic zone. Back in 1956, it used to be the largest canning factory in China, the Yingjinqian Canned Food Factory which produced the iconic but foul tasting, dace in black bean sauce. It reopened in 2009 - displaying art, fashion and culture. Redtory is now home to more than forty establishments including art galleries, themed restaurants and design studios.

Address: 128, Yuancun Si Heng Lu, Zhujiang New Town 天河区员村四横路128号

Contact: 020 8557-4346

Subway Line Five: Exit B, Yuancun Station

Liuhua Bonsai Garden 流花湖公园

In the southern corner of Liuhua Park, just past the bird market, is an area overseen by the World Bonsai Friendship Federation. While nowhere near the standards that one would see in the nurseries of Kyoto or Hiroshima, this still makes an interesting short hour's outing, as a break from the endlessly suffocating wholesale markets. The ancient Chinese practice of penjing (盆景 literally "tray scenery") is actually an early pre-cursor of bonsai, but like so many early Chinese innovations, later turbulence prevented development that continued elsewhere. Perhaps the most amazing aspect of the display in Liuhua is the fact that many of these trees are not miniature at all, but are some of the largest examples of bonsai that I have ever seen. What they lack in terms of delicate care and attention, they certainly make up for in stature and impact. Up by the west wall is the Jingpingyuan, a small closed garden with water features and a collection of fifty prize-winning specimens that are said to exemplify the Lingnan (Southern China Style). For the best experience, try to avoid coming here during weekends or after school hours, when it tends to fill up up with squally kids that spoil the atmosphere with their constant tantrums and bad behaviour.

One interesting corner of the garden is a stunted little oak tree that was planted by Elizabeth II, the Queen of England back in 1986 "as a symbol of the long standing friendship between China and Great Britain." Obviously her hosts did not take her to the "Anti-British Memorial Park" in San Yuan Li or any number of the other Guangzhou monuments where the British are still vilified as invaders and barbarians to this day. Even worse, this stumpy little oak tree is barely taller than many of the bonsai that surround it. Unless there was some kind of hidden agenda, planting an oak in sub-tropical Guangzhou seems to make about as much sense as planting a palm tree in the royal grounds of Balmoral, Scotland.

Address: Dong Feng Xi Lu 东风西路和人民北路

The Museum of the Mausoleum of the Nanyue King 西汉南越王博物馆

Hidden 20 meters (65.6 feet) underground, the tomb is made up of 750 huge stones with colourful murals, and was discovered by construction workers excavating foundations for the five-star China Hotel. It has yielded more than 1,000 burial artefacts, a chariot, gold and silver vessels, musical instruments, and human sacrifices were also found - fifteen courtiers, concubines and servants were buried alive with the King to serve him in death. The Silk-Jade burial shroud of King Zhao Mo (r. 137 BC – 122 BC) second king of Nanyue, a garment made up of 2,291 pieces of jade, is the highlight of the museum. Alongside Chinese artefacts, pieces from the steppes, Iranian and Hellenistic Central Asian regions have been found: a Persian silver box found in the tomb is the earliest imported product found to date in China. The tomb was discovered in 1983 and the museum opened in 1988. The excellent information in English about the each of the relics really enhances the experience. Such a museum could very easily be dry and uninteresting, but the Mausoleum of the Southern Yue King is truly fascinating. Admission: 12RMB   Open: 9:00-17:30.

Address: 867, Jiefang Bei Lu 越秀区解放北路867号

Contact: 020 3618-2920

Directions: From Yuexiu Park Subway Station, Exit D2, follow the street as it veers to the right and keep walking straight. The Mausoleum is about five minutes walk from the subway.

Chen Clan Academy 陈家祠

A massive, luxuriously furnished complex constructed in typical southern architectural style. Financed by the wealthy Chen family for Emperor Guangxi in 1890, the temple contains six courtyards, nine main halls and a collection of art that includes wood carvings, stone carvings, lime carvings, pottery, and cast iron pieces decorated with historical figures and mythical figures. The temple now houses the Provincial Museum of Folk Arts and Crafts. The Chen family is commonly referred to as one of the largest clans in the Pearl River Delta. Admission 10 RMB

Address: 34,   Zhongshan   Qi   Lu 荔湾区中山七路恩龙里34号

Subway Line One: Chen Clan Academy - Exit D

Xiguan Traditional Architecture 龙津西西关大屋区

Traditional Cantonese residences (西关大屋 xi-guan-da-wu) from the Qing Dynasty can be seen on Duobao Road (多宝路), Baohua Road (宝华 路), Longjin West Road (龙津西路) and Shangxiajiu Road (上下九路). One of the most famous is located at 18 Baoyuan North Street (宝源北路18号). These were occupied by the upper-class merchants and are slowly disappearing due to the rapid growth in the city. They make great photo spots.

Address: Longjin Xi Lu 荔湾区龙津西路

Subway: Line One Changshou Lu

Ganding Backstreets

Much of Guangzhou has now been taken over by soulless Dubai style skyscrapers but parts of the old city do still exist. In fact, just like an archaeological dig, there are many layers of history for those willing to dig a little. The mazes and warrens that lie behind the computer markets of Shi Pai Dong Lu are reminiscent of the Hong Kong's infamous walled city. Extremely densely populated, no streets, no yards, no trees; nothing except for cramped and dark apartment buildings. Filled with all kinds of small shops and dodgy beauty salons, this is where migrants from other provinces are forced to make their homes. For me nothing is more than representative of Guangzhou.

Address: Shipai Dong Lu 石牌东路

Canton Tower 广州塔

At 610m (2,000 ft.) and 37 storeys high, this was the tallest building in the world for about five minutes back in 2010. Already it has dropped to ninth position and continues to fall as the building bubble surges on relentlessly. Opened to coincide with the city's hosting of the 16th Asian Games, its anorexic hourglass design looks strangely out of place even among the high-rises of the southern waterfront, facing Zhujiang New Town. Some expats have already begun referring to it as the "mole-hair tower," likening it to an ugly single whisker, sported by Asians of generations past. In addition to the observation deck, the tower features various restaurants, a 4-D theatre and other entertainment venues. Admission ranges from 50 RMB to 240 RMB. Open 9am - 10pm.

Address: 222, Yuexiang West Road, Haizhu District 海珠区阅江西路222号

Contact: 020 8933-8222
Subway Line Three: Chigang Pagoda

Guangzhou Crocpark 广州鳄鱼公园

The world's largest crocodile farm with 60,000 to 70,000 of these prehistoric survivors. Thai crocodile wrestlers perform stunts like reaching down the throat of crocodiles and sticking their heads in the animal's mouth. In 1997 and 1998, taking advantage of low prices caused by the Asian financial crisis, the owners bought 40,000 crocodiles for as little as 75 cents a piece. The crocodiles, ranging in size from a few centimetres to six feet, filled the holds of five 747 cargo jets. The park loses money because it cannot persuade the crocodiles to breed. To make money it has opened its doors to tourists who pay $1.25 for a bamboo pole with two chicken torsos attached to them to feed to the crocodiles.

Address: Dabian Village, Panyu District 番禺区大边村
Contact: 020 8479-6100

Vitamin Creative Space 维他命艺术空间

A small establishment located at the rear of a partially enclosed vegetable market. It is not easy to find, but the artwork inside is some of the most eclectic you will ever see. If you like weird and wacky works of art, this museum is worth the trip. Make sure you call in advance to make sure they are open and to ensure someone will be able to meet you at the gates of the market to help you find the entrance. Opening times: Monday to Saturday, 10 pm - 6 pm

Address: Room 301, 29 Hao, Heng Yi Jie, Chi Gang Xi Lu
广州赤岗西路横一街29号
Contact: 020 8429-6760
Email: mail@vitamincreativespace.com
Website: www.vitamincreativespace.com

The Cathedral of the Sacred Heart of Jesus
耶穌聖心主教座堂

The site of the cathedral was originally the residence of Ye Mingchen, the Viceroy of Guangdong and Guangxi Provinces during the Qing Dynasty. Ye was a tyrant and occultist who relied on spiritual contacts with the Daoist Immortals to forge his policies and military tactics. As well as hating all foreigners, he was also quite happy to execute more than 70,000 native Chinese who were accused of rebellion. In the nineteenth century he was blamed for causing the second opium war. More recently Chinese history has been rewritten to portray him as a patriot. Construction of the foundations concluded in 1863. On December 8, the Feast of the Immaculate Conception, a grand ceremony was held, attended by the Viceroy, all senior Mandarins, and somewhat surprisingly, a detachment of three hundred Tartar warriors. The cathedral was funded by Napoleon III and construction turned out to be very challenging, mostly because of its all-granite structure and the lack of machinery, which meant the cathedral had to be built entirely by hand. None of the Chinese workers at that time had seen a western cathedral before, not to mention have any experience of building one. Communication was another major problem, especially as foreigners had been forbidden to study Chinese for such a long time. It is one of the few churches in the world to be entirely built of granite, including all the walls, pillars and the twin towers. The stones were transported from Kowloon, Hong Kong by sailing ships. For this reason, it is nicknamed "Stone House" (石室) by local people. "Stone House" is pronounced "Shishi" in Mandarin and "Seksat" in Cantonese, hence the name "Shishi Cathedral" in Mandarin or "Seksat Cathedral" in Cantonese. The cathedral was finished in 1888, after 25 years of construction and is now the largest cathedral in the Gothic style in China and South-east Asia. Since its completion, the cathedral has undergone three major repairs. The first time was in the 1920s when the timber roof was replaced with concrete. A second repair took place after the Cultural Revolution in the 1980s when most of the original stained glass was smashed out by Red Guards. Recently between 2004 and 2006, the largest repair works were carried out. Some visitors complain that there are no grounds and that the location is smack in the centre of one of Guangzhou's busiest trading districts. It remains a popular attraction for domestic tourists who see it as a fantastic photo opportunity and is a great place to make Chinese friends on a weekend. There is an English language service at 3.30pm every Sunday.

I personally prefer the lesser known Christian Saviour Church on the other side of Beijing Road at 184 Wanfu Road. Built in 1919 as a focus for Anglicans, the building has a very Cantonese feel with its ornate eaves and wooden eaves. The Church was severely damaged and closed in 1966 at the height of the Cultural Revolution but reopened again in 1985. The Zhuguang Community Health Centre just next door at 190 Wanfu Road is another spectacular example of late Sun Yat Sen Period architecture and well worth a look around.

Address: 56, Yide Road 一德路 56号

Zhujiang In-Bev International Beer Museum 珠江-英博国际啤酒博物馆

On the river front next to the Party Pier, this re-purposed factory is a dull and uninspiring museum. Somehow, the Chinese seem to excel at creating such boring attractions. Even so, the main attraction here is the free beer that they serve all day, down in the attached bar. Entry fee: 50 RMB Opening hours: 8:30-12:00, 13:00-16:45

Address: 118, Modiesha Avenue, Xingang Donglu, Haizhu District 广州市海珠区新港东路磨碟沙大街118号

Contact: 020 8420-2521

Getting there: Metro Line 8 to Chigang Station, exit C1, transfer to Bus No. B7 to Yuejiang Middle Road, walk 200m west. Or, Buses No. 779, 765 to Zhujiang-Inbev International Beer Museum Station.

GMP Skatepark Changzhou Island 广州长洲岛板场

The world's largest (and probably emptiest) skatepark. The ramp copings and grind bars are rusty through lack of use but a little wax would soon solve that. There is a good selection of pools and a gentle mini-ramp for beginners. Open till 10pm when it is completely flood-lit, which is a relief as the whole place is unbearably hot in the afternoon. Cost: 5 RMB per hour. Take a look on the bogdam.com video site for a short video of the site's facilities, filmed at the park by the Bestial Wolf scooter accessory company.

Address: Changzhou Island, Huangpu District 黄浦区长洲岛

Directions: Take the subway (line 4) and get off at the Higher Education Mega Centre N.(大学城北) station, leave the station at exit B, as soon as you go up to the street there is a bus stop, take the 383 bus to the Shenjing Market (深井市场) bus station and it is right beside the market. The bus only comes every 45 minutes so you might be waiting a while in which case you can take one of the many motorcycle taxis that are hanging around at that bus station here.

6 WHERE TO PARTY

There are three main bar clusters in Guangzhou. The most westernised night-life is near the Garden Hotel on Huanshi Dong Lu (near Taojin subway station), especially on Jianshi Liu Ma Lu. Bars such as the Cave Bar and the Gipsy King Bar are still popular but are really showing their age these days.

There is also a cluster of bars and clubs along and

around Yanjiang Xilu, on the north bank of the Pearl River, including BabyFace, BonBon and the Bio Fashion Club. They try to be more upmarket establishments. Unfortunately in Guangzhou this often means that they are more snobby, xenophobic and expensive rather that anything else.

These days, the Zhujiang Party Pier is one of the better locations in town and Zhujiang new city has an up and coming party area too.

Some years ago, the government decided that they would dictate where all the night-life was going to be housed and heavily promoted the Bai-E-Tan bar street in the Fangcun district. It was actually just another property scam and never really got off the ground. It is now closed completely, so ignore anything that that you read on the internet that recommends it.

Anyway, lets look at some of the more active areas in greater detail.

Huan Shi Road Area

Tekila 特其拉墨西哥餐厅

Located smack in the heart of infamous the Jianshi Liu Ma Lu, the preferred playground of the travelling trader, stomping ground of the dodgiest drug dealers and a magnet for the most persistent prostitutes. Despite these setbacks on the streets outside and the over priced drinks, Tekila is a popular weekend haunt of the city's Latin community and always has a vibrant party atmosphere.

Address: Second Floor, 11, Jianshe Liu Ma Lu 广州市越秀区建设六马路11号二楼

Contact: 020 8381-6996

Website: www.vivatekila.com

Getting there: Take Subway Line 5 to Taojin station

The Happy Monk

Located all on one floor with an indoor seating area

and an outdoor terrace, the Happy Monk has a very cosmopolitan feel to it, different from other bars in the area. It also stocks Belgian ales like Liefman's Fruit Beer (40 RMB 400ml) and Maredsous (35 RMB a pint) which cannot be found at any other bars in town. With a snazzy décor, it is a great place to go on a date or to meet up with friends.

Address : Units 107-110, Ground Floor, Peace World Apartments, 29, Jianshe 5 Road 广州市环市东路29号好世界公寓首层107-110单元

Contact: 020 8331-5013

Directions: When at the Garden Hotel, turn left into Jianshe Liu Ma Lu, walk down the street and turn right at Huale Lu, and you will find it on the corner at Jianshe Wu Ma Lu.

The Cave

Cave Bar is a good place to party or pick-up. Later in the evening there are 'erotic' shows on the dance floor. Look out for Joey, the snake dancer and her two metre reticulated python, Cissy.

Address: 360, Huanshi Dong Lu 环市东路360号珠江大厦地下

Contact: 020 8386-3660

Directions: Cave Bar is just west of the intersection between Huanshi Dong Lu and Jianshe Liu Ma Lu, on the west side of Peace Plaza.

Gipsy King Bar 大篷车酒吧

Gipsy King Bar is of a similar mould to Cave Bar but a little seedier and more expensive than its nearby neighbour. Another of Guangzhou's more popular hook-up bars. Unfortunately a shadow of itself since DJ Snoop moved on.

Address: 358-360, Huan Shi East Road, Zhujiang Mansion West Tower Basement 环市东路358-

360号珠江大厦西座

Contact: 020 8387-5177

Directions: Entrance on the west side of the Zhujiang Building. About 100 metres west of the intersection between Huanshi Dong Lu and Jianshe Liu Ma Lu.

The Paddy Field Pub 田野西餐吧

The very first of many Irish Bars in Guangzhou and one that tends to draw a slightly older crowd than its nearby rivals and is also more classy. The Paddy Field does well in the food stakes. Big attractions include a full Irish breakfast for 65 RMB and a Sunday Roast for 85 RMB. Then of course there are the slathered in garlic-cheese Paddy Chips and the Guinness Pie. Now with branches in both Tian He and Foshan.

Address: 2nd Floor (up the escalator), 38, Hua Le Road, Central   Plaza, 越秀区华乐路38号广怡大厦2楼 （上手扶梯）

Duo Club

Another popular choice for the expat community to party. Regular special events and imported DJs make this one of the favourite late night venues.

Address: 16, Jianshe Liu Road 越秀区建设六路16号

Tianhe District

Rebel Rebel Café & Bar 叻宝叻宝咖啡厅

A small but busy British themed bar, with live music and a series of other eclectic regular events, ranging from art exhibitions to parties.

Address: 42, Ti Yu Dong Lu, Tianhe 天河体育东路42号

Next door to Oakwood, between Grand View Plaza and Oggi's

Contact: 020 8520-1579
www.rebelrebelgz.com

W Guangzhou 广州W酒店

FEI, located on the 2nd to 4th floor within the hotel, is the place to see-and-be-seen. Very upmarket with prices to match.

Address: 26, Xian Cun Road, Zhujiang New Town 天河区珠江新城冼村路26号

Contact: 020 6628-6628

Q Bar 广州海航威斯汀酒店

Inside the up scale Westin Hotel, Q Bar offers a Latin American ambiance. Music, dance shows and salsa parties rekindle vibrant pleasures, and a VIP parlour with Cuban cigars provides privileged relaxation. It is a good place for a business hang-out. Many foreign chambers of commerce and companies hold drinks parties here.

Address: 6, Linhe Middle Road, Tianhe 天河区林和中路6号

C:Union 喜窝

It is not easy to find this plain looking bar without some guidance. It lies in the thick shade of trees and at the back of Tianyi Plaza. It is like searching for some mysterious house, and the entrance of the bar is so simple that it can easily be overlooked. Great place to hear atypical live music, like reggae or classic rock. A great place to find unusual live acts such as the recent Flamenco/Guzheng combo. The bar has both an indoor section consisting of a dance floor and couches and an outdoor section with patio seating and recently-added new basement. A wide beer selection and bartenders that measure all drinks out in plain view. Early on the bar is populated mostly by locals, however as the night progresses the bar quickly fills with expats. Patrons tend to be very friendly open to meeting new people. There is usually at least one English speaking bartender at each station. Other than the periodic shows presented by bands from home and abroad, you can also find table football and darts. Popular with those in the know, due to its proximity to places like the Xinghai Conservatory of Music, the Guangdong Provincial Song and Dance Troupe, the Guangzhou Ballet Troupe, the Guangzhou Modern Dance Company and the Guangdong Traditional Music Ensemble. This means that it attracts a far better class of customer than places like New Era and Golf Club, which tend to be rammed with local youngsters that cannot handle their alcohol.

Address: 1st Fl, Chengshi Hui, Shuiyin Road 水荫路115号城市会天溢大厦副大堂1楼

More about C: Union at www.cunionbar.com

Zhujiang New Town

The Zhujiang Party Pier (珠江琶醍啤酒园)

The best emerging late-night party-zone in Guangzhou. The purpose-built riverside bar-street has extended trading hours, limited noise restrictions and a concert stage under the brewery's silos. The electronic club, Suns Bar pioneered the waterside strip in 2011. Now open are party spot Wave Bar, Mexican bar Zapatas and jazz club The Clock. With One Lounge imminently opening, and an a number of lease spaces available, the Party Pier can only get better. The Party Pier is along the riverside, east of the Canton Tower and Liede Bridge – above the Modeisha tunnel on Yuejiang Dado Xi (阅江西路). Access Area A by continuing east through the parking lot. Or for Area B take the exit side road that loops around the top of the tunnel entrance for the taxi rank.

Address: Zhujiang Party Pier Culture & Art Zone, 118, Modiesha Dajie, Xingang Donglu

海珠区新港东路磨碟沙大街118号

Contact:: 020 8420-6636

Web: www.zhujiangbeer.com

How to get there: Metro line 8 to Cigang station (赤岗站), go from C1 exit, then take Bus B7 to Middle Yuejiang Xi Lu (阅江西路中站) or Bus No. 779 to terminal. Metro line 8 to Cigang station (赤岗站), take taxi or walk to Party Pier (珠江琶醍), Zhujiang-Inbev International Beer Museum (珠江啤酒博物馆) or Modiesha Tunnel (磨碟沙隧道口)

Four Seasons Hotel 四季酒店

Head up to the 99th floor Tian Bar at Four Seasons Hotel Guangzhou for spectacular views of the city while sipping drinks at a unique bar made from a 26-foot-long piece of colourful agate. Just watch out for the minimum consumption fees if sitting next to the windows or on the some of the couches.

Address: 5, Zhujiang West Road, Pearl River New City

天河区珠江新城珠江西路5号

Contact: 020 8883-3888

Hooley's

Considering the amount of clubs and discos that seem to be on every corner in Guangzhou, you might be surprised at the relative lack of pub style venues. Fortunately, this is a typical Irish expat joint where where people can just sit and drink and relax after work. There is a 3-level Hooley's in the CBD on the ground floor of Binghua Hotel that meets this criteria as well as sub-branches in Foshan and Zhongshan.

Address: 8, Xingsheng Lu, Zhujiang New Town, Shop 101, behind Baoli Xin Yu

珠江新城兴盛路8号, 101号铺, 保利心语后面

Contact: 020 3886-2675
Website: http://www.hooleys-pub.com/

McCawley's Pub 麦考利酒吧

This joint venture between McCawley's and Delaney's is the largest Western Bar in Guangzhou. Spread out over two floors with an amazing façade that stretches over thirty meters across. Fitted in hard wood and stained antique, it is finished with old lanterns and brass goosenecks. Giant brass letters spelling out McCawley's confirms you have arrived at the right place. Their menu is a mix of traditional pub food and a selection of Tex-Mex favourites. Frozen Margaritas, both traditional and strawberry, mixed continuously in a 'Slurpee' machine.
Address: Shop 101, 16, Huacheng Ave, Zhujiang New Town 广州珠江新城花城大道16号101商铺
Contact: 020 3801-7000
Website: http://www.mccawleys.com/gz/index.html

Pearl River Night Cruise

For the ultimate neon-by-night experience, hop aboard one of the many leisurely river cruises from Tianzi Pier (Beijing Lu; open 6.30pm-10pm daily). The boat ride affords great views of the Guangzhou skyline along the Pearl River. Tickets for the deluxe dinner cruise can be bought from most high-end hotels. Prices from 50 - 200 RMB per person. Higher end cruises usually include dinner buffet. For those on a budget, grab a bottle of wine and bring your own wine glasses, no service charge and you have the best lounge in the city.

7 WHEN TO COME

Guangzhou is much warmer in winter than other cities in China, but you would probably never know it due the the almost complete lack of heating. In terms of climate, the best time to visit Guangzhou is between October and November. Alternatively, April and May are also good months. Guangzhou's sub-tropical climate make humidity levels sky-rocket to almost 40 degrees throughout the long summer and there is little respite from the heat until the National Day holidays in October.

8 LANGUAGE

Cantonese is the first language for half of the residents, while the other half speak mainly Mandarin. The migrant population from other provinces of China account for around forty percent of the city's total population. Most of them are rural immigrants and speak only Mandarin. They have taken on many jobs that the local citizens are unwilling to do.

Do not expect a great deal of English. English is taught at all schools but the reality is that foreign languages are only of any use for Chinese that want to emigrate. There are only a minuscule amount of opportunities for foreign language speakers inside the country. Despite their claims, the Chinese education system is of extremely poor quality. Average public education investment around the world is 5.1% of GNP, with developed countries leading the way at 5.3%. Even sub-Saharan African countries devote 4.6% to education yet China comes in almost last at 2.3%. China, which makes up 1/5th of the world's population receiving education, only makes up 1.5% of the world's total expenditures on education. Kenya, Malawi, Lesotho, Uganda, Tanzania and Mozambique, in fact 2/3rds of African countries have educational expenditures exceeding 4% of their GNPs, almost double that of China. From this perspective, it is clear why Chinese degrees are unrecognised anywhere else in the world and so many Chinese students yearn to study abroad. Beyond the corruption and the institutionalised cheating, it is clear why levels of English are so poor. The general level of sellers' English is also quite low, so it is sometimes advisable to bring an interpreter with you. You can find many of those on-line. If you need any recommendations, feel free to send me an email.

9 BANKING SERVICES

Banks are everywhere in Guangzhou, in fact the cynical locals now have a saying that there are more banks than rice shops, their way of saying that is a definite surplus of financial institutions. Most banks have ATMs that accept foreign credit or debit cards, but withdrawals are available in Chinese currency only. Smaller domestic banks sometimes only accept cards on the Unionpay system. This is sometimes also true for the Agricultural Bank despite being one of the largest banks in the country. Most banks will also exchange local currencies to RMB. Your passport is required for this service.

As with most services in China, long lines, rare English service, and the confusion over paperwork are just the beginning. Still, it is possible to open an account with a valid passport. A minimum of 1 RMB deposit is needed if you are opening an RMB account. After you have filled out an application form, you will be asked to create a six digit PIN number (which is different from the usual four digit PIN number in other parts of the world). You will then be issued a "passbook" in which you can record your withdrawals and deposits, along with a debit card which you can use at any of the bank's branch ATM's in China. Be warned, however, that if you withdraw money from an ATM outside of the city or town in which you opened your account – even if the bank branch is the same – you will likely be charged a small fee of a few RMB.

Opening an account for foreign currency is sometimes a much more difficult task. ICBC (Industrial and Commercial Bank) for example has some of the strictest rules of the Big Four banks. To do so, you must bring your passport and, if applicable, your residency permit. You must also bring a notarized translation of your English name into Chinese, and fill out a basic application form. The bank will then open the account under your officially approved Chinese name. A dual currency account can be opened with only $20

Another popular choice is Bank of China, which happens to be China's oldest bank (founded in 1912). Any money you deposit into the China branch account cannot be accessed in overseas accounts. To open a foreign currency account with BOC, you need your passport and your residence permit (if applicable). You can then fill out an application, deposit the minimum amount required: for USD accounts, the minimum is currently $500 USD. Bank of China is the best bet for using foreign cards. Actually the name Bank of China is very misleading. Every province is separate and they are not connected to each other. I recently lost my bank card in Yunnan. When I went to the bank, I was told I could not access my money because the account was opened in Guangzhou. I even had my bank book and still I could not access my cash or get a replacement card!

Paypal only accepts Union Pay credit card accounts issued by Huaxia Bank, HSBC or Citibank. Most banks offer on-line banking, but generally it is in Chinese language only and does not cover foreign currency and bank-to-(overseas) bank transfers. The PSB now only accepts payments using a Union Pay card. Supposedly this is meant to cut down corruption but a minor tweak like this is going to have a very minor impact on a system that already thoroughly rotten.

If you wish to transfer RMB from China into an overseas account, you will have to physically go to a bank branch with your passport, your work permit and a contract from your employer vouching your employment and income. You will also need a letter on your company's letterhead (and with your company's stamp) verifying the taxes that you have paid on your income. This is a mandatory requirement, as you are not allowed to transfer any Chinese income for which you have not been taxed. In addition, you must bring your monthly pay slips, with your company stamp and government issued tax receipts. Conflicting reports state that customers do not need any tax clearance or tax proof but only a passport and a valid visa to transfer funds to offshore accounts as long as it is within $10,000 and you can state the reason for the transfer.

Alipay is the Chinese on-line payment service of choice and is widely accepted in China but only a handful of foreign on-line enterprises accept it.

The China Merchants' Bank receive consistently good reports regarding their on-line banking and in-branch service. They were incredibly helpful in advising me on how to send money home, entirely in English (this was a fairly large branch in Beijing though).

Foreign Banks in Guangzhou
Many of these are only Representative Offices rather than full service branches. Please check in advance to avoid any confusion.

Asia Banks

Hong Kong
Nanyang Commercial Bank 南洋商业银行
Room 402, Sky Galleria, CITIC Plaza, 233 Tianhe Bei Lu
广州市天河区天河北路233号中信广场商场402铺
Contact: 020 3891-2668

Fax: 020 8384-2726
E-mail: Only available on-line
Website: www.ncb.com.hk

Chong Hing Bank Guangzhou Representative Office
创兴银行广州代表处
Room 302, 7 Yongshengshangsha, Donghu Lu
广州市越秀区东湖路永胜上沙7号302室
Contact: 020 8375-8300
Website: www.chbank.com/en/index.shtml

Bank of East Asia 东亚银行
G/F to 3/F, Metro Plaza, 183 Tianhe Bei Lu
广州市天河北路183号大都会广场一至四层
Contact: 020 8755-1138
Fax: 020 8755-3938
E-mail: Only available on-line
Website: www.hkbea.com.cn

Heng Seng Bank 恒生银行
137-140 of G/F shopping Arcade, No 250 of 2/F and
3701、3708 of 37/F , CITIC Plaza, 233 Tianhe Bei Road
广州市天河区天河北路233号中信广场商场首层137-
140号,2层250号,37层3701和3708号
Contact: 020 3811-0888
Fax: 020 3877-2473
Website: www.hangseng.com

Hong Kong and Shanghai Banking Corporation Ltd.
汇丰银行
HSBC has ATMs that will accept just about any card on
the planet.
G2, G/F, Garden Hotel, 368 Huanshi Dong Road
广州市环市东路368号花园酒店首层G2
Contact: 020 8313-1888

Fax: 020 8365-2368
Website: www.hsbc.com.cn

Singapore
United Overseas Bank 大华银行
Unit 1107-1110, Metro Plaza, 183-187 Tianhebei Lu
广州市天河北路183-187号大都市广场1107-1110室
Contact: 020 8755-8611/8787/8789
Fax: 020 8755-6661
E-mail: Only available on-line
Website: www.uob.com.sg

DBS Bank 星展银行
Unit 1006, 10/F, Fortune Plaza West Tower, Tiyu Dong Lu
广州市天河区体育东路118号财富广场西塔10楼1006室
Contact: 020 3884-8010
Contact: 020 3884-8060
Website: www.dbs.com

India
Bank of Baroda 印度巴鲁达银行
2011-2013, Metro Plaza, 183 Tianhe Bei Lu
广州市天河北路183号大都会广场2011-2013室
Contact: 020 8375-2466
Fax: 020 8375-2285
E-mail: Only available on-line
Website: www.bankofbaroda.com

Korea
Kookmin Bank 国民银行
Room 4602/3, Office Building, CITIC Plaza, 233 Tianhe N. Road 广州市天河北路233号中信广场4602/03室
Contact: 020 3877-0566/3020/3700

Fax: 020 3877-0569
Website: www.kbstar.com

Europe

BMPS – Banca Monte dei Paschi di Siena
Unit 1708, Tower A, Centre Plaza, 161 Linhexi Road,
Tianhe District
Contact: 020 3825-1001, 3825-1002
Fax: 020 3825-1003
E-mail: segr.gen@postacert.gruppo.mps.it
http://www.mps.it

Banque Crédit-Agricole
Room 2501-2503, Guangzhou International Electrical
Tower, 403 Huanshi Dong Lu
Contact: 020 8732-4608
Fax: 020 8732-4272/3
www.credit-agricole.fr

ABN AMRO
Room 1804, Main Tower, Guangdong International Hotel,
339 Huanshidong Lu
Contact: 020 8331-1886
Fax: 020 8331-2029
www.abnamro.com

Banco Commercial Portuguese
Room 2301, 23/F Peace World Plaza, 362-366,
Huanshidong Lu
Contact: 020 8387-4277/ 8387-4377
Fax: 020 8387-4307
www.millenniumbcp.pt

Deutsche Bank AG
Rm 6403-6404 CITIC Plaza, 233 Tianhe Bei Lu
Contact: 020 3877-1618

Fax: 020 3877-1406
www.db.com

Dresdner Bank AG
T.P. Plaza, Office 905, 9/109 Liuhua Lu
Contact: 020 8669-5920
www.dresdner-bank.com

BNP Paribas
Unit 1001-1002, TP Plaza, 109-9 Liuhua Road
Contact: 020 8669-5822
Fax: 020 8669-5733
www.bnpparibas.com.cn

Credit Agricole Indosuez
Rm 2103, Teem Mall, 208 Tianhe Road, Guangzhou
广州市天河路208号粤海天河城大厦2103室
Contact: 020 8732-4608
Fax: 020 8732-4272 / 4273
www.calyon.com

Fortis Bank
Rm.2601, 26/F, Peace World Plaza, 362 Huanshi Dong Lu
Contact: 020 8387-2783
Fax: 020 8387-0086
www.fortis.com
E-mail: milson.lau@fortisbank-gz.com.cn

Standard Chartered Bank PLC
13/F May Flower Plaza, 68 Zhongshan Wu Road
Contact: 020 8391-8822
Fax: 020 8333-9998
www.standardchartered.com.cn/e_index.html

Societe Generale
Booth 3-101, 5-101, 7-101, Unit 9-4201-4205, 4216, 4217-
4221, China Shine Plaza, No 3-15 Linhe Xi Lu, Tianhe

广州市天河区林和西路3-
15号（单号）耀中广场9号第42　　层01-05，16和17-
21号单元，3号101、5号101和7号101复式商铺
Contact: 020 3819-7888
Fax: 020 3819-7666
www.socgen.com

North America

Bank of America 美国银行
The bank has alliance with China Construction Bank.
Unit 2509, 25/F Bank of America Plaza555 Renmin Road
Middle 广州市人民中路555号美国银行中心2509室
Contact: 020 8130-3000
Website: www.bankofamerica.com

Citibank 花旗银行
Rm 7201-7202, Office Tower, CITIC Plaza, 233 Tianhe
Bei Lu 广州市天河北路223号中信广场7201-7202室
Also Unit 101, Fortune Plaza, 118 Tiyu East Road
Contact: 020 3898-1688. This bank has a full service
branch with currency exchange services and 24-hour
ATMs.
Contact: 020 3877-1333/1166
Fax: 020 3877-0990
Website: www.citibank.com

Wachovia Bank, NA 美联银行
 Room 3206, CITIC Plaza, 233 Tianhe Road North
广州市天河北路233号中信广场3206室
Contact: 020 3877-1335
Fax: 020 3877-1336
Website: www.wachovia.com

American Express 美国运通

Room 806, Main Tower, Guangdong International Hotel, 339 Huanshi Road
广州市环市东路339号广东国际大厦主楼806室
Contact: 020 8331-1611
Fax: 020 8331-1616
Website: www.americanexpress.com

Scotiabank 加拿大丰业银行
Unit 1503, 1505, 1506, Tower A, Centre Plaza, 161 Linhexi Road
广州市天河区林和西路161号中泰国际广场A塔1503.1505.1506室
Contact: 020 8396-3668
Fax: 020 8331-1799
E-mail: Only available on-line
Website: www.scotiabank.ca

BMO Bank of Montreal 蒙特利尔银行
Suite 1203, T.P. Plaza, 9/109 Liuhua Road
广州市流花路109号之9达宝广场1023室
Contact: 020 8669-5148 ext 218
Fax: 020 8669-5149
Website: www.bmo.com

10 CHOCOLATEVILLE

Guangzhou's 'Chocolateville' stretches from the Xiaobei Road area all the way up to the far edge of San Yuan Li. Many Arabs and Africans originally settled in these parts of the city because of the large numbers of Chinese Muslims living and working here In the nineties numbers quickly fell after the Han-Uighur conflicts in Xinjiang and other parts of the country, and many Muslims were forced to leave. It is probably now the most cosmopolitan part of the city with French and Arabic commonly being heard as well as English and Chinese. This is especially surprising considering the prejudice held against blacks by most Chinese people. In a recent survey conducted by Dr. Li Zhigang, Professor of Regional and Urban Planning at Sun Yat Sen University, 86% of local white-collar workers reported a dislike of black people. This was in direct contrast to those business people that came into daily contact with the black community who overwhelmingly accepted black people at a level of 88%. These figures will not surprise anybody who has spent a long time in Chinese society, and has experienced first hand the way in which the authorities encourage racial prejudice. When I first arrived in China I was deeply shocked at how everybody hated the Japanese with a vengeance, even though they knew nothing of the culture, had never been to Japan, nor even met a Japanese person. I would often play devil's advocate and tell them that my wife was Japanese, just to provoke some much needed self-examination of their baseless bigotry.

The enormous levels of innate Chinese xenophobia and deep-seated racial resentment raised its ugly head when Lou Jing a half-black, half-Chinese girl sparked off a huge controversy by entering a Chinese X-Factor type TV show. Despite being born in Shanghai to a Chinese mother, netizens blasted her with insults and derogatory epithets, showing quite clearly how closed minded much of the country remains.

Despite these obstacles, there are still at some estimates, up to 200,000 Africans living in Guangzhou, a number that increases 30 - 40 percent each year and now constitutes the largest African community in Asia. This is hardly surprising considering all of the investment that China is making on the African continent to secure its growing appetite for raw materials. When I first arrived in Guangzhou nearly twenty years ago, I enjoyed much of my free time with a group of Congolese doctors who had trained at Zhongshan university. Each one could speak at least half a dozen languages including Cantonese and Mandarin, and could even write complex pharmaceutical prescriptions in Chinese script. Despite their obvious expertise, none were accepted into the local community as physicians, and all have since relocated to more tolerant parts of the globe.

Nowadays the Africans in Guangzhou cover a much broader spectrum. There are still polymath students here to broaden their education, and these can be seen down at the university mega-centre, but the majority are now business people here for the import/export trade. In Xiaobei, the Shishi Catholic Church routinely draws upwards of a 1,000 African patrons for weekly mass. Drug use among the less salubrious elements of the western multinational expat community has encouraged a small number of Nigerian drug dealers to cater to their needs, yet on the whole most of the Africans here are pleasant and friendly.

There have been demonstrations (although tiny in scale when compared to the anti-foreigner protests organised by the Chinese themselves) to protest the suspicious deaths of a number of Africans, who were pursued and imprisoned by the local police. Negative portrayals in the media, have only exacerbated the situation. There is still a certain tenseness in this area, and this is the only part of the city where I have been asked to produce my passport for inspection by the police (I am white by the way). Even so, I very much enjoy the atmosphere that the Africans bring with them and relish the opportunity to sample such a wide range of cuisines and converse with such a broad selection of nationalities.

11 HOLIDAYS

China has different holidays than most other countries. The most important holidays are:

Chinese New Year. For approximately two weeks in January or February every year, all factories and wholesale markets close down. Dates vary each year because of the lunar calendar used to set the date for this holiday.

May Day. At the beginning of May many Chinese factories and wholesale markets are closed, factories for up to a week, but wholesale markets usually only for 2-3 days.

Mid Autumn Festival, or moon cake festival is held on the 15th day of the eighth month in the Chinese calendar, which is in September or early October each year. Usually this is just a one day holiday in factories and wholesale markets.

National Day. The Chinese National day is on October 1st. Usually this is followed by a whole week of vacation for factory workers.

12 SAFETY AND SECURITY

Chinese continue to perpetuate claims that are centuries out of date. Most for example still sincerely believe that London is extremely polluted and foggy. The rest of the country believes that Guangzhou is a hotbed of crime and lawlessness, that anybody walking the street is likely to be assaulted and anything of value will be snatched at the first possible instance. While there are a few Chinese cities that do give that feeling, Guangzhou is not one of them. Guangzhou is no more dangerous than any other large city, anywhere in the world. Cautions about scams and bicycle stealing apply in Guangzhou as much as anywhere else but the most dangerous thing is the traffic. Generally speaking, the more expensive the car, the worse the driver.

While safety in Guangzhou is generally not an issue, there are occasions when the city falls into paroxysms of temporary insanity and absolutely anything can happen. A good example of this were the recent anti-Japanese protests which quickly spiralled out of control until large numbers of PLA soldiers had to be bought in to quell the disturbances. Japanese cars and even stores that were even slightly related to Japan such as 7/11s and Watson's were trashed with impunity. Perhaps because the authorities forbid the kind of peaceful protests that we are familiar with in the West (such as marches and demonstrations), Chinese do not understand how to behave in these situations and simply go on the rampage, throwing all rationality out of the window. Perhaps it is a cultural trait as evidenced by a long history of massacres of foreigners that has repeatedly taken place over the centuries. Whatever the reason, China is not a safe place to be in when this kind of madness takes hold.

There are still many apologists who claim that China is one of the safest places on Earth. Unfortunately these are usually English teachers who rarely lift their heads out of the sand of their campus or expats that only leave their gated-communities by chauffeur-driven limo. The reality is that China is a seething cauldron of tit-for-tat protests where mass violence is the inevitable result. The anti-Chinese riots that recently took place in Vietnam showed the other side of the coin. Every single South East Asian country has experienced similar anti-Chinese protests which usually end up in mass killings.

China has tried to rewrite its history so that its own anti-foreigner protests are swept away from view. For example, few of the expat community in Guangzhou are aware that in back the ninth century some 200,000 foreign merchants were massacred by local residents. This was repeated in Ningbo in 1542 when 3000 Portuguese were killed and again in Yangzhou in 1645 when as many as 800,000 were massacred in the streets. This occurred once more in Guangzhou in 1650 when another 700,000 foreigners were openly slaughtered.

I was unfortunate to be in China during a number of similar periods of media-encouraged unrest. The first time was in May of 1999, when the Chinese were using their embassy in Belgrade as a communications centre for Serbians fighting against the UN in Bosnia. Why the

Chinese were prepared to help Milosevic is a more murky question. One possible explanation is that the Chinese lacked Stealth technology, and the Yugoslavs, having shot down a Stealth fighter in the early days of the air campaign, were in a good position to trade. When the US forces targeted the building with a missile strike, the Chinese government did everything in its power to rouse the fury of the Chinese people. One of my best friends in Guangzhou at the time was a British manager working for a large multi-national food company, and it being Saturday evening he decided to go out for a quiet drink. He was completely unaware of the day's events and simply headed out for the evening as he would any other weekend. As soon as he stepped into the bar, he was jumped by a group of Chinese men who repeatedly bottled him to the floor. He was not given chance to say anything and was immediately attacked simply for appearing to be an American. The reason why I remember the incident so well is because of what happened next. Being a well-paid expat, his company provided him with the best insurance possible and yet when he arrived at the International Hospital they refused to treat him, claiming that his policy did not cover him for 'civil disturbance.' Instead his local girlfriend rushed him to a nearby Chinese military hospital where he received more than seventy stitches in his head and face .I personally know of at least half a dozen foreigners who were hospitalised on that one weekend alone.

Those of us unfortunate to be stuck in Guangzhou at that time spent the next week locked inside our apartments, not daring to step outside the front door. I remember calling some friends from the Foreign Language University who told me that the authorities were deliberately encouraging the action by bussing large numbers of students down to the American Embassy on Shamian Island, where local police encouraged them to stone the building. Each student was paid ten RMB for a full days efforts of pelting the place with stones and bottles. Many stayed behind in the evening to torch the diplomatic vehicles. Others pushed against the lines of police ringing the embassy, shouting: "Don't you protect Americans" and "Pay blood debts in blood"

Chinese media fuelled the protesters' anger, largely ignoring NATO's apologies and its insistence that the embassy attack was an accident. Instead, media outlets like the People's Daily reported that NATO had "spilled Chinese blood" on purpose. Interestingly, several members of the outlawed China Democracy Party were rounded up and ordered to stay away from the protests.

In Chengdu, the US Consulate was forced to evacuate all personnel after thousands of people stormed the grounds and put it to the torch. Chinese authorities later had to send in 2,000 baton-wielding People's Liberation Army (PLA) troops to clear out the protesters. After about a week things eventually returned to normal and I finally plucked up the courage to venture out onto the buses (this was before the days of the subway) and even then the feelings of animosity and hatred were still very palpable. It was especially ironic that during all this time, back in the UK, the Queen and the Prime Minister were hosting a state visit by the then President of China, Jiang Zemin, who was staying at Buckingham Palace. I on the other hand spent most of the week locked in my bathroom.

A few years later the whole situation repeated itself when a Chinese fighter jet crashed into an American reconnaissance aircraft and forced it to make a crash landing in Hainan. Once more the streets were suddenly filled with frenzied mobs baying for the blood of foreigners. Again I locked myself in my apartment, desperate to sink into big city anonymity.

When the first of the major anti-Japanese protests took place about ten years ago, I was in Xiamen, and I just happened to be dating a very pretty Japanese guest relations officer at the local Holiday Inn. When they troubles flared up she narrowly escaped the mob and was very lucky to escape to the sanctuary of her hotel. Of course she was petrified and returned to Japan just a few days later. Needless to say, I never saw her again. The protests quickly got out of control and turned from anti-Japanese to anti-government, which was when the authorities finally stepped in and put an end to the protests in the only way that they know how.

Luckily, I was not in China during the second wave of 2012 anti-Japanese demonstrations. Several thousand protesters managed to break into the Garden Hotel in Guangzhou, which houses the Japanese Consulate General, and completely destroyed the place. A French friend who was still in town sent me very worrying photos of the thousands of PLA troops that were quickly being deployed to protect large business centres such as the Teem Mall. I was very grateful that I was safely ensconced in the relative safety of Thailand.

The fact is that anti-foreigner protests break out unexpectedly, but on a regular basis all over China, and if you happen to be caught up in one of them, China suddenly becomes a very dangerous place. You may have hundreds of Chinese friends but once the ring-leading jingoists start chanting 'kill the foreigner!' I guarantee that your blood will turn to ice.

There is a common perception that China is a very safe place and that there is very little crime. This is partly because the media is so crippled that almost no crime is ever reported. Large corruption cases are reported with political and propaganda motivations, rather than as pieces of carefully uncovered investigative journalism. Enforcement is also very selective and many citizens realise that crimes against ordinary people will not be pursued and therefore they do not bother to report them. Street crime definitely exists and in very large amounts. Even the casual observer can see that most apartments have heavy steel grills on their windows. Cash carrying security vans always have at least two guards armed with shotguns as they fill the ATMs. The ATMs themselves have a much larger number of warnings for customers to be vigilant than in other countries. Each of these is clear evidence that crime is a major threat but because so little is reported in the media, (in global rankings, the Chinese press is fifth from the very bottom in terms of journalistic freedom) the authorities are able to perpetuate a myth that instances of crime are very low.

Kidnappings

Guangzhou, Dongguan, and Shenzhen have seen incidents of kidnapping, ransom, and extortion. Kidnappings occur mostly over business disputes and might better be categorized as "unlawful detentions," often in the office or hotel room of the victim. Victims are generally allowed to use their mobile phones (in order to arrange the resolution of the dispute) and should immediately call the police for assistance.

STDs

It is estimated that 10 million Chinese had some type of a sexually transmitted disease in 1949. After the Communists took power and initiated mandatory screening, free treatment and a crackdown on prostitution, STD's were all but eradicated by the 1970s. The rate of STDs in China has recently sky-rocketed again. According to data from the Chinese Centre for Disease Control (CDC), the number of people living with HIV/AIDS reached close to 800,000 by the end of 2011, even though fewer than 500,000 cases were recorded in 2010. Despite the low prevalence rate of .10% (about the same as Japan and less than the UK), more frightening are current projections that the number of people in China living with HIV/AIDS could potentially jump to 10 million within six years. According to a BBC report, syphilis too has risen at an "alarming rate", from .02 cases per 100,000 to an incredible 20 infected individuals per 100,000 in 2010—thus turning syphilis into something of a modern epidemic. In addition, Chlamydia is still considered the most common sexually transmitted infection in the country, with one 2003 University of Chicago report suggesting that 16% of men and 10% of women living in the coastal provinces had been infected with the disease. Statistics also show that other sexually transmitted infections (STIs) like genital herpes and warts have also proliferated amongst the general population. According to data from a 2008 World Health Organization (WHO) publication, 10%-30% of the individuals residing in developing Asian countries (China included) have genital herpes while an estimated 65% of Chinese prostitutes are infected with this untreatable virus.

13 INTERNET RESOURCES

Internet Censorship and VPNs

Western media is always harping on about the Great Chinese Firewall and the army of censors that police the Chinese intranet. The two things that they usually fail to mention is that firstly, being restricted to Mandarin language only that is the most effective form of censorship for most Chinese users and secondly, the sites that are blocked are of little consequence to expats living full time in the PRC. Facebook and Twitter might indeed be essential if you are in New York or London, but they are of little relevance when you are based in Tianjin or Chengdu. I personally never saw the attraction of Youtube where the noise-to-signal ratio was almost unbearable. The torrent networks have always been practically immune to any form of blocking and so why anybody would use a streaming-video service that is so full of dross is beyond me. It can be frustrating that so many blogs are blocked and the ongoing war between Google and the Communist Party is becoming a real pain for anybody with a Gmail account or those wanting to use Google maps.

According to the VPN service provider IVPN.net, China is listed as the top user-rights violator in the world, though North Korea is notably absent from the list since its citizens only have access to a limited domestic-only Internet. Iran, Syria, Cuba and Egypt round out the top five worst Internet censors in the world.

Fortunately, VPNs are widely available on Taobao starting at 10 kuai per year. There is a constant war of attrition between the authorities and the very nature of the internet that is ongoing. For those who really need access to blocked sites, then the best VPN software that I have seen so far is Panda Pow (https://pandapow.co/) but at US$84 a year it is not the cheapest option available. I have high hopes for the newly released Lantern service that utilizes P2P technology to overcome any restrictions. Distributed networks have been demonised by corporations and copyright cartels but at least their losing battle will be replaced by a much more robust international communications network.

Information on VPNs for China: http://www.greycoder.com/best-vpn-china/

Listed below are 12 well-know blocked websites in China:

1. Facebook

In Mainland China, Facebook was blocked following the July 2009.

2. Twitter

Twitter was blocked from 2009, June to present.

3. YouTube

YouTube was banned in mainland China from 2009, March to present.

4. Blogspot

It was forbidden in China since 2009, May to present.

5. WordPress

This famous blog platform was blocked in mainland

China from 2011, October to present.

6. Picasa

This photo sharing website was blocked in China from 2009, July to present.

7. Technorati

This famous blog search engine was blocked in mainland China from 2008, July to present.

8. Plurk

This social website was blocked in mainland China from 2009, April to present.

9. Hulu

Like many other video streaming sites, Hulu is blocked in China.

10. Dropbox

In May 2010, Dropbox users in China were unable to access Dropbox. Later, Dropbox confirmed they had been blocked by the Chinese government.

11. Wikileaks

China has blocked access to WikiLeaks since Nov 2010.

12. Google+

Google+ was blocked in China since July 2011.

China Related Websites

Chinasmack.com

This website gives an interesting insight into how the "fenqing" or angry young men and women of China, see the rest of us. To balance out its dreary pre-processed state media, there exists a huge Chinese blogosphere which chatters and twitters much as ours does. One topic which is always safe, representing no conceivable threat to the Communist Party, is foreigners and what dirty dogs we all are. One should not, of course, regard one website as the voice of a nation. You really have to take everything at Chinasmack with a grain of salt - in many ways it is a superb insight into the Chinese internet and blog scene but remember that the Chinese comments are cherry-picked; usually to try and squeeze in both sides of the argument, but more often than not the intention is to invoke sympathy, opposition or anger with the Chinese readers and see the contrast that results with the English comments on the site. Treat Chinasmack like a tabloid newspaper that most people read for controversy. Expect absurd comments from the Chinese, because it would be boring to only pick the most sensible ones. Do not presume that the comments represent the opinion of every Chinese commenting on the topic.

Thenanfang.com

For a slightly less sensationalist approach to news in China, this Hong Kong run website is always filled with fascinating articles that never make it into the state-run media. The English is much better that most of the locally run news websites and is regularly updated with the latest stories.

GZStuff.com

What started out as a very promising forum site has since degenerated into in chat site, dominated by trolls and relationship talk. There are still some very knowledgeable posters on site but they are struggling to keep their heads above water these days. The most useful part of the site are the events listings which are always very thorough and up to date.

Expat-blog.com

The Guangzhou forum of this site is not so active these days with only maybe thirty or so posts per month. Even so, it can be a useful resource for those seeking local knowledge.

Quora.com

This massive site has a large number of old-China-hands that are willing to provide interesting and enlightening answers to questions regarding the PRC. Unfortunately there are also growing numbers of local youngsters who probably could not find their own arse even if they had a map. Be selective about who you follow and whose opinions you take on board and this can be a very useful site for all kinds of China related information. China does now have its own Quora equivalent at Zhihu.com but as of yet it is still Chinese language only.

Fiverr.com

This is actually an Israeli micro-tasking site, but there are many China-based service providers here that can provide valuable services in the PRC. Chinese copy-cat sites such as lisili.com have not really taken off and Fiverr remains a useful resource when looking for leads local information.

Guerrillainchina.com

A quick plug here for my own nascent website, which I have set up so that readers have their own business discussion forum to share insights, tips and knowledge. Things are a bit sparse at the moment but stop by for a visit to introduce yourself and hopefully we can build up some momentum.

14 TRANSPORTATION

Flights

Guangzhou Baiyun International Airport (广州白云国际机场) is a major hub in Southern China, second only to Hong Kong. The airport is the base for China Southern Airlines, now the third largest airline in the world. It is 28 km north from central Guangzhou. The most convenient way into the city is by Metro Line 3. The lower level of the airport terminal leads to the Airport South Metro station. A journey to the East Railway Station, or to Tiyu Xilu Metro station (both 12 RMB) takes about 50 minutes. Trains run every seven minutes, with the first train leaving the airport at 6am and the last train departing at 11pm.

Taxis are also available and take about the same time, although a taxi ride to central Guangzhou will cost about 120 RMB. Taxis are available outside Arrival Hall Section A Gate 5 and Arrival Hall Section B Gate 6. There have been a number of reports about taxi scams at the Guangzhou airport. Beware uniformed officials who approach you and offer taxis or claim that you are supposed to change money. There have also been reports of men taking new arrivals to a different part of the airport, into a small room, and exchanging money. The bills were not counterfeit, but the men gave exactly 50% of the proper exchange rate. Avoid any unsolicited assistance and head straight for the official taxi rank.   There   are also express airport buses that run to and from various locations in the city (for locations of buses see http://newsgd.com/specials/airportguide/airportqna/200 407300080.htm). Line 1 (16 RMB) departs every 10-15 minutes from 7am until the last flight and takes 45 minutes to reach the Guangzhou Railway Station and Central Hotel. Lines 1 to 6 are travelling within the metropolitan area, while lines 7-11 go to outer districts. There are also direct Airport Express buses to some cities in the Pearl River Delta region, such as Zhuhai and Foshan.

Many visitors fly into Hong Kong and then cross the border through Shenzhen and onto Guangzhou. From the Hong Kong International Airport, you can take cross-boundary coach to Guangzhou and other cities in Guangdong. Service providers include China Travel Service, Trans-Island Chinalink and Eternal East. Fares range from HK$220-250 one way.

To get from Hong Kong to Guangzhou by train head for Hung Hom where there are direct trains through to Guangzhou East Station almost every hour.

Chinese Airlines

Commercial planes in China have the worst delays in the world. Beijing's airport ranks dead last among the world's top 35, with fully 82% of flights failing to leave on time. Second worst was Shanghai, at 71%. Since being overrun by Mainland travellers, Hong Kong is now ranked 29th among the top 35 international airports, with only 64% of flights departing on time. Most flight delays are not as punishing as the one in Shanghai last year that stranded Newark-bound United Airlines passengers for three days. In a separate incident the airport took three days to unload the luggage for ten arriving flights. Still,

42% of Beijing's delays were considered "excessive," defined as 45 minutes or more. And 5% of all flights were simply cancelled. None of China's provincial airports surveyed by FlightStats -- including Guangzhou, Kunming, Nanjing, Chengdu, Changsha and Urumqi -- could manage to get half of their flights on time. Eight of the ten worst-performing Asian airlines in terms of delays were Chinese carriers.

China's airports simply can not keep up with commercial airline growth. The total number of airports in China is expected to reach 244 in 2020, compared to 80 in 2011. As the aviation industry has expanded, so have the crowds but not the air space that planes are allowed to fly in, in part because China's military still commands most of the skies. Nearly 80% of China's airspace has been reserved for military use. In other countries, such as the U.S., the situation is exactly the opposite. Some airlines say that inexperienced passengers who do not understand the logistical issues involved are the real problem, but the appalling attitudes of staff and distinct lack of customer service skills regularly causes passenger meltdowns. In February 2014 during the Golden Week holiday mayhem, more than 2,000 delayed passengers stormed check-in counters at an airport in Henan province, smashing computers and equipment, in response to the airport's five-hour long shut-down because of snow. Henan Radio said that airport patrons were fed up not only with the delays, but the staff's attitude. Last summer, there were over two dozen fights at airports, while in March last year a British businessman recounted witnessing an elderly man being applauded by other passengers after he attacked a stewardess in response to a four hour delay. "He went completely mental and stormed up the plane and into the business class. I heard a punch and looked up and he was attacking the stewardess," Graham Fewkes told the media. "What surprised me was that passengers were applauding as the man was hitting her." Such attacks have prompted drastic measures. Hong Kong Airlines now requires its staff to undergo six hours mandatory training in Wing Chun Kung Fu, the martial art made famous by Bruce Lee. In October, a mob of passengers held an Australian pilot hostage for six hours when their flight was diverted from Beijing to Shanghai because of bad weather. Having seen the infamous traffic jams outside, they were probably afraid that they would have to make their journey by road.

Most Chinese flights are filled at least 95% and the behaviour of the passengers indicates that there are many first time fliers taking advantage of all the new aircraft in the Chinese skies. I personally gave up flying many years ago and now take advantage of the country having the world's largest rail network. I would advise most people to do the same whenever possible.

Trains

Trains cover the 182 kilometres from Hong Kong in about two hours, including a stop at Dongguan. Through trains to Guangzhou East Railway Station depart from Hong Kong at Hung Hom railway station in Kowloon and arrive in Guangzhou at the East station. Through train services are operated by Hong Kong MTR. The one-way journey price starts from 210HKD - 250HKD.

It is cheaper to take the Guangshen intercity train service (广深城际列车) from Shenzhen to Guangzhou East Railway Station. Shenzhen is right across the border from Hong Kong and thousands of people walk over the bridge between the two every day through Luohu (罗湖). Tickets can be bought at the Shenzhen Rail Station in Luohu. The one-way journey price starts from 80 RMB. Bear in mind there are now three major train stations in Guangzhou. Countless travellers have gone to the wrong station and missed their scheduled trips, so be sure of your departing station, which is specified on the ticket.

The MTR (KCR no longer exists) trains terminate at Lo Wu. Immigration and customs controls take place between

Lo Wu and Shenzhen and the foot journey between trains is now entirely undercover.

The two rail options between Hong Kong and Guangzhou are:

As above to Shenzhen then by train every 15-20 minutes to Guangzhou Dong (East) with about 25% of the trains continuing to the Guangzhou main station. Fares are 75-100 RMB and the journey time is around an hour.

Further details can be found on the MTR website: http://www.mtr.com.hk/eng/train/intro_index.html

By direct train from Hung Hom (Hong Kong) to Guangzhou East, with twelve trains each way daily. Fares are HKD210-250 and journey time is just under two hours. The through trains are more expensive and generally not faster, but may well be considered more convenient. Immigration facilities are at Guangzhou East Station and passengers are required to fill out an arrival card and go through customs. Follow the crowds out and down the escalators to the taxi terminals at the front. Do not be tempted by the various travel desks offering taxis. They will often quote visitors 200 RMB for what turns out to be a 50 RMB fare. Make sure you have your hotel written in Chinese and the address and phone number. You can copy it off any Chinese hotel website and hand to the driver. They always use a meter with the foreigners, which may have something to do with the soldiers monitoring the queues with fully automatic machine guns.

On the other side of the city, Guangzhou Railway Station (广州站) is one of the biggest in the country and has services routes that go all the way to Harbin. Metro lines 2 and 5 have a connection stop here. Here is a rare chance to see what China is undoubtedly most famous for: its enormous population. While other tourist highlights such as Tian'anmen Square are usually devoid of life, here is a large public square that perpetually teems with humanity. Certainly one of the best opportunities to visualize what a population of 1.6 billion really looks like. At Chinese New Year, this square is awash with more than 100,000 people a day, and ticket queues stretch kilometres away into the suburbs. Even at the non-peak times, being in this area is like being outside the stadium doors as a rock concert finishes and the audience pours out, and is a great place to see what a human super-organism might look like. The area has a bad reputation for crime but this is rather undeserved, especially compared to the new East Station and the central business district of Tian He, where gangs of pickpockets roam openly and arrogant motorists make the simple act of crossing the road one of the most high-risk events of your entire trip. Here at the old station, there are at least 18 kinds of uniformed security as well as patrol cars ranging from converted golf carts to oversize SUVs. Simply find a vantage point and look on in awe, as immense flows of human traffic surge endlessly by.

China Rail Expert Duncan Peattie has a very useful Quick Reference Chinese Railway Timetable available as a free .pdf download from his website.
http://www.chinatt.org

Guangzhou East Railway Station (广州东站) services routes to Hong Kong and some mainland cities. Metro line 1 ends here.

Guangzhou South Railway Station (广州南站) serves the high-speed rail network.

Although some signs are available in English, staff may not understand English, except at the Guangzhou-Kowloon counter. It is ironic that if you decide to travel back to Hong Kong by train, this is the only route in China that does not demand any form of ID from foreigners. Buying tickets domestically requires a passport at both the time of purchase and boarding, and yet buying tickets to get back to Hong Kong is a cash only transaction. There are two kiosks up on the second floor, one for Chinese

Renminbi and one for Hong Kong Dollars. There is usually a long queue at the RMB counter while the HKD counter is nearly always queue free. Trains leave every hour or so but this route is busy so try to buy tickets in advance unless you want to sit around in the station for two or three hours.

Coaches

Coach services are available to bring passengers from Hong Kong International Airport to several locations in Guangzhou. Among the destinations are recognizable landmarks like Jinan University (暨南大学) on Huangpu Avenue (黄埔大道), Garden Hotel (花园酒店) and China Hotel (中国大酒店). The trip takes about 3+ hours and costs 250 HKD. There are also cross border bus terminals throughout Hong Kong. One of the Stations is at Austin Road and Canton Road near Kowloon Park. A one way ticket costs about 100 HKD.

Many buses terminate at the Provincial Station (省汽车客运站) (145-149 Huanshi West Road 环市西路145-149号) (Metro 2 & 5 Guangzhou Railway Station Exit F1, F2, H1, H2). The station serves mostly long distance lines outside the Guangdong Province. Liuhua Station (流花站) (Metro 2 & 5 Guangzhou Railway Station Exit D4) across from Provincial Station, mostly serves nearby cities in the province. Tianhe Station (天河客运站) (633 Yanling Road 燕岭路633号) (Metro 3) services Southern and central China, reaching as far as Gansu Province. There are also many routes to cities in Guangdong. Haizhu Station (海珠客运站) (182 Nanzhou Road 南洲路182号) (Metro 2 Nanzhou Station Exit A) is located in the southern part of Haizhu, servicing major cities in the province and other Southern China provinces, including Hainan. Fangcun Station (芳村客运站) (51 Huadi Middle Avenue) (Metro 1 Kengkou Exit B) serves similar routes as the Haizhu Station. Yuexiu Nan Station (越秀南汽车站) (越秀南东园横2号) serves other destinations in the province and other provinces, it also has lines to Macau and Hong Kong. Guangzhou South (广州南汽车客运站) mainly services nearby cities. There is a bus to Lo Wu, a commonly used border crossing between Hong Kong and mainland China. The fare is 65 RMB and it runs every hour.

Ferries from Hong Kong to Guangzhou

There is a fast catamaran ferry from Hong Kong to Guangzhou, New Nansha Port (南沙港客运). The trip costs 200 HKD and takes about 75 minutes. There are also first class and VIP tickets that cost 50 HKD and 100 HKD more respectively. Ferries leave from the China Ferry Terminal on Canton Road, past the Ocean Terminal and the Marco Polo Hotel. The ferries themselves are huge and the main deck with its three to four hundred seats feels more like a football pitch than a ship. The windows at the sides are usually tinted but the unobstructed views at the front are very impressive. The only complaint that I had was the annoyingly repetitive pre-recorded safety announcements that drone on endlessly before departure, but these that easily be blocked out with a pair of headphones. This is a spectacular route overlooked by most travellers, which passes through some of the busiest shipping lanes in the world, and it is not uncommon to see the world's largest oil tankers and container ships up-close and personal. These vessels are incredible and some of the wonders of the industrial world. I personally have seen the Emma Maersk, the world's largest container ship on this route and I felt like a minnow swimming next to a blue whale in comparison. There are huge container ports, vast deep-sea drilling-rig construction docks and many other interesting sites on this route. It certainly beats the endless drab factories that line the bus and train routes to Guangzhou.

The port of arrival at Nansha is very modern and the immigration facilities are fast and efficient. Nansha is still quite a long way from the city centre, and about 1.6km south of Humen Bridge. There is no subway station at the port but there are free mini-buses that take passengers to the nearest station at Jiaomen. From here it takes about an hour on line four to Chenbeinan which in turn connects with line five, connecting to most downtown locations.

There is also a ferry service from Hong Kong international Airport to Nansha but it currently only runs on Tuesday, Thursday and Saturday. From HKIA to Nansha ranges from RMB 265 to RMB350. The official website of NS ferry http://www.nskyg.com/

The only minor annoyance that I encountered was that Nansha is not listed as a point of entry on the Public Security Bureau computer system. This can sometimes cause difficulties when registering at hotels, especially if the staff are unwilling to risk losing face by asking for confirmation.

Guangzhou Metro

Opened in 1999, the ever-growing Guangzhou Metro system covers much of the city centre. The fare ranges from 2 RMB to 12 RMB. Most of the signs and announcements are in Chinese and English. There are currently 8 lines in operation

If you are staying in Guangzhou for any length of time it is well worth purchasing a multi-purpose Ling Nan Tong - Yang Cheng Tong (岭南通-羊城通) stored value card, which can be used to pay fares in metro, bus and ferries and used for many convenience stores, public phones and vending machines. It also avoids the horrendous queues for tickets at the larger stations. Cards can be recharged at 7/11 stores along the subway and at laundry shops on the underground network. The same card can only be returned for a refund of the deposit at only one location: Gongyuanqian (Exit J) and Tiyu Xi Exit

G, and East Railway Station. (Exit HJ).

Buses

There is also a comprehensive public bus service that covers Guangzhou from end to end. It is the cheapest way to move around but can be a challenge for visitors unfamiliar with the city and the language. Bus fares are 1 RMB for the older buses and 2 RMB for the air-conditioned ones, although the older buses have been mostly retired. Information at bus stops is mostly written in Chinese, although the current stop's name is also written in either pinyin or English (not always consistent with the recorded announcement in English), and stops close to subway stations are (usually) marked with the Guangzhou Metro logo, which is handy if you are lost. On-board announcements are made in Mandarin, Cantonese and sometimes English but are usually unintelligible. Exact fare or a Yang Cheng Tong card is needed when boarding. If travelling on a quiet bus, it is advisable to signal to the driver that you wish to get off when approaching your stop by pressing the red buzzer next to the exit door or by saying "yau lok" (有落) which is Cantonese for getting off. Heavy traffic means that buses can be a very slow alternative to the subway, although trolley bus lines (Routes 101-109) are handy for exploring Liwan and Yuexiu districts.

BRT

The Bus Rapid Transit system went into service in early 2010. It is essentially a long segregated bus lane (not an elevated bus way like in Xiamen) running along the Tianhe Road and Zhongshan Avenue corridor towards the eastern suburbs. As with normal bus routes, there is almost no English at BRT stations, and only the current station name is in pinyin.

Taxis

Taxis start at 10 RMB for the first 2.6 kilometres and 2.6 RMB for each kilometre thereafter. A 50% surcharge is automatically added when the trip reaches 35 kilometres. The taxi hotline is 96900 in case you forget your valuables in a taxi. Save your receipt because it contains the taxi's identification number. Most taxi drivers do not speak English or any other foreign languages, so be sure to have the name and address of your destination written in Chinese to show your taxi driver. If your destination is not well known, have a nearby landmark included in the address, e.g. "across from the Garden Hotel."

Whilst the majority of taxis are the regular VWs and Hyundais found in almost all Chinese cities, there are an increasing number of 'London taxis' on the streets of Guangzhou (which comes as no surprise as the latest generation of London black cabs are built by Geely Motors in China). They are wheelchair accessible and can carry up to six passengers.

Self Drive

In 2008 Guangzhou announced that the number of cars on its roads had reached 1 million (New York has 2 million). There are now 16 million residents and 2.4 million vehicles. The metropolis has several auto factories, and aspires to be China's Detroit. Last year, 180,000 new vehicles hit the city's roads. That is nearly 500 a day. After Shanghai, Beijing and Guiyang, Guangzhou has become the fourth Chinese city to limit car sales in a bid to reduce traffic jams and improve air quality. Traffic jams in Guangzhou have worsened recently. Average speeds during rush hours have slowed to 20 km per hour and are expected to become even slower. Growing motor vehicle emissions have also worsened the city's air quality. Driving in Guangzhou is an extremely daunting and potentially dangerous option. However, it is common in Guangzhou to rent a car that comes with a driver.

Motorcycles

Petrol powered motorcycles are banned in the city centre but you will often see electric bikes outside subway stations where the drivers actively call out for customers. Fares generally start at 10 RMB for foreigners and are a convenient way of avoiding the stifling summer heat on selected routes, such as in the new embassy district just south of the river.

15 CHINA POST OFFICE

Do not overlook the regular China Post Office as valuable shipping service, especially if you are sending home, low volume, high-margin items. Although there are some limitations, generally speaking the Post Office service in China is excellent and an absolute bargain. Staff will first inspect everything that you wish to send to ensure that there are no restricted items. These include the usual dangerous chemicals, explosives etc., but also CDs and DVDs. Replica firearms such as lighters and decorative pieces will not be accepted, but in reality very few products will be rejected. Packaging is all done on site, with sturdy cardboard cases in a variety of sizes available at minimum cost. The staff use quality own-brand sellotape and usually have a plastic banding machine for added security. Pens are available at the desk but it is handy to bring along your own marker pen for writing the address on the box. The Chinese write the sender's address in the top left hand corner and then the addressee in the lower right. Staff will require you to write a sender's address on the form and it is handy to have a business card of your hotel for this purpose. The staff will invariably have some form of packing materials for use inside the parcel but there is no harm in bringing your own. Bubble wrap is cheap and widely available and far superior to the excess card and polystyrene that will likely be available at the Post Office. Do not use Chinese newspaper to wrap individual items as a law still exists that forbids the international mailing of Chinese printed media. This is a hangover from the Mao era when authorities worried that Chinese newspapers might be used by overseas agencies for espionage. Obviously they have never read the propaganda drivel that is a Chinese newspaper. Note also that writing in red ink is not allowed when addressing envelopes and parcels.

There are three forms of shipping, air, air and surface combination and surface. Air takes between a week and two weeks to overseas destinations. Air and surface combined will take a month or more. The official time stated for surface is three months but I find that parcels for the States usually take between a month and six weeks. Insurance is a available at a cost of 1 RMB per 1000 RMB insured but of all the hundreds, maybe thousands of parcels that I have sent out of China, I do not recall losing a single one. This may not however be the case when sending to non-western destinations however. I have heard that parcels to South East Asia regularly go missing. Because post offices are so well priced in China, there are often long queues for service. Avoid lunch times and weekends and be patient, knowing that Chinese rarely deviate from the rules, no matter how stringent or time consuming they may be. Simply take a few extra moments to relish the bargain that you are purchasing, especially compared to the outrageous postal charges in the west.

China Post Offices, with their striking green logo can be found in all districts. In Guangzhou the main post office is directly next to the train station, but there are dozens others dispersed at useful points throughout the city. Opening times are usually 8:00am to 6:00pm during the week. Some smaller offices and post offices in remote areas may be closed on weekends.

Some individual offices are better than others. I have never had any problems whatsoever at the Dongshankou Branch on Shuiyin Lu. Others are less reliable. I specifically remember having lots of problems at the Wushan branch when trying to send a box of one-sixth scale GI Joe/Action Man type collectibles. Included in the parcel were a few tiny miniature rifles from the WWII era. The staff insisted that I could not send firearms through the post and I had one helluva time trying to explain that these were only scale models. Eventually they called down the branch manager from her office. I will never forget the sheer idiocy of this women trying to fire the triggers on these tiny plastic models.

Some items may be confiscated by Chinese customs if you do manage to get them past the beady eyes of the Post Office staff. These include the following:

Over 4,000 varieties of plants that are on China's endangered list (that is 1/5 of the country's entire plants species)

Chinese currency

DVDs: technically, it is not just DVDs. It also includes CDs, and magnetic tape.

Meat and animal products

Aerosol spray cans or pressurized bottles. Due to dramatic and frequent changes in temperature and air pressure during the actual shipping process, these sorts of items can easily burst, potentially harming package handlers and recipients.

Nail polish may seem a bit random, but nail polish is considered a "combustible product" by the post office

Alcoholic Beverages

Tobacco and tobacco products: This not only includes cigarettes but also lighters too.

Counterfeit Items: mailing fake watches, bags, sunglasses, etc. through the post can be a risky operation – and will most likely result in you never seeing those items again.

I have to admit that over the years I have managed to get away with most of these, depending on who is at the Post Office at the time. Sometimes I have even received a note inserted by China Customs saying that the package has been opened and inspected.

16 VISAS

Visitors to mainland China must acquire their visas in advance. A passport with at least 6 months' validity and two blank pages is a minimum requirement. Applications typically take 3 to 5 working days to process, although the payment of extra fees can speed this up to as little as 1 day when applying in person. "L" (tourist) visas are valid for between 2 weeks and 3 months depending upon political events in China at the time. These include high level meetings such as the National Party Congress in Beijing. Double-entry tourist visas are also available. One passport photograph on a blue background is required, as well as one for any child travelling on a parent's passport.

Apply to your nearest consulate and your visit must begin within 90 days of the date of issue. Applying for a visa requires completion of an application form that can be downloaded from many consular websites or acquired by mail. Visas are valid for the whole country, although some small areas require an extra permit from the local police. Temporary restrictions may also be placed, sometimes for years at a time, on areas where there is unrest, and a further permit may be required. This is currently the case with Tibetan areas where, until recently, travellers were required to form groups before entering the region. In general, do not mention Tibet or Xinjiang on your visa application, or it may be refused. Some consulates indicate that sight of an airline ticket or itinerary is required, or that you give proof of sufficient funds, or that you must be travelling with a group. These regulations can usually be temporarily be circumvented by local travel agencies who are skilled at supplying all the correct temporary documentation for a small fee.

Once inside China, single-entry tourist visas only can usually be extended for a maximum of thirty days at the Aliens Entry-Exit department of the Public Security Bureau (PSB) in most towns and cities. Extensions within China now typically take five working days to process. The PSB in Guangzhou is like a zoo, with angry foreigners constantly frustrated by grim, robotic officers .Look out for the riot shields and helmets as evidence of how often these clowns enrage applicants so badly that they lose it completely. The authorities here make many more demands than their counterparts in cities favoured by tourists. Requirements in Guangzhou require at least proof of funds and often a great deal more.

A complete list of all Chinese embassies and consulates overseas can be found at the Chinese foreign ministry's website: www.fmprc.gov.cn/eng (or various mirror sites around the world). Click on "Missions Overseas."

Another option is to obtain a visa from an agency in Hong Kong. Depending on your passport, a 30 day single or double entry is available for around 1000 Hong Kong Dollars. Email them directly for the latest prices and application requirements.

Forever Bright Trading Limited.
Rm. 916-917, New Mandarin Plaza Tower B, 14 Science

Museum Rd., T.S.T. East, Kowloon, HK.
九龍尖東科學館道14號新文華中心B座9樓916-917室
Contact: 852 2369-3188
Fax: 852 2312-2989
E-mail: fbtravel@fbt-chinavisa.com.hk
8:30am ~ 18:30pm (Monday – Friday)
8:30am ~ 13:30pm (Saturday)
Closed on Sundays and Holiday
Directions from Tsim Sha Tsui MTR station: Take exit P1 towards the Nikko Hotel. Nearby is the Duty Free Shop in the China Chem Plaza. New Mandarin Plaza is just next door.
From Hung Hom train station: Take the exit D and follow the pedestrian footbridge all the way onto Science Museum Road where the New Mandarin Plaza is located.

Japan Travel Agency
Room 509-513, 5/F, East Ocean Centre, 98 Granville Road, Tsim Sha Tsui East, Kowloon, Hong Kong
Contact: 852 2368-7767 Fax: 852 2724-8551
8:30am ~ 18:00pm (Monday – Friday)
Closed on Saturdays, Sundays and public holidays
Email: visa_hkg@jta.biz
Directions from Tsim Sha Tsui MTR Station: Exit B2 (Cameron Road Exit), walk down the Cameron Road until you find Park Hotel at the left hand corner. From the Park Hotel, you can see the foot-bridge at your left hand side. Cross the footbridge and walk 20m to the East Ocean Centre.
Directions from KCR Hung Hom Station: Exit-D from the main concourse. Pass the taxi stand and turn right opposite HKG coliseum and walk down between the concourse and the Coliseum to the pedestrian underpass. Once inside turn quickly left for only 10 metres, and enter the pedestrian footbridge to TST EAST with the Cross-Harbour-Tunnel on your left hand side. Bear left, go past the basketball court and down the stairs. Look for Circle-

K on your left and 7-Eleven on your right. Look for Genki Sushi and HSBC bank on the right. This is East Ocean Centre Building.

A third option, no longer as popular as it once was is the Grand Profit International Travel Agency, 711AA, seventh floor, New East Ocean Centre, 9 Science Museum Rd., Tsimshatsui
Contact: 852 2723-3288

Hong Kong visas

U.S., Canadian, Australian, and New Zealand citizens, and those of most other developed nations, are granted 90-day stays free on arrival. British citizens are granted 180 days. Passports should be valid for 1 month longer than the planned return date. In theory, proof of sufficient funds and an onward ticket may be demanded, but this request is almost unheard of.

17 MAPS

In order to keep the costs of this book down to a minimum, I decided not to include location maps in this book. In the internet age there is now a plethora of interactive map services available on line.

Thanks to the Chinese Great Firewall, Google Maps is generally unavailable in China unless you have a strong VPN service. The easiest way around this is to access Google Maps through one of the major hotel booking sites. For example, the following page at booking.com (http://www.booking.com/city/cn/guangzhou.html#map _closed) offers a large map of Guangzhou that is not much different in practical terms from the original Google version.

China does have its own on-line map services but unfortunately, the largest, such as Baidu and QQ do not have English language versions. For a Chinese equivalent to Google Streetview, the website http://gz.city8.com/ is an interesting locally produced alternative, although at the moment it is only available in Chinese.

Sogou (http://map.sogou.com/#) also has a local equivalent of Google Maps but again is only available in Chinese.

Better than both of these is a website called lbs.amap.com.

Type the URL http://lbs.amap.com/api/javascript-api/example/a/0106-2/

You will see three small blue rectangles with Chinese writing at the bottom right hand corner of the page. The first changes the map descriptions to English, the second to Chinese and English and the last to Chinese only. Maps within China are reasonably up-to-date, especially in the bigger cities, although overseas coverage is pretty worthless, so it is probably better to go back to Google Maps once you are back on the other side of the Great Firewall.

18 TRAVELLING BEYOND GUANGZHOU

A business trip to Guangzhou is a great excuse to enjoy an extended stay and see some other parts of the country. Most of the big cities are quite similar to modern metropolises the world over. It is nature and spectacular vistas where China really excels.

Guangdong province certainly has some interesting locations, but most of these are better read about than actually visited. These include the New South China Mall (新华南 Mall) in Dongguan and Hallstatt in Huizhou.

In 2001, Dongguan's richest man, Hu Guirong, kicked off one of the largest commercial retail projects in the world - South China Mall. Today it still stands empty and derelict. There is no train, no subway, and the place was built without any highway off-ramps

The Chinese Hallstatt (广东惠州山寨奥地利村庄哈尔斯塔特) is a direct copy of the famous Austrian hamlet of the same name. The town was developed by Minmetals Land Limited Company. Staying true to China's wanton disregard for intellectual property rights, the town is a near-verbatim copy of the original in Austria. While at first there were some hard feelings from the actual Hallstatters (Hallstattanians?), they were eventually won over (likely with a liberal dose of cash filled hongbaos). Even the Mayor of Hallstatt, Alexander Scheutz, flew in to take part in the opening ceremony in June 2012. The whole place remains a series of concrete shells with very few visitors, partly because it is so difficult to find.

Along with disappointing let-downs such as Danxia and Kaiping, most of Guangdong province is probably best avoided. Here instead are three locations that are further afield and far more rewarding.

Jingdezhen 景德镇

The English word "china" probably derives from Jingdezhen's former name, Changnan. The place got its big break in the first year in Jingde Reign of Song dynasty (1004–07), when the potters of the town, picked up a juicy commission from the Zhen Zong emperor. The royal court decreed that local artisans stamp their bowls and vases with the wording "Made during the Jingde Reign" printed on the bottom of every piece. Hence the city assumed the name of its imperial patron "Jingde Zhen." Porcelain now runs deep in Jingdezhen's history. The layer of discarded porcelain shards and kiln debris under its streets is said to be 9m (30 ft.) thick in places.

Industrialization of the area, which employed around half the town's workforce, soon stripped the hills bare and enough coal was fired to turn the skies black. Just 10 years ago, mass-production kilns began to be converted from coal to gas. The air is much better now and even the porcelain quality has improved thanks to this change in technology.

If you are still in shopping mode from your Guangzhou adventures, Jingdezhen can be a lot of fun. There are a number of museums such as the Porcelain Culture Exhibition, with its workshops and enormous duck's-egg-shaped kiln, one of Jingdezhen's oldest, but far more interesting than all the museums put together are the thousands of porcelain shops that fill the city. The North Bus Station is surrounded by wholesale shops. But I prefer the artisan studios just to the south of Renmin Square where the large five-floor ceramics market showcases some very creative artists among the mass-produced stuff. Even more interesting are the back streets behind Zhejiang Lu near the train station. Here you will find the more exotic lines such as the Cultural Revolution reproductions, where the Red Guards stand atop kneeling intellectuals wearing dunce caps and placards, with slogans such as 'Kill the Capitalist'. Coolies dragging back-breaking carts of pots and plates are a common sight. Expect to see everything here from faux antique phones to porcelain weighing scales. Poison bottles make especially good gifts and look out for the Red Leaf Brand which the government uses as gifts for visiting foreign heads of state. Rail services are much less common than you might expect for its central location. Nanchang and Jiujiang, both best reached by express bus from Jingdezhen, have far more trains.

If you are looking for a break from commerce, then the region encompassing the provinces of Yunnan, and Guangxi, is home to some of China's most spectacular mountain scenery. As the Yunnan-Guizhou plateau in the south-east gives way to the Himalayan mountain range in north west Yunnan , the scenery changes from the famed limestone hills of eastern Guangxi to the awesome 5,000m-high glacier peaks of the Jade Dragon Snow Mountain range. Three of Asia's mighty rivers—the Salween, the Mekong, and the Yangtze - cut parallel paths all within 150km of each other in the northwest mountains before they flow their separate ways, creating in their passage some of the most breathtaking gorges and lush river valleys in the country.

Yangshuo 阳朔

65km south of Guilin, is now a Mecca for backpackers, but has long been a geomancer's delight. Here the vast landscape is reduced to a garden scale, nature in microcosm, where hills, mountains, oceans, and rivers are reduced to rocks, karsts, streams, and pools. Set amid an awesome cluster of limestone pinnacles - a zigzag, serrated skyline superior even to that of Manhattan - Yangshuo is more beautiful, less expensive, and significantly less crowded than Guilin. With its inexpensive hostels and Western-style cafés, some foreigners have been known to stay for months, sometimes even years.

The train route from Guilin to Guangzhou is a flagship journey for overseas tourists and so the staff are hand-picked and the carriages are spotless. If you want to try the comforts of a Chinese train, then this is one of the best routes to choose. There is even a "special soft sleeper" class, consisting of just two bunks with their own private bathroom for 700 RMB. Apart from the Wholesale Carving Market, Guilin is probably best avoided. Taxis from Guilin will make the trip in an hour at a cost of around 300 RMB. If heading straight to Yangshuo, call ahead and your hotel can arrange a taxi for around 200 RMB.

The Li River cruise from Guilin to Yangshuo remains

one of the top river journeys in the world. The 83km stretch between the two towns affords some of the country's most breathtaking scenery as the river snakes gracefully through tall karst mountains, gigantic bamboo sprays, and picturesque villages - sights that have inspired countless poets and painters for generations. With so many karst hills and caves around the area, Yangshuo has become outdoor sports centre, especially for rock climbing, with around a hundred climbing circuits. Companies like Terratribes organize adventure sports trips in the area including caving, rafting and kayaking. Magnolia Hotel is one of the best choices of accommodations, a great-value boutique hotel run by an Australian entrepreneur who also owns a selection of great local eateries including Café China and Pure Lotus Vegetarian Restaurant.

Dali, Lijiang and Shangri La 大理 丽江 香格里拉

The trifecta of Dali, Lijiang and Shangri La are some of the most popular destinations in this region and travel is a lot less arduous than it used to be. Dali (大理) 392km NW of Kunming, is located in a mountain valley at an elevation of 1,948m. It is sunny year-round, though winter nights can be chilly. The express way from Kunming has brought the nine hour journey down to just over four hours. Back in the 1980s, this route took a good two days, although for Marco Polo it was nearly two weeks. The trains here are excellent with numerous overnight sleeper services. Old town Dali, with its 9m-high battlements, dates from the Ming dynasty (1368–1644), but the current wall was restored and extended only in 1998. In one of the villages nearby, the Linden Cultural Centre is definitely one of the top three places to stay in all of China. The Centre is intended as a sort of cultural retreat and boasts sweeping views of Xizhou's rice fields. The Lindens deal in Asian antiquities and contemporary Chinese art at their gallery in Wisconsin, and have an impressive selection of their collection on display at the Centre. The gardens are especially relaxing, the library makes most Chinese public libraries look sad, and the rooms themselves are filled with endless little details that transform a regular stay into a genuine experience.

A side trip to the Tea Horse Road town of Shaxi (沙溪) to see the forest covered hills of Shibaoshan is always a popular option. The Baoxiang Temple hangs spectacularly but precariously on the cliff face with a colony of three hundred or so wild macaques that make the steep inclines look like child's play. You might even want to take some fruit with you for these guys. In fact, I always have a few carrots or apples with me for the many goats, cows and donkeys that I meet around the valley.

Lijiang (丽江) was hit by an earthquake in 1996 and became a UNESCO World Heritage town in 1999. The old town, with its cobblestone streets, gurgling streams, and Naxi architecture is located on the road to Tibet in a region widely regarded as being one of the most beautiful in the world. At an elevation of 2,146 metres, it has a pleasant year round climate and offers a plethora of fascinating side trips including Tiger Leaping Gorge and Jade Dragon Snow Mountain that can easily take up to a week or more of your time. Lijiang has a pleasant climate year-round with average temperatures in the spring, summer, and fall. Lijiang also has a vast array of accommodation, from traditional Naxi courtyard guest houses to up scale resorts.These range from the budget priced Garden Inn, through to the mid range Bivou, and the newly opened boutique Arro Khampa at the higher end of the scale.

Just over 100 miles north of of Lijiang, the Tibetan town of Zhongdian was officially renamed Shangri La 2002. Although the Ancient Town was all but destroyed in a devastating fire in 2012, it remains a world apart from the rest of homogeneous Han China. The locals are colourfully dressed and the streets are filled with exotic looking Gelugpa (yellow hat sect) monks. When night falls tourists to join in the giant carousels that form the Tibetan folk dance Guozhuang that are often comprised of over a thousand people. For a once in a lifetime experience Caravane-liotard organises multi-day horse treks with a dedicated team of wranglers and horses up in to the reaches of the Himamlayan Foothills with luxury tents. A more reasonable option for all of the Yunnan locations is kiwi guide, Keith Lyons (Tel:13769001439) and his lovable highland collie, Lassie. Keith was here as an NGO just after the quake and knows the area like the back of his hand. Lassie loves hiking and will jump at the chance to take visitors to Haba Snow Mountain or Stone Mountain Village.

SECTION TWO

WHOLESALE MARKETS

1 ANTIQUES MARKETS

Yuansheng Xijie 加和饰品城

The open-market area of Yuansheng Xijie is bordered by four main historical thoroughfares, Kangwang Lu, Changshou Xi Lu, Wenchang Bei Lu and Longjin Zhong Lu, all in the Liwan District. It is from this area that all the domestic tourist-town shops source their so-called antique souvenirs. Whether they are actually genuine antiques is open to question but there certainly is plenty of selection.

When shopping in these areas, some vendors will try to convince you that an item is very old and very valuable. When you explain that you are not interested in anything old, because it is illegal for you to take antiques home with you, they will likely quickly shift gears to say that the items are not really old, after all, but just made to look old. At this and many other markets, I noticed people buffing their merchandise and doing nasty things with urine to put a nice patina on the porcelain to give it the aged look. Antiques "created while you wait"!

The most obvious entrance to this vast labyrinth of market stalls is just north of the Hualin International Building, marked with a traditional Chinese gate that leads right into the heart of the action. The gate is made from wood and stone with a roof of green tiles. The steps lead down below nine carved characters that read "源胜陶瓷玉石工艺街." This route leads directly through the market and out onto Tianliao Gudao (田料古道) which emerges on Wenchang Lu. Inside the market is a warren of tiny cramped alleyways, often as old as the goods being sold and with exotic names such as Hexi Tongxin Er Xiang (荷溪通津二巷) and Xingguan Li (兴光里). Expect to see all kinds of strangeness, from clocks and woodcarvings to swords and poison bottles.

Address: Kangwang Lu 康王中路

Wenchang Lu Antiques Market 文昌陶瓷玉石工艺市场

As well as all the small market stalls, there are at least two large market buildings here that have been populated by antiques vendors. The first and oldest of these is the Antiques Market (文昌陶瓷玉石工艺市场) on Wenchang Beilu. At the top end of the road, look for the public toilets on the left hand side. The market is opposite number 279 and looks extremely run down. Inside there are two floors of old swords, classic watches and highly suspect porcelain. Apart from the permanent stores, there are a number of temporary vendors pitched out on the veranda, displaying their wares on laid out tarpaulins.

Address: Wenchang Beilu 广州市荔湾区文昌北路

Xiguan Antique City 西关古玩城

Just south of here is the second and much newer Antiques Market (元邦工艺城), sometimes also known as Xiguan Antique City (西关古玩城). This is the only antique market approved by cultural relic management departments but I am not really convinced that counts for much. It has three floors and over 160 sellers, and attracts dealers from across the province. Antiques on offer range from the Tang Dynasty era up until the Republic of China era. The area is well-known for antique collectors who mainly deal in old pottery and porcelain, famous scripts and paintings, the four treasures of traditional study (writing brush, ink stick, ink slab and paper) and jade articles. To put it politely, not all the antiques available are originals, so it will challenge your appraising abilities.

Address: Yaohua Dongjie, Wenchang Beilu 广州市荔湾区文昌北路耀华东街(近文昌北路)

Getting there: Take the subway to Changshou Lu, exit on to Changshou Lu, take the first left onto Wenchang Lu.

Guangdong Arts House 广东艺海堂

On the Kangwang Lu side of this quadrangle, the authorities have built a number of huge mall buildings to house the exploding jade trade. The oldest of these is the Huicheng Garden Complex, opposite the Guangzhou Elizabeth Women's Hospital. Look out for the unusual carvings outside of stylised camels and rhinos, or the English sign for the Dong Hong Hotel (惠城花园). This is a run down mall that has seen much better days, with as many porcelain dealers as there are jade carvers. Even so, at least 70% of the stores are now abandoned.

Address: 181, Kangwang Lu 康王中路181号

Directions: Look out for a large run down, brown glass exterior. There are few English signs, so look instead for the Dong Hong Guest House (东宏宾馆) which is clearly marked. At the ground floor entrance is a sign for the Guangdong Arts House (广东艺海堂) behind the abstract sculptured elephant.

Collectibles Markets

There were until recently two main collectibles markets in Guangzhou. Unfortunately, as well as being the most fascinating, they are also the most challenging of buying environments. Vendors here are especially hardened, and dealing with them will likely be some of the most frustrating interchanges that you will experience. These markets receive far less foreign visitors than the various commodity markets, and many of the stall holders are much older, often with prejudices that date back to times when China was a still a very closed country. I personally love seeing what these markets sell, but hate dealing with the vendors. Like a giant flea-market full of oriental exotica, browsing here is enthralling, especially if like me, you have a strong interest in Chinese history and geography. The downsides are that unlike sales people in the regular markets, these vendors have had few dealings with western business people and therefore see them as stereotypes rather than real people. They tend to think that we are all ultra-wealthy, and put ridiculous prices on items that only a clueless millionaire would pay. Almost zero English is spoken here, and so they are nervous about communication, often refusing to even make an attempt, rather than risk losing face in front of their peers. Another problem is that due to the unending turmoil and destruction that been visited upon Chinese society in the last one hundred years, there simply are far fewer collectibles here than in western countries, where recent history has been far more stable, even uneventful in comparison. So much of China's cultural legacy has been burned, destroyed, looted and pillaged, that there is honestly not a great deal of authentic material that has survived. Civil wars, cultural revolutions, great famines, all of these events have ensured that many items just did not make it though to today. In addition, much of their recent output has been practical necessities, rather than luxury items that become collectibles over time. Then of course, there are cultural misunderstandings. What we in the West would consider junk or garbage, might in fact be so rare here in China that the price asked might seem insulting in our eyes.

Haizhu　　　Lu　　　Collectors'　　　Market
广州市纵原邮币卡收藏品中心

The larger of the two Guangzhou collectors markets is situated on the first three floors of the Zhongyuan Building on Haizhu Lu. The beginning of the street contains a handful of stamp and currency dealers to let you know that you are heading in the right direction. The ground floor is filled mainly with numismatists and philatelists. Obviously this is a very specialist market and you really need to be an expert here to be able to turn a profit. That being said, the collectors market in China is certainly one of the fastest growing and so this could be a very profitable business. One only has to look at how the prices of Chinese art and antique porcelain have jumped to incredible levels in the last few years, to see the potential here. I do not claim to be an expert here, but my own limited research has shown that stamps and old money related to the province of Yunnan seem to be the best performers on eBay. Perhaps if you can find good deals on those items down here in Guangzhou, then you might do well back in the States or in Europe. For more details on China's burgeoning stamp market, please see the special section below. In one corner is a shop that specialises in beautifully artistic, antique stock certificates. In 1905 for example, the underground resistance movement T'ung-Meng Hui issued bonds to raise money for military development. As a member of the secret society, Sun Yat-Sen signed on the bonds and affixed his seals, which has increased their historical value in recent years. Less important certificates still make wonderful decorative items in Chinese offices and studies. Other dealers here specialise in coins, phone cards and even valuation guides. The latter do well abroad, but obviously only if they an English and unfortunately, here the vast majority are in Chinese.

Up some dirty escalators that have not functioned since Deng Xiao Ping was alive, the second floor holds a more eclectic range of goods. A number of shops specialise in ration tickets, while others trade in Communist Party medals and badges. Much of the floor is taken up with huge piles of printed matter that has been rescued from the garbage. Occasionally I have found books in here that have been useful for travelling in the rest of the country, but most of it might have well stayed in the rubbish. Among all this paper ephemera there are old magazines, advertising materials, letters and postcards. It has been picked over in great detail, and just about anything of real value has been removed, but this will not stop vendors quoting offensively outrageous prices if they see that something catches your eye. In any other country most of this stuff would have been tossed out for recycling, even by charity shops and thrift stores.

One exceptional shop on this floor is a small, cramped booth that deals mainly in Communist propaganda posters (欣欣藏品 Room 208A contact: 赖小姐 13533849381.) Most of her supplies are destined for obsessive French collectors, but she has amazing domestic resources and is always hunting down quality new examples. Of all the items for sale in the collectibles market, these are my absolute favourites. Heavy on Socialist Realism, they feature huge, brightly coloured images of leaders such as Mao, surrounded by adoring schoolchildren or contented workers. Each one beautifully portrays a fantasy world that only existed in the minds of the rulers, and are therefore very collectible both at home and overseas. Unfortunately, demand completely outstrips supply of these wonderful items and so it is very difficult to find a bargain. Collectors are lined up all over the world, just waiting to pay exorbitant prices for the very best examples. Even so, if I was going to seriously invest in a form of Chinese art, I think this would be the area that I would choose, as these are examples that I know will continue to appreciate over time.

Propaganda posters of the Cultural Revolution (文化大革命, Wenhua Dageming, 1966-1976) were the mouth piece of a mass campaign of enormous dimensions. After the foundation of the People's Republic of China in 1949, posters became an important means of getting the message across from the Communist Party to the people. These posters were probably the most influential means of propaganda. This is hardly surprising considering that especially in the rural areas, most people were illiterate. Radio or television did not exist for the majority of the population in the 50s, 60s and were still rather rare in the 70s. Posters were easy and cheap to produce. The total output has been estimated at several billion over a period of thirty to forty years.

Some of the earlier examples are bucolic scenes of agricultural efficiency. The colourfully dressed minorities were shown celebrating newly installed irrigation projects or agricultural machinery. These are my favourites and in the past I have helped guest-house owners purchase examples to decorate their premises. With the beginning of the Cultural Revolution in 1966, the scenes became aggressive and ugly, with many faces expressing hate showing up. Even the children are shown with fierce and hateful looks, as little grown-ups who actively take part in hunting down the "Four Old Evils" (old ideas, old culture, old customs and old habits).

The posters were designed by professional artists and artisans trained at China's academies and publishing houses. They were produced by nationalized companies like Shanghai Peoples' Art Publishing House. The artistic roots for the designs came from three major sources. First to be mentioned is the so-called social realism that had developed in the Communist Soviet Union. Another important root was the old, traditional Chinese folk art prints, known as New Year Prints.

Chinese propaganda posters have developed into a serious section of art collecting - comparable to art works from the period of Russian Realism. Prices for posters are still modest. For rare examples several hundred dollars is a common price. Even now fakes do exist. It may sound a bit ironic, but this is always a sign of a sound and interesting art market. If you want to get first-hand information about fake Chinese propaganda posters, the web site of Chris To, an expert collector from Hong Kong is a good place to start. Next to Chris To, Stefan Landsberger should also be mentioned. He has an outstanding web site with a plethora of information and images from his collection. Most of the value criteria used for art prints, are also applied to Chinese propaganda posters. An early edition counts more than a later one.

Serious collectors try to describe their objects with the publishing house and with the date of publication.

Up on the third floor, a few scattered shops sell more assorted junk and cultural paraphernalia. One specialises in militaria, another in old phonographic recordings, while the rest have a similar stock of what can only charitably be described as ephemera. Most of it is simply paper junk. Worth a browse, but probably not worth buying.

Address: 288, Haizhu Zhong Lu 海珠中路288号

Directions: From the Ximenkou subway station, take exit A, head east along Zhongshan Liu Lu and take the first right onto Haizhu Zhong Lu. The Collectibles Market is about a hundred metres down on the left.

Yingyuan Tower Collectibles Market 顺邮坊邮币卡市场

The second collectors market over on Yingyuan Lu (应元路), just off Xiaobei Lu, which was much more focussed on stamps and currency, has now closed down and relocated. Up on the second floor of the Yingyuan Tower, hidden away from view of the road, dealers hoarded vast quantities of commemorative coin sets and first day postage covers. Seeking out bargains here for later resale in the West was always a real challenge. To most western collectors, the majority of this stuff is simply too exotic. The adventurous might want to try dabbling in silver pandas, but make sure that you have a testing kit with you as fake items are just as prevalent here as they are in the rest of the country. Many of the dealers have now relocated to a new mall (广州宝贝城藏品) opposite Guangzhou Museum on Yuexiu Zhong Lu (越秀中路60号), near Peasant Movement Institute (Nong Jiang Suo 农讲所). As of yet, the place has not really gained any traction, and Haizhu Zhong Lu is still a better bet if you are interested in collectibles.

Stamps as Collectibles

One reason that the dealers in the wholesale market are so arrogant and condescending might well be the relative vicinity of Hong Kong. As everybody knows, there is an enormous wealth gap in China and most of the riches are funnelled into the cities. Of these, Hong Kong is by far the most attractive and is a magnet for newly wealthy Chinese. It is estimated that the very first thing that 80 percent of the country's newly-minted millionaires want to do is emigrate, and Hong Kong is the perfect stepping stone. It is for this reason that there are unimaginable amounts of Mainland money sloshing around Central, Kowloon and the New Territories. The real estate market bubbles and bursts on a regular basis, and the stock market is probably more rigged than the casinos in Macau. This means that a great deal of money flows out into alternative investments. Apart from antiques and art, another popular choice among the Chinese is stamps.

China's first stamps were printed by the British colonial postal system in Shanghai in 1865. British colonists wishing to send letters home were the target audience for these stamps, and their adoption spurred other Chinese municipalities with large international communities to quickly follow suit. The country's first national stamps, the "Haiguan Dalong" or "Large Dragons" series, were created in 1878 for the Chinese Imperial Customs service, run by an Englishman named Robert Hart, who organized the Chinese Imperial Post in 1897. His service ended with a stamp celebrating the first anniversary of Emperor Hsuan T'ung's ascension to the throne in 1909.

During the Japanese occupation of China in the 1930s, complex underground postal systems developed among networks of Chinese communists, who printed many small runs of crudely designed stamps. After the Japanese were defeated in 1945, China's postal service was still not centrally organized, so most stamps were designed only for specific regions. These stamps generally featured portraits of Mao Zedong or patriotic military emblems. The first official stamps for the National Republic of China were also printed in 1945, some featuring Sun Yat-sen, the rebel leader who helped depose the Manchu dynasty. A single pair of 1941 Sun Yat-sen stamps recently sold for HK$5.5 million ($709,000) in Hong Kong. Before a standing-room-only crowd in the auction room, as well as hundreds of mail, telephone and internet bidders from around the world, the sale was a clear example that unprecedented economic growth of Mainland China had brought a whole new group of collectors to serious Chinese stamp collecting. Price increases of 300% over the past few years have not been uncommon.

During the 1950s and '60s, Chinese stamps most commonly portrayed communist heroes and symbols, like the popular series inscribed with quotes from Mao's "Little Red Book." Some of the most interesting communist-era stamps are from a 40-part series depicting poses for a radio gymnastics program that all citizens were expected to practice. Another popular set among collectors is the 1964 series of traditional tree peonies, long cultivated for the Chinese aristocracy.

What happens when economies open up and there's an expanding middle class is that people start buying their stamps back? A lot of stamps from China, the Middle East and India are all leaving Europe and going back to the countries they originated from and when this happens, prices rise. Of course, Mainland collectors are not regular philatelists and they have very little interest in perennial favourites such as Kangaroos, Penny Blacks or USA Zeppelins.Stamps with Chinese language inscriptions are the main preference, but certainly not country overprints from Germany, Britain, the USA, and all those other despised colonials that made them suffer 'one hundred years of shame and humiliation.' Very few of China's newly wealthy are educated. Even the Standing Committee of the Politburo, the very highest circle of government only accepted its very first university degree holder in 2013. The accumulation of wealth in China has more to do with connections and corruption than intellectual ability, just as it is in the rest of the world. That said, Chinese investors dislike complicated specialist material. To them the Cultural Revolution is easy to follow, and is now old enough to not be sensitive, so it has become a very popular era to collect. Supply is very limited of the key pieces, and demand is sky high. Some collectors estimate that the key pieces from this period are likely to double or even treble in value in the space of just one year. Two distinct groups of collectors seem to be emerging. The first focuses on "new China" (post 1949) stamps, while the second hold a fascination for the Cultural Revolution, ironically a time when stamp collecting was actually banned by the Party. Stamps from this period are extremely popular because of the great political story behind them. Since the death of Chairman Mao in 1976 the pastime has gained considerably in popularity, with the country now boasting around twenty-five million philatelists.

On particularly famous stamp with an error printing, issued in 1968 now has an estimated value of nearly half a million US dollars. The stamp features a red map of China imprinted with the golden words "The Whole Country is Red", plus a picture of a worker, a farmer and a soldier holding the "Selected Works of Chairman Mao." The face value of the stamp is 8 fen (1 US cent). The stamp was originally issued for less than half day. An editor of SinoMaps Press found that the map on the stamp was not accurate and reported it to the Ministry of Post and Telecommunications. As a result, all Chinese post offices were forced to stop selling the stamp and return all the copies. Only a small quantity of the stamp went to private collections.

Even more valuable is the unique 1968 Mao's Inscription to Japanese Worker Friends corner block of four, which recently sold for a staggering HK$8,970,000 (US$1,151,630), setting a new world record for a Chinese stamp lot at auction. The record-setting block, bought by an unidentified collector in Hong Kong, features a design known as Mao Zedong's 1968 Inscription to Japanese Worker Friends. They were never issued, because the Japanese government, worried that the revolutionary message from Mao would cause Japanese people to riot, objected to Beijing. Stamps are now important cultural icons and treasures - just like art and hold a special place in Chinese culture

For a good overview of philately in China, have a look at this page which answers many frequently asked questions.
http://www.fidelitytc.com/faq.htm

Wende Lu Artworks Street 文德路文化艺术品街

This part of Guangzhou is currently undergoing significant redevelopment, with many of the older properties being demolished and then replaced by monster high-rises. Even so there are still a number of artwork outlets featuring paintings that are popular on the domestic market. These range from calligraphy and classical Chinese mountain and water paintings (Shan Sui) to oil reproductions of famous western artists. Other local handicrafts available include Foshan ceramics and gong-fu tea sets from Shantou.

Some of the newer buildings include the Guangzhou Antique Store (广州文物总店), the Culture and Arts Expo Trade Centre, the Oriental Wende Plaza and the Guangzhou Cultural Relics Store (广州市文物总店) which house ancillary services such as the Guangfu Culture Research Centre, antique identification services and auction sale-rooms. Opened in 1960, this is one of China's official top four cultural relic stores, and is comprised of two sections, the Yueya Hall (粵雅堂) and the Zhai Antique (博古斋) area. Goods on sale mainly consist of antiques and jade, though shoppers can also browse the calligraphy section on the second floor. Due to its status, the store has precious items from the Yuan and Sui Dynasty eras on sale for those interested in Chinese history.

Address: Wende Bei Road 文德北路

Getting There: Take metro line 1 or 2 to Gongyuanqian station (公园前站) near Beijing Lu (北京路). From Beijing Lu walk east along Zhongshan Lu (中山路) then turn right on Wende Lu (文德路).

Dafen Art Market, Shenzhen 大芬油画村

Unfortunately the stores of Wende Lu pale into insignificance when compared to the hundreds of reproduction art stores that are crammed into Dafen Artists Village in Shenzhen. This small but tight knit community has risen to prominence as the 'copy capital of the world', and is host to thousands of painters who supply the world with reproductions of Renoir, Rembrandt, Raphael and many more.

Back in 1988, Hong Kong Businessman Huang Jiang set up the very first reproduction studio amongst what was then paddy fields. These days Dafen houses more that 10,000 artists of all kinds, and it is estimated that they churn out at least five million assorted Klimts, Bouguereaus, and Fragonards every single year, an estimated sixty percent of all the world's oil paintings. Multi-national hotel chains are some of the biggest customers, purchasing hundreds of pieces to hang in the individual rooms of every single property.

Artists will happily take commissions to copy photos or pictures, so that you can immortalise that landscape of your childhood, or even have yourself painted into your favourite Botticelli. I know an expat in Guangzhou that had his entire extended family painted into The Last Supper, and I myself have used them to custom paint leather biker jackets. While China as a whole suffers from an incredible dearth of good quality museums and galleries, this area is a very refreshing change. So many treasures have been looted or destroyed in China's turbulent past, that there is almost nothing left for tourists and yet Dafen is packed to the rafters with all kinds of interesting art.

Some people claim that the output of Dafen is about as close to art as Kraft cheese slices are to fine French Roquefort. Others recall that in the times of the Old Masters, all of an artist's training was done by copying, and that apprentices can often learn a whole lot more from carefully reproducing a single Van Gogh than from any two-year college art course. True artists obviously emerge from this environment, just as they do in Greenwich or Essaouria or the seaside towns of Western Ireland, all with similar albeit smaller scale communities. Even so, the majority of artists here are simply the taxi drivers of the painting world, they get you where you want to go for a couple of dollars, but it is the Formula One racers that receive the fame and fortune.

There are some 600 galleries in Dafen whose highly convincing reproductions grace homes and offices across the globe, and more than a thousand newly-graduated artists arrive every year. And with it only being a couple of hours away in Shenzhen, anybody seriously looking at purchasing reproduction art would be better off skipping Wende Lu completely.

Chinese Contemporary Art

Five of the top-ten traded artists in the world are now Chinese, pushing out well known icons such as Warhol and Picasso. Fifteen of the most expensive living artists in the world are Chinese. Many would argue that this does not necessarily reflect the quality of contemporary Chinese art, nor does it hide the fact that the only people left with any spare cash to splash out on multi-million canvasses are the nouveau riche millionaires coming out of the Mainland who probably could not tell a Breugel from a Banksy. Nevertheless, Chinese art is hot property.

A look at the current crop of contemporary Chinese art shows that style and even skill is relatively unimportant. Being memorable and even sensational is far more necessary. If the artist is an outspoken political underdog that can express themselves in English such as Ai Wei Wei, then that is an added bonus. It is always difficult to promote a new personality when they are unable to express themselves to a Western audience and need an interpreter present to be interviewed. Extra points if they are visibly photogenic, have straight teeth and display a sense of iconoclasm that sets them apart from the average Chinese citizen.

Finding a future talent is one thing, but exposing them to the rest of the world is something else completely. The chances of stumbling across the next 'Star Group' or 'No Name Group' is unlikely but if you have a talent for international marketing and the right connections, it is not impossible. Before you arrive in China, research local galleries and artist collectives. Make some contacts at local art schools so that you can offer to arrange a contemporary Chinese art showing once you have developed a portfolio of upcoming artists. Familiarize yourself with the art press and make notes of those writers that have already expressed an interest in the Chinese art scene. Make sure that you are up to speed on Chinese art. This means knowing the difference between political pop and cynical realism at the very least. If you can properly pronounce Cao Fei then you will be well ahead of most of the so-called experts. Once you have found your unknown prodigy, these will be the guys with whom you will want to share your valuable new secret about the next big thing in Chinese art.

There are certainly very talented artists hidden away

in China but one of the main reasons that they remain undiscovered is that they have absolutely no contacts in the outside world. If you prepare well in advance, then once you do find tomorrow's shining new star, then you will be able to make the rest of the world aware of his multi-million dollar talents.

Well known locations such as 798 in Beijing and the Loft area in Shenzhen are already full of scouts looking for the next big thing. In the nineties, there were just five art galleries in Beijing and now there are coming on for more than three hundred. Many of the most successful artists have become prolific one-man production lines. Yue Ming Jun is a good example of this, churning out endless grinning mannequins, but this is unfortunately what the market now demands. Although commerce undoubtedly stifles creativity, a steady stream of work is essential to meets the needs of collectors and speculators alike. Some would say that many of the most popular artists including Fang Li Jun and Zhang Xiao Gang are now past their prime, even Ai Wei Wei no longer has the urge to shock and cause controversy like he once did. Many of the younger artists have grown up implicitly understanding their boundaries and perhaps unknowingly self-censor themselves. The likelihood of finding work related to proscribed subjects such as Tibet, Uighur separatism, sexual deviance or contemporary political satire is becoming less and less. It is subjects like these that expand the boundaries of art, but who is willing to move out of their comfort zone and risk jail time to push the envelope of modern art? Instead, younger artists are using nostalgia to appeal to a growing domestic audience. Chu An Xiong's work harks back to early television animation and classical ink brush styles, making it more accessible to a larger and larger market.

Fortunately, prices are a reflection of the market rather than inherent quality. High artistic standards are not as important as the ability to capture attention and then reproduce a similar theme that has generated appeal in the market. The downside is that you might have difficulty in finding art that you really like. When foreigners criticise Chinese art, accusations of 'not understanding Chinese culture' become an easy get out clause; Chinese are in effect are playing their patriotism joker in order to defend their efforts. I personally think that Cao Fei's work is infantile and weak compared to the real masters of the genre such as Reggio, Fricke and Burtynsky, but my Chinese colleagues will often use the 'cultural difference' trump card to simply ignore my opinion.

If you still have any doubts about the potential of contemporary Chinese art, consider that both Sotheby's and Christies have now been given permission to operate in Mainland China. Museums too have been launching major initiatives. The Guggenheim announced in April that it will partner with the Robert H. N. Ho Family Foundation to acquire Chinese contemporary art for the museum's permanent collection. In New York, the Metropolitan Museum of Art has opened its first ever major exhibition of Chinese contemporary art, featuring 35 artists and 70 works. In Paris, the Musee d'Art Moderne offered the first major retrospective of the celebrated Chinese artist, Zeng Fanzhi. These are significant events.

International collectors are also putting their money where their mouths are. Don and Mera Rubell, influential American collectors, have used their entire museum space in Miami to showcase 28 Chinese contemporary artists. In Europe, collectors Dominique and Sylvain Levy have extensively added artworks to their existing 200 artists-strong collection. New and young collectors outside Asia are also actively starting to buy young Chinese contemporary artists. This is without mentioning the already established collectors from within China who are putting their efforts (and heavy wallets) to considerably build up their collections, and show them in private museums, such as in the Long Museum in Shanghai. What about biennales and art fairs? The latest Venice Biennale featured nearly 350 Chinese artists. Yes, that's 350 artists, compared to 150 artists from 38 other countries in the Central Pavilion and the Arsenale. This prompted Art in America magazine to call the Biennale "a giant survey of Chinese contemporary art, with some Western work mixed in for a balance."

Of course, in a country where faking is so common place, there are inevitably forgeries and copies running rampant. Some even claim that they are the rule rather than the exception. These fakes are so good that even the experts cannot tell the difference. Take the example of an ink painting by Chinese master Qi Baishi, which "sold" for $65.4 million at the China Guardian 2011 Spring Auctions in Beijing, but still sits in a warehouse because of doubts over its authenticity. In turn, this creates inflated numbers for the market.

With prices jumping up at such crazy rates this area is rife with fraud and forgeries.One only has to look at the recent scandal involving Beijing Tranthy International Auction Company to see the the instability of the Chinese auction market. Famed Chinese painter Zhang Xiaogang has said that a painting sold in a recent modern and contemporary sale was not, in fact, his. "It's a bad fake at first sight. Poorly done. How dare someone put it up for auction," Zhang wrote on Sina Weibo, a Chinese social media platform. Tranthy Auction has withdrawn the piece from possible auction and apologized to the artist. But as it turns out, the work, a portrait of a young girl, had already been sold earlier in the year at Beijing Yinqianshan International auction for $278,000. The Yinqianshan buyer then put the work up for sale at Tranthy.

An even more bizarre development occurred when Wang Xinghua, the president of Yinqianshan, stated that it was not up to Zhang to say which paintings are real and which were not. "The artist's opinion doesn't necessarily make the final verdict for the appraisal of an artwork," he says. "Also, the auction house gives no guarantee for the authenticity, quality or defect of the auctioned item." Wang then challenged the painter: "Does Zhang remember clearly how many paintings he has done through his life?" The entire saga is a clear illustration of the weaknesses of China's art auction system.

Below is a list of the ten most expensive Chinese works of art recently sold at auction.

1.   Qianlong   Dynasty   Porcelain   Vase 清乾隆粉彩镂空"吉庆有余"转心瓶
This Chinese 18th century Qianlong dynasty porcelain vase, sold for US$85,921,461 at Bainbridges auction house in London, 12 November 2010

2. Dizhuming 砥柱铭
Dizhuming, a Chinese calligraphy masterpiece composed by Huang Tingjian from the Song Dynasty set a new high bid. The final price was US$70m at Poly Auction in Beijing.

3. Mount Wansui Painting Manuscript万岁山图稿本
The painting was composed by Fang Danian and Emperor Wenzong. This scroll painting sold for US$54m at Beijing Jiuge International Auction.

4. Ping An Tie 平安帖
Wang Xizhi's cursive-hand scroll Ping'an Tie (Peace Note) was auctioned out at US$50m at China Guardian Auction. Wang Xizhi lived about 1600 years ago, he is acknowledged as the founder of the art of calligraphy in China.

5. Qianlong "Wanshou Lianyan" long-neck gourd-shaped vase 清乾隆"万寿连延"长颈葫芦瓶
This Qianlong long-neck gourd-shaped vase was sold for

US$35m at Sotheby's Auction in Hong Kong

6.Baren Jishui 巴人汲水图

Xu Beihong's Baren Jishui (The Sichuan People Draw Water) sold for US$28.4m at Beijing Hanhai Auction.

7. Suihan Sanyou 岁寒三友

Bada Shanren's Suhan Sanyou or Three Friends of Winter sold for US$27m at Beijing Jiuge International Auction.

8. Autumn in Han Palace 汉宫秋图

This painting is composed by an unknown artist Song Dynasty sold for US$27m at Beijing Poly Auction

9. Songchuang Gaoshi 松窗高士

Shen Zhou's superb landscape measuring 3.36 metres high by 1 metre wide that sold for $20.4m at Beijing Jiuge Art Auction.

10. Songshi Jianyi Lyre 宋徽宗御制 "松石间意" 琴

This lyre was made by the order of emperor Huizong sold for US$22m at Beijing Poly Auction.

Auction Catalogues

While not everybody has the budget for antique porcelain and big name contemporary painters, one area of interest that I would like to share with you is that of auction catalogues. Just as Chinese art is becoming more and more collectible, so are the catalogues that are used to promote them. Not many people realise this and they can sometimes still be found in house clearances and second-hand junk stores. Just to give you and idea of what I am talking about, here are a few examples of some of the most popular catalogues and the prices that they have recently fetched on eBay.

Sotheby's 1980/1 Edward Chow Collection Chinese Art 3 volumes: US $1,056.00

Chinese porcelain, the S.C. Ko Tianminlou Collection, Hong Kong: US $900.

The˙Eumorfopoulos Collections Sotheby's Chinese Ceramics 1940: US $770.00

Ceramics and porcelain catalogues from Christie's and Sotheby's seem to be in most demand, but it is easy to do a little research to see what is currently selling well. Other auction houses are not yet commanding the same high prices but might possibly increase in the future.

One of the most fascinating ways that I managed to educate myself about Chinese fine art was through the medium of auction catalogues. One of my regular stops when making visa runs to Hong Kong was the Oxfam charity store in the basement of the Prince's Building, just opposite the Central Post Office. At first, I was just looking for some cheap reading material to take on my travels. Book stores on the Mainland are all state-controlled and the choice of English language material is pretty dire unless you are a die hard fan of Dickens, Plato or Aesculapius. On the bottom shelf of all the donated paperbacks, I noticed a large selection of auction catalogues from the local offices of Christie's and Sotheby's. It was only when I checked on eBay that I realized that some of these glossy brochures were fetching hundreds of dollars a piece. As the market for Chinese art has been hugely inflated by Mainland speculators, even the price of catalogues has gone through the roof.

There used to be a great deal of catalogues available at low prices in the second-hand book stores that have started springing up around universities in China, but shop owners are forever savvy to new markets and have started using Taobao and other websites as price guides, so finding bargains is certainly not as easy as it once was, but I find that these places are always worth a browse, just in case. Catalogues for the two big houses seem to fetch the best prices, but it is also worth looking out for Bonham's and the Mayfair specialist Eskenazi. Chinese language catalogues from Mainland auction houses such as Poly International and China Guardian unfortunately do not seem to command the same levels of market interest.

2 AQUARIA

Yihe Fish, Bird and Stonework Market
艺和鱼鸟石艺市场

Yihe Market is one of the biggest wholesale and retail markets for fish, bird and stone products in China. It is also a popular leisure travel destination for various age-groups. Better known as the Huadiwan market, it is located south of the river in Fangcun District, but is not a wholesale market in the strictest sense of the term. Even so, it certainly is interesting to take a wander around. Many of the stores are factory representatives but a large majority of them are more used to offering retail prices to walk in customers. To make matters even more confusing, it is sometimes also known as the Yuehe Market (越和花鸟鱼艺大世界 or 越和花鸟鱼虫市场).

For aquaria, there is a vast choice available from the very smallest goldfish bowls to the most enormous hotel lobby tanks that would make even Deuce Bigelow's jaw drop. Every possible accessory is available, including nets, filters, pumps and backdrops of all sizes and descriptions. In addition, a vast range of underwater denizens is also for sale, from baby guppies to spectacular scorpion fish. In between, there are miniature sharks, giant sturgeon and Little Nemo lookalikes. Enormous arowana that cost more than a small apartment vie with king-size koi in gigantic tanks. Of course, arowana are just the tip of the iceberg, and there are many export restrictions surrounding these kinds of products. Few Chinese aquarists are aware of the damage that is caused to the environment that their hobby can cause and therefore you will see plenty of shops openly selling plundered coral. (For more information on this subject, I recommend Michele Benson's Miss Scuba website – http://www.miss-scuba.com/coral-or-not.html.) One species that surprised me by its absence was the octopus. I personally would have thought that these super intelligent creatures would have made ideal pets, but nobody at this market seemed to agree with me. One especially impressive store is the reptile shop (洛青宠物器材批发) which stocks all kind of scalies and eight-legged beasties, including some beautiful tarantulas.

One area that is a little lacking in this market is that of aquarium ornaments. Many of the examples display are of a distinctly oriental nature and obviously aimed at the domestic market. An avenue of aquatic plants at the rear leads into the pet area proper, where customers can purchase anything from scorpions to Saint Bernards. Be warned though, animal lovers may be distressed at the mercenary puppy farming and the sight of row upon row of cats and dogs in cages so small that they can barely turn around. In addition, the stench is appalling. Aside from the yelps and whines, this huge expanse becomes a Chinese garden centre with a clear emphasis on shanshui (mountain and water) features, viewing stones (oddly shaped rocks to the uninitiated), and forests of bonsai. Finally, the bird market showcases just about every kind of avian from plain homing pigeons to imported parakeets and full-display peacocks. Huadiwan is a spectacular array of sounds and colours but at the same time locals have little respect for concepts such as conservation and the protection of endangered species. Profit comes first, and so you will see stores piled high with coral and exotic animals of all shapes and sizes. My advice is to keep your hands firmly in your pocket and make a large donation to the WWF when you get home.

Address: 271, Huadiwan Xique Lu, Liwan District
广州市荔湾区花地湾喜鹊路271号

Directions: Take the subway line 1 to Huadiwan and look for exit C. The market is the large Mall directly outside, beginning with art and furniture stores and then continuing to pets and garden landscaping.

Arowana

For those of you unfamiliar with this strange looking fish, the Asian arowana, also known as the dragon fish or the Asian bony tongue, was listed as endangered by the 2006 IUCN Red List, so its trade is controlled under the Convention on the International Trade in Endangered

Species of Wild Flora and Fauna. Despite this, it remains a highly sought after fish in the illicit aquarium fish trade. In 2011, a Malaysian smuggler was sent to prison for twelve months and fined $4000 for attempting to conceal sixteen water-filled plastic bags in his luggage. In the USA, attractive specimens command up to $10,000 each. Ironically the fish (nine of which died in transit) would likely not have been discovered had his baggage not been misplaced in Hong Kong. The contraband was only found when the bag arrived on a later flight. They are especially popular in China where they are considered a rare and noble fish, bearing a close resemblance to the traditional dragon of ancient China. It is believed to be auspicious and symbolises strength, prosperity, luck and wealth - and provides any aquarist with good Feng Shui. Renown across Asia for their symbol of wealth, these fish have a life span in excess of twenty years.

Shufang Jie Aquatic Animal Market 书房水族市场

This is a tiny market in comparison to Huadiwan, which stretches only a hundred meters or so the city's centre located off Danan Road (越秀区大南路书坊街) near the city centre, still has few dealers but is now mainly retail as is the largely sanitised Qingping Market.

Address: Danan Lu 大南路

Qingping Aquatic and Pet Market 清平水族宠物市场

A reasonably-sized retail district that deals in all kinds of pets and related products, including plenty of aquatic animals, equipment, and fodder. This is a popular haunt for wealthy American tourists who stay on Shamian Island nearby, so do not be surprised if you can only get expensive foreigner prices here.

Address: Qingping Lu, north of Shamian Island, Liwan District 清平路

Directions: From Shangxiajiu Pedestrian Shopping Street, look for the Holiday Inn Shifu Guangzhou

(十甫假日酒店) located at 188 Di Shu Fu Road (荔湾区第十甫路188号). The Qingping Aquatic and Pet Market begins at the main entrance to the hotel and leads south.

Chengnan Pet Market 沥新城南宠物市场

The nearest wholesale pet market is out in Nanhai, but is probably worth a trip if you cannot find what you are looking for downtown. Look for full details and directions in the Pet Products section.

3 AUTO PARTS

Auto accessory suppliers stretch from one side of the city to the other across the length of Guangyuan Road. Some of the older markets are still located on the San Yuan Li side of Airport Road. The greatest concentration are in the Yongfu Road Area, close by to the Huanghuagang Subway Station. Many moved here recently from the Baiyun Avenue area when the new subway opened. This means that there is still a lot of confusion on the internet regarding current market names and locations. This is the most reliable and up-to-date information currently available.

Yongfu Automobile Market 永福汽车配件专业街
Heading out of the Huanghuagang Subway Station and onto Yongfu Lu, this is the first large market complex that visitors see on the right, situated in between the Bank of China and a large Moutai Rice Liquor outlet. Unfortunately this plaza is closed at the time of writing.
Address: 40, Yongfu Road 广州市永福路40号

140

Contact: 020 8771-2123

Jinzhong Mingpinghui Automobile Accessory Plaza
金中名品汇汽车用品城

Opposite Yongfu Tower, on the right hand side as you come up from the subway station, featuring four floors of accessory dealers. The fourth floor is mainly office space with a large sales showroom devoted to the Tidelion Electronics Company. The third and second floor are the most active areas, with a wide range of accessory suppliers ranging from wiper blade manufacturers to decal and sticker designers. I was also impressed by a number of 4x4 off road auto specialist shops. The ground floor is only half the size of the other floors and might be a little disappointing at first sight. Up on the second floor there is even a Muslim prayer room.

Address: 48, Yongfu Road, Yuexiu District
广州市永福路48号
Contact: 020 3781-3165

Guangdong Yong Fu International Car Parts Centre
广东永福国际汽车用品城

Sometimes also known as the Shengda International Auto Accessories Plaza (盛大国际) or the Exhibition Centre of Car Accessories. This is perhaps the most popular of all the auto markets, is filled from top to bottom with all kinds of auto accessories that will have any gear head foaming at the mouth. All kinds of fancy upgrades, add-ons and refits are available here. From simple replacement wipers to to most fashionable seat and steering covers. There are bucket seats, anodised exhaust tips and even racing coveralls. All kinds of seat covers, luggage racks, HID light sets, hub caps, seat covers and solar protective films. There are high end cameras, audio/video and GPS, all the way down to stores that specialise in plastic ice scrapers and cleaning brushes.

Some shops focus on only one product, while others are Aladdin's caves for any auto enthusiast. There are very few replacement internal components here but for add-ons and accessories this place is paradise. Six storeys plus a large basement. Approximately 40 stores on each floor. Very busy with very few vacant stores.

Address: 60, Yongfu Lu 广州市永福路60号
Contact: 020 3781-3144

Yongfu Tower Auto Electronics Market 永福大厦汽车电子城

Three floors of auto electronics specialists, from xenons, LEDs and headlamp units up to can bus and in car audio systems. The lower floors feature a strange circular staircase that is also lined with electronics dealers. The third floor is decorated as if it were once the reception area for a swanky nightclub but is now mostly warehousing space.

Address: 35, Yongfu Lu 广州市永福路35号
Contact: 020 3781-3354

Guangdong Yongfu International Auto Supplies City广东永福国际汽车用品城

Directly facing the end of Yongfu Road at the junction with Hengfu Road, this is a irregular shaped courtyard complex surrounding a large parking area. As well as ground floor shops, there is also a second floor that stretches around the perimeter of the market. This one even extends onto a footbridge that crosses the main entrance but ends in a dead end going nowhere else. It stretches back around the market giving access to a wide range of accessory shops on an undulating, winding second floor.

Address: 70, Hengfu Road 广州市恒福路 70号
Contact: 020 3781-3171

Lihong Auto Accessories Plaza 利泓汽车用品城

Directly below the Guangdong Yongfu International Auto Supplies City is the Lihong Auto Accessories Plaza. There is a ground floor entrance next to the main archway as well as a lower entrance on the side road next door. Lots of upgrades available down here from Recaro racing seats and multi-coloured power racing hose sets to compressors and pressure washers to keep all the boy racers in tip-top condition.

Address: 45, Yongfu Road 广州市永福路45号
Contact: 020 3781-1256

Jinyongfu Auto City 金永福汽配城

Farther east along Hengfu Lu, this is the main wholesale distribution centre for automotive products in Guangzhou, mainly car and engine components rather than add-ons and accessories.

This area is so tightly packed with car parts suppliers that almost every inch of pavement is taken up with packaging, crating and delivery companies. All shapes and sizes of components are wrapped and packed on the pavement by delivery agents who will then weigh and calculate the cost for customers. Whatever space is not being used by delivery firms is used as temporary parking space for motor vehicles. In terms of traffic safety, remember that the simple pedestrian is way down the hierarchy in this part of the city. Do not expect any polite, gentlemanly drivers and you will not be disappointed, or even be shocked when they try to bully and intimidate you off the pavement in their flashy motors.

Address: 48, Hengfu Road 广州市恒福路 48号
Contact: 020 8771-4634

Li Yuan Plaza Yongfu Auto City 利远广场永福汽配城

One of the oldest looking buildings along this strip, the interior looks suspiciously like a converted fruit and vegetable market. Inside there is a selection of car accessory suppliers with a large number of upholstery manufacturers producing foot wells and car mats to order on large scale cutting machines.

Address: 45, Hengfu Road 广州市恒福路 45号
Contact: 020 8763-6199☐

Guangzhou Yi Yun Automobile Accessories Square 倚云汽配广场

More than 150 manufacturers of every kind of automotive accessories. The entrance leads up into a rear area that is directly behind the Yongfu Auto City, but one that houses some of the largest showrooms in the area, many of which carry huge ranges of stock.

Address: 79, Hengfu Lu 广州市恒福路 79号
Contact: 020 3781-3177

Fuyi Automobile Accessory Centre 福怡汽配中心

Just next door to Yiyun is the now rather dated Fuyi Mansion. Four floors of stores, with about twenty stores per floor. Above this is mainly admin and office space. The stores are located around the edge of a central atrium. There is is the usual mix of assorted accessory makers but the most memorable aspect of this building is the fact that it has the most foul smelling toilet facilities on all of Yongfu Lu. This would not be so bad if it were not for the central atrium design which allows the horrible odours to waft throughout the entire building.

Address: Fuyi Mansion, 49, Yongfu Road, Yuexiu District 广州市永福路49号福怡大厦
Contact: 020 3728-9754

Longfu Auto Parts Centre 隆福汽配城

This is the closest of the auto markets to Taojin Road on Hengfu Lu. It is just past the main Cancer Centre and just before a large military restricted area. It is approximately five minutes walk down to Yongfu Lu from here. There are two vehicle entrances on Hengfu Lu and a rear entrance on Henzhigang Bei Lu. Inside the plaza is split into two main courtyards, with four or five floors of parts suppliers, selling all kinds of internals, from clutches and brakes to transmissions and turbo chargers.

Address: Hengfu Road 广州市恒福路

Contact: 020 3339-6273

Jingtai International Auto Parts Factory Brand Trade and Exhibition Centre 景泰国际汽配工厂品牌展贸中心

Squeezed in between the military Administration Area and Danjingzhong Lu on Guangyuan Lu, just east of the Guangyuan Bus Station this small market is well past its glory days. It used to be the number one area for parts for luxury European brands such as BMW and Mercedes but these days half of the stores are empty and much of the office space abandoned. There are now just twenty stores here that deal in auto components and about the same amount of support offices up on the upper floors of the seven story building.

Address: Guangyuan Dong Lu 广园东路

Contact: 020 3637- 6111

Southern China City Auto Parts E. C. Park 华南汽配城

A large new complex of auto parts suppliers directly opposite the Paco Business Hotel, which remains mostly empty at the time of writing. A handful of suppliers sell transmissions, ignition coils and other assorted engine parts' but the second floor is completely empty and even the first floor is taking a while to fill up with vendors.

Address: 2003, Guangyuan Dong Road 广园东路2003号

Contact: 020 8721-3313

San Yuan Li Area

Hong Yun Auto Parts Market 鸿运汽车配件广场

Situated directly opposite the San Yuan Li Temple and Anti British Memorial Park. This is a propaganda memorial where history has been completely rewritten to unite the Chinese against an imagined common enemy, but unfortunately all of the displays are in Chinese only. If you are white like me and look like a typical buttoned-down civil servant do not be surprised if you get some funny looks. Of course, one country's beloved martyrs are another's reviled terrorists, so do not pay too much attention to the propaganda.

Like all the auto markets on this stretch of Guang Yuan Lu, there are only signs in Chinese at the main entrances. Inside, an old gated community has been converted with large wholesalers on the ground floor of most buildings. Hong Yun has a good selection of internal components with a special focus on air-conditioning systems and related items such as thermostats and blowers.

Address: 60, Guang Yuan Xi Lu 广园东西路2003号

Contact: 020 8234-1565

Wanli Auto Parts Plaza 万里汽配厂

Next door to Hong Yun, this market is especially popular for air conditioning systems for larger forms of transport such as HGVs and public buses.

Address: 61, Guang Yuan Xi Lu 广园东西路2003号

Contact: 020 8756-4534

Behind Guangyuan Bus Station Area

Jing Dian Car Accessory Market 经典市场汽配区

The markets in the area range from sprawling and obvious to hidden and compact. Just opposite the Jingtai Junior High School, near the Keziling (Hetian Lu) Bus Terminal 柯子岭（河田路）总站, is the archway sign (经典市场汽配区.) This is only a small collection of thirty or forty spare parts dealers. Still, it is always useful to know the Kezeling stop is the origin on the 546 bus line, which is always handy for getting back downtown.

Address: Hetian Lu (Behind the Guang Yuan Bus Passenger Terminal) 河田路（广园客运站后）

Contact: 020 8633-5523

Guangzhou Zong Ding Qi Pei Guang Chang 广州众鼎汽配广场

This is a much larger parts market that is located just before the flyover on Baiyun Da Dao. It is sometimes also known as the Chen Tian Zhan Long Auto Parts Market 广源湛隆汽配交易中心 or 广州市白云区白云大道北陈田湛隆汽配城

Address: 78, Baiyun Avenue North, behind the Guang Yuan Bus Passenger Terminal (广园客运站后)

Contact: 020 8656-2988

Xi Chang Dian Qi Zhong Hui 西场电器总汇

This is a small market specialising in car audio that is located at the Songnan Interchange among the Luochongwei cluster of motorcycle accessory markets.

Address: Songnan Lukou, Luochongwei 松南路口罗冲围

Contact: 020 8176-5369

Guangzhou Used Car Market 广州旧机动车市场

Located in the Luoxi area, south of the city proper, what was the largest motor vehicle trading centre in Guangdong has since been over taken by many individual dealerships. There is now a much larger at the race track on Tian He Nan Lu in the Shi Pai district. Considering the enormous tax changes on cars in China, they are hardly ideal export products.

Address: 1601, Guangzhou Dadao Nan, Haizhu District

Contact: 020 8429-0229

Christian D. Taulkinghorn

4 BEAUTY PRODUCTS AND COSMETICS

The main wholesale markets in Guangzhou for beauty and cosmetic products are located in the Jichang Lu (which is sometimes directly translated as Airport Road) and Guangyuan Lu areas. Collectively, this area is known locally as the Guangzhou Baiyun Business Cosmetic Circle (广州白云化妆品商圈) and includes a number of large wholesale markets.

Cosmetics and toiletries are rapidly growing market segments in China and ones which have boomed in the last two decades as the rural populations have moved en-masse into the cities. When I first lived in Shanghai some twenty years ago, it was impossible to find deodorant anywhere and cosmetics courses were all the rage for young women that were arriving in droves from the hinterland peasant villages. This is also an area that is very susceptible to fake products and so is an area where buyers need to be extra careful. Bear in mind that the trend in China is for skin whitening rather than tanning and so this will greatly affect the number of western type products available

Guangzhou Mei Bo Cheng Beauty and Cosmetic Wholesale Market 廣州美博城

The largest beauty and cosmetic wholesale market in the Asia Pacific region and probably the world.

Building A plays hosts to a number of banks, offices and other businesses but very few actual cosmetics wholesalers. Building B is most popular with overseas buyers. The fourth floor is mainly underwear wholesalers. The third floor is dominated by exotic beauty salon equipment much of it looking to the untrained eye like some exotic machinery from a science fiction movie. Lots of laser treatment contraptions aimed at high end salons as well as more questionable items such as magic belts for slimmers. The second floor is mainly packaging items, all shapes and sizes made from all kinds of materials. Every kind of glass and plastic perfume bottle that you can imagine, but mainly OEM and made to order. The ground floor has large numbers of hairdressers outfitters, supplying everything needed to set up a new salon. Everything from hair-dryers and scissors to staff uniforms, salon chairs and barbers poles. It is the basement which is busiest with foreign buyers as here there are many shops that specialise in wigs and hair. As well as synthetic wigs of every colour (especially now that cosplay is becoming so big in China), the is also a large number of what seems to known in the trade as virgin hair, with stock from Peru and Brazil seeming to be especially popular. There are always lots of Africa buyers down here buying up large quantities of hair extension. The choice is vast and the only thing that I was unable to find was synthetic dreadfalls that are popular within the rave and cybergoth community. I am reliably informed that many of the virgin hair suppliers are from the provinces of Henan and Qingdao, but if you travel in the the more rural parts of any province, there are always dealers at small local markets whose business is buying hair from peasant women. Most of the time it is cut there and there and then purchased by weight and length. Stores numbers down here are a complete jumble. Numbers are not consecutive and seem to be assigned to shops completely at random.

Building C covers products aimed mainly at the domestic market. On the fourth floor is located the property management office and the third floor houses numerous offices of the stores below. The second floor is mainly shops selling packaging and perfume bottles. All kinds of containers, bottles, atomisers and fancy cosmetics containers are available here, as well as very high end gift boxes for the most expensive items. The second floor focuses on daily necessities. These include shampoos, perfumes, eye shadows, curlers, lipsticks, facial masks and eyelashes. There are one stop shops here where it is possible to completely outfit a nail salon or tattoo parlour. The basement has large amounts of aromatherapy oils and products aimed at massage parlours and spas. The lower basement area is unhelpfully described on the sign-age as the 'Sandwich Health Museum' but is mainly supplies for Chinese beauty salons, including exotic treatments such as cupping and moxibustion.

Address: 121, Guangyuan W. Road 广园西路121号
Contact: 020 6114-9830 / 6114-9831
Transportation: Metro: Get off at San Yuan Li metro station, Line 2, Exit D, walk along Guangyuan Xi Lu along a very narrow pavement, towards Guangzhou Railway Station direction for about 600 meters.

Eva   International   Cosmetics   Centre
怡发国际化妆品采购中心

This is the large three storey building on the southern corner of Jichang Lu and Xingtai Lu. Until about a year ago, this was actually a CD and DVD centre, but thanks to streaming video websites like Youku, that market had a major coronary and never recovered. Cosmetics have begun to take up the slack in this particular location but the third floor still remains largely empty for the time being. The only remnants of the DVD market exists at the rear of the building where there are still a large number AV packaging manufacturers, selling all manner of CD cases and DVD boxes. Much of the first floor is filled with local brand make up and perfumes, but more interesting is the second floor where all the packaging manufacturers have gathered. Here is possible to find almost any shape or size container related to cosmetics, from tiny perfume samplers to large family sized shampoo bottles.

Address: 1, Xingtai Lu 兴泰路1号

Contact: 020 8235-6672

Guangdong Audio and Video City 广东音像城/中国国际音像博览会

Despite the name, this is now much more a cosmetics market than anything else. A few CD and CD wholesale hold-outs cling on to life with their last gasps on the third floor, but it does look like they will last very long. Only five years ago, I can remember attending an exciting and vibrant AV fair in this building and discovering a great selection of music and video from all around the world that had been mostly ignored by western companies, but the few shops that remain are now almost devoid of customers. All that remain are bargain bins and groups of vendors with little else to do all day except play cards.

The second floor has only a handful of cosmetics stores at the moment but the first floor has become a hive of thriving activity, with nearly almost as great a selection as Eva across the road.

Address: 124 – 128, Jichang Lu 机场路124-182号

Contact: 020 8798-7667

Yifa Plaza (Eva Plaza) 怡发国际化妆品采购中心

Xingfa Plaza and Yifa Plaza are all gathered on the edge of the old city airport site. Most of the products here are orientated towards the domestic market, and includes mainly local brands of cosmetics products, cleaning products, hair and beauty equipment. Stores spread out over 50,000 square meters and connects directly with Xinfa Square, Guangdong Video City, Tianlong Circuit City (Tian Long AV 天龙音像包材中心) and Yifa Square

Address: 138, Ji Chang Rd 机场路138号

Contact: 020 8655-1837

By Metro: Line 2 , Get off at Feixiang Park

Xingfa Plaza 兴发广场化妆品展览中心

This is the largest of the beauty products markets and is located just off Jichang Lu, in an area that is directly south of the old Baiyun Airport facility. When I first lived in Guangzhou around two decades ago, arriving planes used to fly spectacularly low over the main road before landing on the old airport runway. There would always a big group of immigrant workers making a day out of it, some even having a picnic by the big wire fence. Every time another jet flew in they would all shout and cheer as it landed successfully. The entrance to the cosmetics market is actually on Xingtai Lu just around the corner, on the same side as the AV city, just a little further along. Apart from cosmetics and hair care products there is also a wide selection of make up tools, including brushes, applicators, manicure sets etc.

The vast majority of products here is locally made and aimed at the domestic market although there are obviously many cheap knock offs of famous international brands. Clearly this is an area where the buyer beware rule is absolutely imperative, especially when taking into considerations China's poor health and safety record in some many others of manufacturing.

Address: 96-98, Airport Road 机场路96-98 号

By Metro: Line 2, Feixiang Park

Zhongren Cosmetic City 中人化妆品城

Located on the second floor of the 2nd phase of Xingfa Plaza, Zhongren Cosmetic market mainly engages in the wholesale and retail of cosmetic, cleaning products, hair and beauty equipment. cosmetics products, cleaning products, hair and beauty equipment.

Address: Second Floor of Home 2 in Xingfa Square, 138, Airport Road, 机场路138号

By Metro: Line 2, Feixiang Park

Tai An Plaza 泰安美容美发用品广场

Further along Xingtai Lu, away from the airport road, Tai An Plaza is a new location to which a number of cosmetics suppliers are now gravitating. While many of the shops in this new area have not yet been rented, it is starting to fill up quickly and is worth a look for overseas buyers. Some of the company names such as Blackhead International seem less than appropriate for the beauty industry but this is China.

Address: 60, Xingtai Lu 兴泰路60号

Contact: 020 8658-3150

By Metro: Line 2, Feixiang Park

Changshou Donglu Beauty and Hairdressing Products Wholesale Market 长寿东路美容美发用品

On the section between Renmin Zhong Lu and the rear of Liwan Plaza, Changshou Lu is filled with beauty salon equipment wholesalers. Many stock a hundred different kinds of hair dryers and hair dressing scissors as well as salon chairs, foot massage tubs along with industrial sized containers of shampoos and conditioners. Towards the western end of the road the beauty products peter out and the shops stock professional gemmology tools and workshop equipment.

Address: Changshou Dong Lu 长寿东路

Contact: 020 8658-5682

By Metro: Line 1, get off at Changshou Lu and walk

towards Renmin Zhong Lu

A number of small boutique type wholesale markets are springing up east along Wanfu Lu. The first of these is the Trendy Wholesale Market at the junction of Taikang, Beijing and Wanfu Roads.

Trendy Plaza Guangzhou 骏田批发广场

Nearly all of the stores here have relocated from the old Haizhu Square Power Station site which is currently being demolished as I write this. The only business left in that whole area is the ever popular expat haunt the 1920 restaurant, named after the power station building itself. While that are is all being transformed in riverside park, much of the commerce moved up to Trendy Plaza, among other places.

Basement – lots of cross stitch packs, mainly Chinese calligraphy and scenery designed to appeal mainly to the domestic market rather than subjects such as Disney that appeal to overseas buyers.

1st floor – Fashion accessories consisting mainly of hair clips, barrettes and scrunchies rather than imitation jewellery that is found further down the road in the Taikang Jewellery Market. Lots of bags, hats and miscellaneous gift items such as watches, with a good crossover of cross stitch and cosmetics from the floors above and below.

2nd floor – Lots more fashion accessories, as well as a smattering of toys, and a great deal of budget cosmetics.

3rd floor – Focussing mainly on cosmetics now, from nail polish to face scrubs and exfoliation masks. No big brands here and a lot of retail traffic from Beijing Road customers, and so prices are not as low as you might find up in the large San Yuan Li wholesale cosmetics markets. Even so, prices are very reasonable compared to other countries and so I always pick up a few gifts for lady friends here, and find that the three packs of varnish remover are especially appreciated for some reason.

4th floor – More cosmetics are mixed in with a growing number of underwear and swimwear stores, mainly for ladies.

5th floor and above – despite the signs, the fifth floor and above remain empty for the time being.

Address: Beijing Nan Lu 北京南路

Contact: 020-8564-4724

By Metro: Line 6, get off at Beijing Road

Taikang Cheng Special Cosmetics Zone 泰康城美容美妆用品

An addition to the Taikang Jewellery Market, but not as well established as its predecessor. This is a city centre market that is well worth watching for future developments.

Address: 44, Taikang Lu 泰康路44号

Contact: 020 8656-7234

By Metro: Line 2, get off at Beijing Road

Asia Pacific Boutique Trading Centre 广州亚太精品交易中心

Situated directly opposite the 1916 Christian Saviour Church on Wanfu Lu, this looks promising but only has a half a dozen open stores on the ground floor and an escalator that leads to a completely deserted second floor. It is best to keep moving East along Wanfu Lu until you reach the busier markets.

Address: 60, Wanfu Lu 万福路60号

Contact: 020 8657-7688

By Metro: Line 6, get off at Tuanyida Square Station 团一大广场站

Yue He Market 越和仰忠批发商城

A converted wet market in a very basic single story building. Expect lots of stores selling products aimed at young ladies. These include hair accessories, low end fashion jewellery, scarves etc. There are even a couple of specialist wig stores here. Small cosmetics and jewellery stores spread out into the nearby streets.

Rather than walking all the way from Beijing Lu, it is slightly easier to catch the metro to Tuanyida Square on line 6. Take exit A which will bring you out opposite the China Telecom Building. From here head west along Dong Yuan Heng Lu past the bus station until you reach the Police Station. Turn right here and it will bring you out directly between Yue He Market and Wanfu Market.

Address: At the junction of Dezheng Lu and Wanfu Lu
德政路和万福路交汇处

Contact: 020 8745-5632

By Metro: Line 6, get off at Tuanyida Square Station
团一大广场站

Guangzhou Wanfu Exquisite Commodity Place
广州万福精品广场

Nearly as large as the Trendy Plaza and significantly cheaper, few foreign buyers make it this far by themselves, which is a shame because there are lots of bargains to be had here.

Much of the ground floor is devoted to hats of all kinds. Baseball caps for gangster rappers to big floppy hats that Chinese girls like to wear on the holidays. There are dozens of hat shops on the ground floor but Dino Brothers at 70-71-72 is especially impressive in terms of breadth of stock.

Up on the second and third floors, there are stores filled with all kinds of fashion jewellery, cosmetics, belts, bags and hair accessories, as well a packaging and display items.

Address: 60, Wanfu Lu 万福路60号

Contact: 020 8658-3150

By Metro: Line 6, get off at Tuanyida Square Station
团一大广场站

Miscellaneous

Tianxu Hotel 天秀大厦

There is a second cluster of hair stores inside the old Tianxu Hotel (天秀大厦) that has been largely taken over buy African and Arab Traders. This is a much smaller market with many other commodities mixed in to serve the bustling Chocolateville community of the area. There are also a few interesting wig shops on the third floor of the Shun Zhao Commerce City (顺兆商贸城) at number 272 on the same road.

Address: 300, Huan Shi Zhong Road 越秀越秀区环市中路300号

Contact: 020 6233-8188

Metro: Line 5, Xiao Bei 小北站

Renmin Nan Lu Chemical Products Equipment Wholesale Market 人民南化工产品仪器批发一条街

This might be the place to come if you are looking for raw materials to create your own cosmetics. Many of these stores focus on lab equipment for education and business purposes but there are a few shops here that go beyond test tubes and retorts to sell chemical components in wholesale quantities. The stores are located on the right hand side of Renmin Nan Lu, just before the Shisanhang/Yide Lu junction. It can hardly be a coincidence that so many small shops have now sprung up on the left hand side of the street offering drug dealing paraphernalia. Buy supplies for your methamphetamine lab on one side and then cross over to stock up on all kinds of pipes, tools and personal security gear.

Address: 90-100, Renmin Nan Lu 人民南路 90-100号

Contact: 020 6233-8189

Metro: Line 6, Yide Lu 德西站

5 CLOTHING

Introduction

There are a number of different areas with clusters of apparel wholesale markets. Therefore I have separated these into eleven main areas. The first is the concentration of markets around the main Railway Station (广州火车站). This is followed by the nearby Zhanqian Lu Area (站前路), the Zhanxi Lu area (站西路) and the Guang Yuan Lu area (广园西) that stretches up to San Yuan Li. Guangda (广大), Sha He (沙河) and Shi San Hang (十三行) are all dealt with separately. This is then followed by sections that focus on childrenswear, underwear, sportswear and wedding attire.

Guangzhou Railway Station 广州火车站

The area surrounding the West Railway Station boasts one of the highest concentrations of clothing wholesale markets anywhere in the world. The Guangzhou wholesale markets are clustered around a number of provincial transportation centres including the train station and the provincial bus station, as well as a large number of shipping companies who also take advantage of this key logistical location. The largest markets are named after horses, ('ma' in Chinese), and so we have White Horse (Bai Ma), Silver Horse (Yi Ma) and Heavenly Horse (Tian Ma) all concentrated together.

Three of the largest are clustered in the same block just behind the Liuhua Bus Terminal, where Zhanqian Lu intersects with Huanshi Lu. This is where exit D4 emerges from the main subway station and there is a large pedestrian footbridge which crosses over to the Liuhua Hotel on the eastern side of Zhanqian Lu. This is the busiest section of the area and consists of the Hongmian, Bai Ma and Tian Ma markets all backing onto each other, a location known to locals as the golden triangle centre of Guangzhou's clothing wholesale market area.

Guangzhou Hongmian Clothing Wholesale Square 红棉批发市场 or 红棉国际时装城

Originally opened in 1993, and also known by its English name, the Kapok International Fashion City, this remains the busiest market for domestic buyers, with more than 100,000 small shop owners from all over the country and the rest of the world visiting nearly 2,000 outlets daily on nine floors, covering more than 60,000 square metres. The main entrance is flanked by large statues, fake Romanesque columns, and huge speakers blaring out deafening techno music. Clothing factories and companies from around the region including the Pearl River Delta, the Yangtze River Delta, Hong Kong, Macau, Japan, and Korea are gathered here, making it the number one wholesale market centre for middle and high quality fashion clothes.

The market is more popular with domestic shoppers than overseas purchasers and the lower floors especially are filled with fashionably-garbed female shop-owners from all over Guangdong Province who have come to buy large job lots of new stock

Floors:

1st Floor: Officially described as the "Top 100 Fashion

Brands," large boutique style shops are packed with locals buying teenager fashions in bulk amounts. Disco music blares out of the speakers and the shop floors are littered with huge bags of orders. Models stand on central benches in each store trying on outfits while dozens of their colleagues run around in circles, picking and packing.

2nd Floor: High street fashions for young women, lots of hand-clapping to attract the attention of buyers but generally smaller stores than on the ground floor.

3rd Floor: As well as clothing, this floor has a large range of cosmetics, accessories, hand bags, shoes and fashion jewellery.

4th Floor: Described as European and Korean brands, this is actually more of the same young women's fashion produced by domestic suppliers, but in European and Korean styles. Korean pop music and Korean TV dramas are massively popular among young Chinese women and so vendors try to accentuate this connection whenever possible. There is even a 'Dosilac Korean Fusion Cafe' on this floor as well as a McDonald's' and an SPD bank. Fashions here are more for ladies in their twenties rather than all the teenage styles on the first two floors.

5th Floor: Listed on the elevators as European and Korean brands for men, this is actually a floor for ladies that are slightly older. Lots of relatively conservative skirts and dresses for married women and young mothers. Around fifty percent of shops are currently vacant on this intermediate floor.

6th Floor: Now we start to see more men's fashion, especially young casual styles that are so popular in the domestic market. Outlets pretend to be international brands, but names like Rique Martin, Wisdom Boy, Falcao Lovsaesar and F+ Homme quickly give the game away that these are Mainland wannabes.

7th Floor: More boutique style outlets for men's fashions, mainly casual and very little in the way of suits or formal wear.

8th Floor: Stylish interior design makes for elegant looking shops, many of which display only a handful of men's garments. This alone gives some insight into the huge profits that these factories are making from just a small range of items.

9th Floor: Fashionable menswear, but very much to a domestic taste with lots of seemingly high-end t-shirts and casual slacks.

10th Floor: Customer service and building management for not shops or outlets.

Address: 184, Huanshixi Lu, Yuexiu District 广州市越秀区环市西路184号

Contact: 020 6213-6611

Transportation: Take Line 2 or Line 5, to Guangzhou Railway Station. From Exit D4 walk around the corner past the Liuhua Coach Terminal and the Hongmian entrance is first on the right. Look for the huge gold pillars and the huge speakers pumping out techno music.

Bai Ma Garment Wholesale Market 白马商务大厦

Also opened in 1993, there are more than 2,000 outlets in this one building alone, with representatives of factories from not only the Pearl River Delta region, but Zhejiang, Fujian and other garment enterprises throughout the Mainland, as well as manufacturers from Hong Kong and Taiwan manufacturers. In total there is 45,000 m2 of floor space with eight floors, including an underground parking lot, five floors for stores and two floors for office use.

Both retail and wholesale are acceptable for the majority of vendors, although most people come here for wholesale. With special orders, MOQ tends to be a hundred pieces with a lead time of seven to fourteen days.

This one building alone boasts an annual turnover of more than thirty billion yuan while occupying six stories of a ten-story office building. White Horse Market may not be in the most pleasant of neighbourhoods or in an easy walking area, but it makes up for it with volume and variety.

The floor descriptions can be a little confusing because the building is lower at one end than the other. This means that the ground floor entrance at the rear adjacent to Hong Mian appears to be the basement when approaching from the front entrance on Zhannan Lu.

Floors:

1st Floor: The ground floor is mainly women's pants, shirts, skirts and accessories. Prices are some of the lowest in the building, anywhere from 5-100 RMB. Expect poor quality and plenty of rough imitations. The prices here are among the highest in Guangzhou clothes wholesale markets. Some of the clothes on the first floor of Baima clothes markets are indeed sourced from Shahe and Shisanhang garment markets.

2nd Floor: Accessed by steps from the front entrance, this also appears to be the 1st floor or even the ground floor, and is officially described as the 'Women's Trendy Zone."

3rd Floor: Confusingly, this is mainly men's smart casual around the edges of the floor with mid-range ladies styles clustered right in the very centre.

4th Floor: Women's clothing and apparel, with a focus on more mature women and even the elderly, especially domestic Chinese styles.

5th Floor: More fashionable women's clothes mostly from smaller scale factories in the region.

6th Floor: Another 120 or so female fashion outlets all crammed in, and all competing like crazy.

7th Floor: The upper floors are much smaller than anything below, perhaps less than a quarter of the overall building size. This floor claims to be international men's fashion but with brand names like Yves Zegnoa, Leyudn Polo Pas, Valaznoo and Leveaus Jeans only the most uneducated of hinterland buyers are going to be fooled.

8th Floor: This is listed as being the floor for ladies' foreign fashion brands but again there was nothing that I, as a European recognised.

A great deal of the clothes in Baima are low standard goods from Shahe clothing wholesale markets and Shisanhang wholesale markets. These are sold at 50, 80 or 100 RMB or more, even though they are bought wholesale at about 10 RMB per piece at Shahe or Shisanhang. Most of the stores are targeted at foreigners and out-of-towners, and it can be difficult to negotiate a good price because many of the nearby stores all belong to the same boss and they try to fix prices.

As to the wholesale price, there are two terms to bear in mind, the "wholesale price" and the "package price." Most stores offer mixed wholesale, which means that you can enjoy the wholesale price as long as your order reaches the minimum quantity. With the "package price", this means you can obtain a lower price than normal wholesale, as long as you order the same style of clothes, and the quantity reaches the store's minimum purchase quantity requirement.

As with all the other markets, most floors have representatives of the local logistics companies who will transport goods to their company offices or cargo companies nearby for very reasonable prices, often less than 10 RMB for small to medium quantities.

Address: 16, Zhan'nan Lu, Yuexiu District 广州市站南路16号白马服装批发市场
Transportation: Take Metro Line 2 or Line 5, to Guangzhou Railway Station, Exit D4 and walk 250 meters along the first underground tunnel to F exit.

Tianma Clothing Wholesale Market 天马服装批发市场

Opened slightly later than its neighbours in 1998, Tianma houses more than a thousand shops on ten floors.
B1 Floor: A very busy mainly retail arcade for the very latest fashions in shoes, bags, sunglasses and accessories. This area is always filled with off-duty KTV hostesses haggling like crazy for the latest style of imitation high

heels or the current must have fake designer handbags.

1st Floor: Young men's smart casual fashion styles.

2nd Floor: Men's and women's leisure wear, coats, jackets, fur clothing, business wear, etc.

3rd Floor: Clothes for mature Chinese women, there are even a couple of traditional qipao stores on this floor. There are also eating options here including a Real Kung Fu Fast Food and a Chinese style canteen as well as a bank of ATMs in the centre.

4th Floor: The fourth floor and above are about half the size of their lower counterparts. This is the beginning of the men's casual apparel, but most of the brand names are Chinglish bastardisations of Dunhill, Aquascutum and the like.

5th Floor: More men's casual along with a few business suit outfitters. Look for domestic brands as well as those from from Taiwan and Hong Kong, including Seven Wolves, Tamrac, Ancient Tino, Champion family, etc. The rental fees per square meter up here drop to as little as 250 RMB.

6th Floor: More men's casual styles, lots of golf shirts and polo shirts

7th Floor: Higher-end smart casual styles for men, housed in expensive looking boutiques.

8th Floor: A few offices and showrooms for men's clothing factories but more than half empty at the moment.

9th Floor: Offices for the property holding company.

Address: 168,   Huanshixi   Lu
广州市环市西路１６８号天马服装批发市场

Contact: 020 8622-9866

Transportation: Take Metro Line 2 or Line 5 to Guangzhou Railway Station. G Exit is just opposite to Yima Clothing Wholesale Market and adjacent to Baima Clothing Wholesale Market. The main entrance is on the corner of Zhan'nan Lu and Huanshi Lu with access to a large pedestrian overpass that goes across the road to the

Provincial Bus Station.

Guangzhou World Trade Clothing City Store
越和仰忠精品批发商城

A vast new Avenue Complex located right next door to the Yima Market and just opposite Baima Market on Zhan'nan Lu. A large concourse, leads into a vast mall type building that is located directly behind the Provincial Bus Centre. As yet, only the stores on the ground floor have attracted the beginnings of rental interest, while the second, third and fourth floors are still mainly empty. It is difficult to see this place filling up with so many businesses in more established market buildings already being forced to close their businesses.

Address: 26-28, Zhannan Lu 广州世贸服装城
站前路站前一街26-28号

Yima Clothing Wholesale Market 壹马服装批发市场

Located directly opposite Baima Clothing Wholesale Market, expect ten floors of clothing and accessories. The top floor is an atrium exhibition area with the offices of just three manufacturers, Times, MawangsJ and Souveran Homme. The upper floors are mainly office/showroom space for local knock-off brands. Giorgio Amanda for example is located on the ninth floor while Bosbinry and Woody Ellen are situated on the eighth floor. By the time we reach the sixth floor, at least half of the stores are now vacant.

On the fifth floor, where the building connects with the Provincial Bus Station next door, the stock changes to fashions for older females with about forty different stores competing for attention. Ladies' brands in showroom set-ups continue onto the fourth floor. The internal escalators reach up as far as the third floor and this is the top of the main market area, with a good scattering of stores selling all kinds of ladies' fashion clothes. Up here is also a branch of the ICBC bank. The second floor has a similar market stall feel to it, along with some strange store names such as the unusual Likey Dog. Eighty percent of the stores here focus on female clothes but the only stores that have been rented are clustered around the escalators and the periphery areas are empty. The ground floor is filled with budget shops, with quality approaching that of Bai Ma across the road but nowhere near Huimei over on Zhan'xi Lu.

Address: 158, Huan Shi Xi Lu, Yuexiu District 广州市越秀区环市西路158号壹马服装批发市场

How to Get There: Take Metro line 2 or line 5, and get off at Guangzhou railway station, then go to exit G.

Guangzhou Bubugao Wholesale Square 红棉步步高批发市场

On the east side of Zhanqian Lu, opposite Hongmian on the corner with Zhan'nan Lu, this is the main wholesale market for woollen items, even though the main sign describes it as a leather market. There are some cheap luggage and bag shops of the ground floor. Up on the first and second floors the building is packed with every conceivable kind of knitted dress, skirt and cardigan, with a very distinctive small market-stall layout, and many vendors all crammed in together. A great deal of Muslim traders come here to source shawls and head scarves. Up on the third floor, medium-sized outlets with glass fronts offer similar styles at slightly higher prices. The fourth and fifth floors stores are larger again, mainly offices and showrooms for large-scale knitwear manufacturers.

Address: Zhanqian Lu 站前路

Transportation: Take Metro Line 2 or Line 5 to Guangzhou Railway Station, then go to Exit D4. Bubugao is just behind Liuhua Hotel on Zhanqian Lu, at the first intersection with Zhanqian Lu.

Liuhua Clothing Wholesale Market 流花宾馆南楼 or 流花服装批发市场

Situated in the South Tower of Guangzhou Liuhua Hotel, this is perhaps the most popular market in the area for visiting overseas buyers, especially those from Africa and the Middle East. Thousands of factories have located their stores in Liuhua Clothing Wholesale Market with glittering arrays of fashionable clothes at extremely competitive prices.

The entire building is a converted hotel and the previous usage is still very clear on the upper floors. The architectural style is very 80's Chinese Five Star, with lots of marble and huge leather sofas at the central lobby and on the upper floors. The smell of stale smoke is especially reminiscent of older Chinese hotels. There is an abundance of elevators, including a glass observation lift at the east entrance.

1st Floor: Due to the slope of Zhan'nan Lu, this floor begins as the basement at the west end of the building but emerges at pavement level at the eastern end. Small market-type stores and crammed in at enormous density selling a huge selection and men's and ladies' fashions.

2nd Floor: More of the same vast choice. Five tightly packed aisles of at least a thousand outlets, all with sales girls shouting "Hello Boss!" and selling everything from cheap twenty RMB shell suits to exotic evening-wear that would probably look better in Pattaya than St. Petersburg. Large numbers of oversized mannequins displaying big djellaba-type dresses.

3rd Floor: Glass fronted office outlets and showrooms. Slightly more upmarket then the lower floors but with similar products available in much larger quantities.

4th Floor: Ladies' medium range fashion, with an emphasis on Middle Eastern and African customers, made clear by names like Yasmin, The Goddess and The Fine Lady. Approximately half the size of the lower three floors.

5th Floor: Men's casual wear, especially sports shorts and

dress shirts.

6th Floor: Ladies wear and dresses mainly in African and Muslim styles.

7th Floor: Men's casual wear on the eastern half of the building with the western half taken up by more ladies' wear.

Address: South Building of Liuhua Hotel, 194, Huanshixi Lu 广州市环市西路194号流花宾馆南楼

Contact: 020 8666-8428

Transportation: Metro: Take Metro line 2 or line 5, to Guangzhou Railway Station. Take exit D4, walk along Zhanqian Lu to the first intersection and turn left at the Bubugao Wholesale Market. Liuhua Clothing Wholesale Market is situated on the left.

Changjiang Jeans City 长江牛仔城

This is the successor to the Guangzhou-Kang Le Jeans Wholesale Market (康乐牛仔服装批发市场) that was located next door along Renmin Bei Lu, but is now scheduled for demolition. Many of the shops have relocated here in the last couple of years but it is still very empty on many of the upper floors.

The basement is little more than an unfinished construction site and best avoided. The first floor houses a large number of denim fashion specialists, mainly ladies' fashion wear but menswear too. Once up onto the second floor, shop occupancy drops to about 20%, a story that is repeated on the remaining 17 floors. For reference purposes, I have included all the floors here even though most of them are extremely quiet.

3rd Floor: Jeans wear, 20% occupancy.

4th Floor: Sportswear and children's wear, completely empty.

5th Floor: Men's casual wear, especially sports shorts and dress shirts, 20% occupancy.

6th to 8th Floors: Ladies wear but only 20% shops still open.

10th and 11th Floors: Just a handful of men's casual clothing stores.

12th Floor: A small amount of men's and ladies wear stores.

13th to 16th Floors: Mostly empty.

17th Floor: Customer Service.

Address: Renmin Bei Lu 广州市 人民北路

Contact: 020 8668-8564

Transportation: Metro: Take Metro line 2 or line 5, to Guangzhou Railway Station. Take exit D4, walk along Zhanqian Lu to the first intersection and turn left at the Bubugao Wholesale Market. Changjiang is situated on the right hand corner of the first interchange i.e. Renmin Bei Lu.

Guangzhou Fu Li Building Foreign Trade Clothing Wholesale Market 富骊服装批发市场

Originally opened by Hong Kong billionaire Li Ka Shing, Fuli is now one of the more mature wholesale buildings in the district. There is a total of eleven floors, all focusing on men's casual clothing. The very top two floors are taken up by large office spaces with showrooms in the rear. Each office has a reception desk, a large sofa and as would be expected in a building owned by a Chaozhou native, every table has an elaborate gong-fu tea service. Products here are generally shirts, slacks, denims and the occasional leather item. Floors nine down to five have a very similar set up of around twenty five or thirty office showrooms per floor. The escalators only reach the third floor. Below this point there is a lot more cold-weather items with many stores selling thick coats, woollen sweaters and thick pants. The outside areas of the ground floor has a number of label and packaging design specialists.

Address: Zhanqian Bei Lu 广州市环市 站前北路

Contact: 020 8656-7865

Transportation: Metro: Take Metro line 2 or line 5, to Guangzhou Railway Station. Take exit D4, walk along Zhannan Lu to the first intersection and turn left at the Bubugao Wholesale Market. Fu Li is on the opposite side of the road, past all the mannequin shops.

Friendship Pants City 友谊裤都

On the opposite side of Renmin Bei Lu from Liuhua Garment Market. The third and fourth floors each contain half a dozen large office showrooms for very well-established manufacturers. The second floor is mostly empty at the moment while the ground floor has around sixty individual store vendors, all specialising in jeans and slacks.

Address: 921, Renmin Bei Road 人民北921路
Contact: 020 8666-9555

China Fashion Trade Centre 中国服装贸易城

Regular visitors to Guangzhou will recognise this building as part of the original trade fair complex before it moved to its new location in Pazhou. It seems that the owners thought that they could transform this massive space into yet another garment market. They were completely wrong. The small sections that have opened up are almost a ghost town in terms of buyers. A few vendors do some trade on the outside steps but this is mainly small scale surplus stock rather than large scale wholesale. To be honest, is probably is not even worth venturing across the road to pay a visit.

Address: Renmin Bei Road, 人民北
Contact: 020 8663-3434

Guang Kong Leisure Clothing Wholesale Market 广控休闲服装批发市场

Although first opened in 2001, the entire building is now derelict and all of the vendors have moved elsewhere.

It is likely that the entire building will soon be demolished and rebuilt as part of the military hospital that is being constructed on the corner of Liuhua Road.

Address: Renmin Bei Road, 人民北

Zhanqian Lu Area 站前路

`Beginning at the junction of Zhannan Lu and Zhanqian Lu, the first concentration of shops are devoted to store fittings and store mannequins. After this follows a number of clothing markets followed by some of the largest jewellery markets in the city.

Mannequin Display Centre 麒龙模特道具总汇

Surrounding the Zhannan Lu and Zhanqian Lu junction are a large number of stores specialising in all kinds of shop dummies and associated store fittings.

Jinxiang Lyla Underwear Market Place 站前内衣袜业批发市场 or 金象服装批发市场

The is the most professional underwear and socks wholesale markets in China and consists of two large floors of socks, knickers, bras, underpants etc. It is clearly visible with English and Arabic signs as well as Chinese above the main entrance. The left side of the second floor has a large selection of shops that focus on glamour wear. Lots of sexy nurses' outfits and peekaboo play-sets but with quality that reflects the low prices. When buying for export, remember that much of the stock on display is destined for the domestic market. Much of this would be considered children's only sizes in many western countries, so be very specific about the sizes that you need for your particular market.

Address: Jinxiang Building, 193, Zhanqian Lu Road 站前路193号金祥大厦

Jindu Clothing Market 金都服装城

In the same building as the Yingshang Hotel (迎商酒店), what used to be a packed hub of men's clothing is now more than half empty. The second and third floor is still a good location for factory-made formal menswear but with so many shops having been left vacant there is not the choice that there once was.

Address: Zhanqian Lu 站前路

Xin Da Di Clothing Wholesale Market 新大地服装批发城

Opened in 1994 with more than 350 shops, this is the best location for upmarket fashion knitwear. Previously a specially developed location for the Chinese Export Commodities Fair, this has since been expanded to incorporate the Xin Da Di Fashion Plaza. All kinds of dresses, cardigans, skirts and sweaters in many kinds of wool.This is the largest wool textiles market in Guangzhou or even in China, with factories represented from all over the Pearl River Delta.

Address: 166, Zhanqian Road广州市越秀区站前路166号

Transportation: Take Line 2 or Line 5, and get off at Guangzhou Railway Station.Walk 500 metres along Zhanqian Lu and look for Xin Da Di on the left. Look for the car park in front filled with high-end Benz's and Range Rovers.

Xin Da Di Fashion Plaza 新大地服装城

Eight more floors of high quality knitwear designers and manufacturers in a pleasant and modern atrium setting. Perhaps the most comfortable of all the markets in this area.

Xin Da Di Building 2, 108-122 Zhanqian Road广州市越秀区站前路108-122号

First Tunnel Clothing Wholesale Centre

广州第一大道服装批发中心

Three subterranean levels of converted nuclear shelters dating back to the hard-line communist era. Nowadays it is impossible to tell that this was once all bunkers, as the walkways are lined with hundreds of fashion outlets and then a number of branded coffee shops at the intersections. More than thirty entrances pop up unexpectedly all over the Liuhua area and once you get to know your way around this is a good way to take an air-conditioned short-cut all the way from the Provincial Bus Station to the Train Station to the Metro. Exits 18, 22 and 24 form a cross, running under the lengths of Zhannan Lu and Zhanqian Lu. Exit 18 comes up in the far east, outside the two stone elephants guarding the entrance to Changjiang Jeans City. Exit 24 is way across at the Bus Station and exit 24 is down at the Liuhua Hotel. Good to know for underground short-cuts between the various markets.

First Tunnel is one of Guangzhou's largest underground markets. The shopping area is a 2 full kilometres (1.24 miles) long with 24 entrances, exits and 18 elevators. There are two main floors, with more than 1,200 shops divided into seven sections: fashionable women's wear, export leisure wear, men's clothing, Korean styles, local leisure wear, children's clothes and socks and underwear. Many shops on the first level specialise in styles made specifically for Middle Eastern tastes. Levels to the south focus on clothing for infants and children. Most of the stores are the factory outlets. There are also several coffee shops in case hunger strikes while you are shopping. Address: 10, Zhannan Road站南路10号亚洲首席地下服装批发中心

Transportation: get off at Exit F of Metro Line 5 Guangzhou Railway Station, turn right and walk straight until you see a bridge, do not cross the bridge and turn right, walk straight for about 20 meters, then you'll see the underground market. Look carefully as you explore and

173

you will see the market emerging from the pavement in more than twenty different locations. If entering from the Guangzhou Bus Terminal at basement level, look for the entrance that has the gold characters 西郊商场 directly overhead.

Zhanxi Lu Area 站西路

Zhan Xi Lu is very famous as one of the main fake products areas in Guangzhou.

Zhanxifu Fashion Wholesale Centre 站西服装批发市场

Opened in 1992, with some 600 shops and even more offices, this market is spread out onto just three floors. The third floor is mainly young men's styles, cheap but exciting. The second floor is young ladies wear, small shops piled high with stock. The first floor has many accessories thrown into the clothing mix, with plenty of belts, handbags and even luggage thrown in for good measure.

Address: 1-4, Zhan Xi Road, Yuexiu District
广州市越秀区站西路1-4号

Guangzhou Huimei International Clothing Market 汇美国际服装采购批发中心

Guangzhou Huimei International Clothing Market first opened in August, 2008. It is one of the more upmarket wholesale centres and is very popular with fashion savvy local shoppers on the weekend.

Floors:

11th to 7th Floors: Offices and showrooms for Men's Fashion Manufacturers

6th Floor: Food Court.

4th to 5th Floor: Approximately one hundred men's fashion outlets, often with suspect names such as Amananna and Cole Kein. Plenty of shop window signs, stating no retail.

3rd Floor: With names like Mr. Korea, Korea Boy and Korea+8090, this floor is more Gangnam than Guangzhou with some seriously stylish boutiques. Some of the stores are distinctly 'pimp' style with huge fur coats, bright yellow suits and crushed velvet ensembles. I was quite taken with a full length Arctic-fox fur coat which was half Vin Diesel and half Huggy Bear but at 7,800 RMB, was a little bit over my budget. This is clearly where a section of the city's well paid ducks (male escorts) come to buy the latest styles. The B Section is devoted to menswear while the A section is given over to ladies wear.

B1 Floor to the 2nd Floor: Fashionable women's clothes, shoes and fashion accessories, children's clothes, hats, socks, etc. The basement has the feel of a teenagers' disco with all the very latest trends on display.

Address: 50, Zhanxi Rd 站西路50号

Metro: Take line 1 or 5 to Guangzhou Railway station, exit F. Walk alongside traffic for about 150 meters past the Bus Station. The building is orange on the side.

Kinbo Foreign Trade Fashion City 金都国际服装城

This market has a confusing floor plan, with many different levels on each floor and low ceilings, suggesting that it was once converted from a very different use.

The eighth floor has a Real Kung Fu fast food outlet along with a number of other local eateries. Floor 7, 6 and 5 are focussed mainly on smart menswear showrooms, with the fourth floor having a number of stores that specialise in larger sizes. The third and second floors focus on more casual styles, while the ground floor has a number of accessory shops thrown in for good measure, including many kinds of shoes and sunglasses. There is also a basement that is half-and-half menswear and children's wear.

Address: Zhanxi Rd 广州市越秀区站西路50号

Kai Rong Du Wholesale Costume Centre
广州凯荣都服装批发中心

The seventh floor is only vacant shops and a large empty atrium area. Floors 6, 5 and 4 are devoted to offices. The third second and first and basement floors are dedicated to ladies' western fashion styles

Address: Zhanxi Rd 广州市越秀区站西路50号

Guangzhou Kinsun Fashion City 广州金象时尚城

Floors five and four are office space only. The third floor stretches across to join up with the International Watch Centre. Expect plenty of western style casual wear, with a huge selection of fake Kenzo T-Shirts and other dubious looking counterfeits.

Address: Zhanxi Rd 广州市越秀区站西路

Gold Elephant Fashion Commercial Centre
金象时装商业中心

More of the same fake styles, much of which is made to appeal to East European and Russian buyers.

Address: Zhanxi Rd 广州市越秀区站西路

Kintan 金炭

One of the smaller markets in the area, but with mostly the same men's casual styles.

Address: Zhanxi Rd 广州市越秀区站西路

Kai Xin Yin 开心印

A compact little market all on the first floor of a single building, all specialising in baseball caps destined for overseas markets.

Address: Zhanxi Rd 广州市越秀区站西路

Panbo 潘博

A varied mix of menswear, ladies wear, accessories

and children's wear, all aimed mainly at overseas buyers. The stores themselves are divided into areas that are named after large fashion centres. These include Milan Street, Taiwan, Seoul, Paris and Tokyo.

Address: Zhanxi Rd 广州市越秀区站西路

Wantong Foreign Trade Clothing Wholesale Market 万通服装批发市场

Wantong is now a shadow of its old self. The main front entrance on the corner of Guangyuan Road is largely boarded up, with a few shops that look more like squatter's dens than legitimate clothing wholesalers. The rear entrance gives access to a number of dirty run-down floors with stores that seem to be aimed mainly at African customers. There is a smattering of shoes and bag stores that are rather isolated up on the six floor. From there down to the third floor, almost every shop has been vacated. On the third floor I found just one store open on this visit that focussed mainly on army-surplus type clothing of a very dubious nature. The second floor is mainly vacant store space with just a few stores carrying more of the same from the basement. This is mainly gangster-style bling, basketball and soccer strips as well as lots of baseball caps. Expect lots of cannabis designs, menacing hoodies and low quality shell suits. Some of the stores look more like thrift stores than genuine wholesale outlets. I did see a store that had some rather nice Harrington Bomber Jackets but they looked about as second-hand as the stock found at Chatuchak weekend market in Bangkok.

Address: Wantong Building, 135, Huanshi Xi Road 广州环市西路135号

Guang Yuan Xi Lu area 广园西路

While the sales assistants down on Beijing Lu now

solicit customers with the phrase 'Hello Boss,' this is the only part of China where a Chinese saleswoman has ever greeted me with the phrase, 'How are you, brother?' Most of the customers here are from West African countries such as Ghana and Nigeria.

There are print shops with T-shirts in the window imploring people to vote for provincial African candidates such as the 'Hon. Nana Amoako' as MP for Upper Dankyira East Constituency, a former district of Ghana. Items here, are tailored for African buyers. Fake Versace is popular, as are leopard prints, denim shirts with brown shoulder patches and reddish gold costume jewellery. There are black T-shirts and hoodies printed with text reading 'Alobam' and '#NGNG' in gold. 'Alobam' is a track by Nigerian rapper Phyno, #NGNG is the title of Phyno's 2014 album, an acronym for 'no guts, no glory.'

Jianan Clothes Wholesale Market (Canaan Export Wholesale Clothes Market) 迦南商贸城

Beneath the main sign for the Canaan market is a banner that says 'Let's say no to counterfeit and shoddy goods and build up a store of civilization and honesty together'. What a joke! A huge selection of clothes in here as well as a wide range of products including jewellery, shoes, handbags, jeans, kids wear, etc. Large numbers of African style clothes and almost 99% of the buyers are from African countries. This means that there is a lot of bling and bright colours, the kind of styles that remind me of millionaire Nigerian preachers, which is quite different from the subdued pastel shades that are preferred in the domestic markets. The ground floor is also the top floor and the lower floors descend to the level of the railways tracks which is well below the level of Guang Yuan Road. The first basement level is mainly jeans and dresses, while the lower basement is a wide variety of all kinds of clothing.

Address: 94-122, Guangyuan West Road, near Yaotai Xi Jie 广州广园西路94-122号, 近瑶台西街

Look for Wanshengtang Bus Stop (王圣堂站)

This area is filled with wholesale markets that cater predominantly too African buyers. Most of the shops are clothing outlets but there are plenty of items thrown in the mix for good measure, along with a few African Restaurants to make the customers feel at home. On the same stretch of Guangyuan Xi Lu you will find the following:

Tianen Trade Plaza 天恩服装市场

Wufu International Garment Market 伍福服装城

Yingfu Export Clothes Trade Plaza 盈富外贸服装城

Bole Trade City 柏乐商贸城

Tong Tong Trading City 通通商贸城

Mei Tai Cheng Clothes Wholesale Foreign Trade 美泰城

Down the road that is directly behind Mei Bo Cheng Beauty and Cosmetic Wholesale Market is a small wholesalers that many buyers overlook. Look out for the Min Tai Hospital (民泰医疗) and the Kwangguan Police Stain which is directly opposite. On the same side of the road is a smaller two-floor market for clothing. The second floor is almost solely devoted to jeans and denim wear, while the first floor is a mixed bag of various clothing, all at relatively low prices.

Address: Yaotai Xi Lu 瑶台西路

Tangqi Plaza 唐旗服装城

Just over the railway tracks from Canaan, Tangqi has a very similar feel, although with much more emphasis on smart formal wear, especially on the upper floors. The seventh floor is given over to management offices for the property owner. The sixth and fifth floors are mainly shirts and suits. Lots of vibrant colours that are meant to appeal to African tastes. Even the suits are often the kind of safari styles with short sleeves that are rarely seen in European countries. Expect lots of interestingly designed tuxedos and plenty of Afrobeat rhythms in the background. The fourth floor has more shorts and suits with a smattering of casual slacks thrown in for good measure. On the third floor are men's T-shirts and ladies wear, while the second floor includes accessories and jewellery. The ground floor is mainly shoe shops and a large African restaurant called Mama's Kitchen. The basement is largely empty with a scattering of logistics offices and cargo forwarders. At the rear is a partially populated second building. The second and first floors house a number of shoe wholesalers, along with a few bag manufacturers. The basement is mainly shipping specialists, while the lower basement is a large covered car park.

Address: 130, Guangyuan Xi Lu 广州广园西路130号
Contact: 020 6124-2398 6218-3588

Guangda Area 广大

Guangda Clothing Wholesale Market 广大服装商贸城

Visitors to the Liuhua Clothing Market Area might be amazed to learned that there is another wholesale market that still dwarfs this area. The market at Guangda is so large that it has its own internal bus routes. Built in 2005 many of the buildings are certainly starting to show their age. The concentration of stores is not as dense as it is around the Railway Station but this market has a reputation for some of the cheapest prices in town.

Guangda is a long way out of town, at least 35 RMB by taxi from the downtown areas such as the train station or San Yuan Li. It is located on Fenggang Road, which leads off Zengcha Road, which in itself is home to a large range of different but huge wholesale markets.

Guangda has its own internal bus station known as

Magang (Guangda Fenghuangcheng) Bus Terminal where the number 757 which serves the rest of the market. In addition, a number of oversized golf carts roam the complex. These can be flagged down and will take buyers from one section to the next. Guangda has its own Public Security Bureau or Police Station although it looked as though it had been long deserted on my visit. Perhaps more tellingly, the market has its own African restaurant.

The layout of the market can be quite confusing for first time visitors. The main entrances to the market are on Shitan West Road and most of the major landmarks are listed inaccurately on Google maps. The bus stop at the front of the market is Jianle Hospital (健乐医院站) but this is marked on Google as the Guangdong Judicial Police Hospital. Fortunately most taxi drivers know Guangda, and the frontage extends so far that unless your guide for the day is Mr Magoo, it is pretty much impossible to miss.

There is no pretence here. Most of the vendors have small undecorated lock ups. No glass windows, mannequins or expensive displays, just cardboard boxes overflowing with surplus stock of all kinds. Much of it is clothing but there are also bags, belts and even some shoes, all going cheap, cheap cheap.

The rear boundary of the market is bounded by Zhaofeng Road with the ugly, outdated-looking Hongshi Hotel (宏致大酒店 Address: 广州市白云区石井街兆丰路38号) on the opposite side of the road. Just beside this is the Bu Pi Fu Liao Market (布匹辅料), where off cuts and waste materials are sorted and sold off in bulk. The rear of the market is signed as the Guangda Leather Clothing Centre (广大皮具服装城) but in fact this is now dedicated to jeans vendors and is now the Guangda Jeans City (广大牛仔城站). Only the first and second floors are populated with shops and much of the second floor is still vacant.

Some of the company names are in amusingly poor

Chinglish such as the Hong Niu Cowboy Foreign Trade Firm. Still with so many cowboys operating in Guangzhou, it is perhaps a change to see some honest descriptions for once. At the near end of the Guangda market is the Meng Jia Baiyun Kids World (盟佳白云童装世界) which is covered in the children's clothing section below.
Address: Fenggang Lukou, Zengcha Lu, Baiyun District
增槎路 凤岗路 交汇处
Contact: 020 6116-2181

Guoda Fashion City 国大时装城

Opposite the Police School bus stop (警察学校站) on Shitan Road (again confusingly listed on Google as the Guangdong Justice Police Vocational College), Guoda consists of a front two storey building and a strange dog leg structure that stretches away behind. Here the vendors are slightly more upmarket than Guangda, with window displays and much nicer fittings and this state of affairs is obviously reflected in the prices charged. The front building has about twenty stores on each of its two occupied floors, all selling similar low end ladies wear. At the rear of the car park, slightly up a hill at the rear, is a long curving covered arcade of more ladies fashion wholesalers, again at the lower end of the market scale.

Guangda Part II

Directly beside the Guoda Market is a second Guangda market, not quite as large as the original but surprisingly spacious all the same. To enter, pass under the overhead sign, past the security box and the open garbage tip, through the car park and the first shops are approximately two hundred metres inside. Expect more of the same here: casual clothes, ladies fashion lines, sweaters, underwear, children's clothing and sportswear. The market stretches all the way through to connect up with the main Zengcha Road at the other end. Just across the road from the main entrance is a stark reminder of why everything here is so cheap. Next to the blackened buildings of the Hutian Cargo Terminal is a repugnant smelling creek with water so foul that it could probably poison fish at hundred yards. Even the river Styx could not have looked or smelled this bad and reminded me very much of the cover of the disturbing account of failed environmentalism in China, 'The River Runs Black' by Elizabeth C Economy.

Address: Fenggang Lu 凤岗路

Contact: 020 3633-9228

Other Areas

Highsun Binbin Plaza 海印滨滨广场

The plaza was built in 1959 by one of the largest property holding companies in the region. The Highsun brand can be seen all over the city from very early buildings such as this one, to the very latest malls such as the underground shopping centre at the Zhujiang New City Central Plaza. Originally Binbin Plaza hosted the Canton Fair between 1959 and 1972, when Haizhu Square was still the beating heart of Guangzhou. At the time, the Guangzhou Hotel directly opposite was one of the smartest hotels in town, and for a long time enjoyed a reputation as the number one place for rich local businessmen and the glamorous Tai Tai wives to go shopping for designer and imported brands. Unfortunately those days are long gone and the Guangzhou Hotel is now a shadow of its former self. Even so, remnants of this past can still be seen in Binbin Plaza, with its large collection of high end ladies fashions, especially the large number of fur coats on the 3rd floor.

The building sits directly above the Haizhu Square subway station, providing important access to areas such as One Link, Yide Road and Taikang Road. The first floor is now filled with Chinese designer fashion outlets, many of which relocated from the Guangzhou Hotel. Apart from the international brands around the Friendship Store and the Garden Hotel, these are some of the most upmarket fashion outlets in the city. The second floor is home to a McDonald's that is very popular with overseas buyers, who have not yet had the courage to come to grips with Cantonese food. Its presence alone is slightly out of place to western eyes, alongside all the designer fashion stores.

Up on the third floor, ladies fashion begins to give way to leather outerwear, and then morphs into a large number of fur coat vendors on the fourth floor. PETA supporters are in the distinct minority here, as many shops will not only have a wide range of seal furs, but even a stuffed baby seal or two also on display to suggest authenticity. This is a perfect example of the huge cultural divides between western and oriental consumers. At the rear of the fourth floor are a number of large artificial flower stores, selling associated items such as large vases and urns. The fifth floor reveals a small number of quite large fashion designer showrooms. Above this and accessible by elevator only is a large KTV emporium.

Address: 1, Qiyi Road, Haizhu Square 起义路1号, 海珠广场

Contact: 020 0802-8328/0801

The focus of Haizhu Square is the 11.5 meter tall Guangzhou Liberation Monument. An enormous PLA soldier stands with a rifle in one hand and a bunch of flowers in the other. The inscription rather ironically reads "All power belongs to the people". The granite statue was erected in 1959, exactly ten years after Liberation, only to be pulled down during the Cultural Revolution, and rebuilt again in July, 1980.

Shahe Clothing Wholesale Market 沙河服装批发市场

This area has exploded in the last ten years. When I lived in Guangzhou during the nineties, there were only a few small markets here, focussing on jeans and other denim-wear. Nowadays, this is probably the busiest clothing district in all of China, if not the world. Lianquan Lu is almost entirely filled with large wholesale clothing markets. Rents here have always been cheap as there are two rail lines that cross this road.

As well as being some of the largest clothing wholesale markets in Guangzhou, Shahe also has some of the earliest opening times. Hoping to find special promotions and amazing bargains, the area is busiest between 3 and 4am. Since the stores open early in the morning, they also close early, usually between 11am and 2pm, although there will be many stores open until 6pm in the busy periods.

The market has a reputation for low quality but this is not always the case. Store owners in Shisanhang, Zhanxi, Baima often go to Shahe for cheap clothes to be resold in their own stores. These vendors use their guanxi and connections to find the real bargains. You will need to exercise patience to find the same deals but it is possible. Perseverance will pay off in the end and you might even find some vendors selling garments by weight. In this case it is often possible to pick up T-shirts at just 1 RMB per piece. Most of the clothing in Shahe is sold directly from the manufacturers.

As in other large scale garment markets, ask the vendor for two tickets whenever you make a purchase. You can then leave all your items at the stores where you bought them and later have a carrier collect it all up and package it for you.

Meili Dong Fang 魅力东方

Shadong Youli International Clothing Wholesale Market mainly consists of three market areas including North Market, South Market and Hengli Market. It is mainly used as warehouse and office building to assist with the business in north market and south market. The front portion of the building houses a number of underwear wholesalers.

Address: 149, Xianlie Dong Lu 广州市先烈东路149号

Wanjia Children's Garments Wholesale Centre 万佳童装批发市场

As you walk from the Shahe subway station entrance, north along Xianlie Lu, there is a small annex market that is part of the Wanjia complex and the first market to be encountered. Inside are three floors, each with twenty or so stores, all stacked high with black bags filled with ladies clothing. As with most of the other markets, it is about all over except for the shouting by 10 am.

The main section of Wanjia Market is much, much larger. Although it was originally children's wear market, there is now a much greater range of garments. The third and second floors focus mainly on ladies wear with each store displaying a dozen or so items, all individually bagged and ready for packing. The main focus here used to be on jeans but these days the ground floor has much more of an eclectic mix and larger individual stores, with lots of jeans and menswear thrown in for good measure. At the rear of the building, shops focus mainly of nightgowns and pyjamas. Here at the rear the market merges into the Changyun Menswear Market.

Address: 115-116, Xianlie Dong Lu 广州市先烈东路115-116号

Changyun Centre Clothing Plaza 长运中心服装城

Three floors of mainly menswear, everything from singlets to silk ties. Lots of vacant stores on the upper floors, with only about thirty percent occupancy up on the third floor. The first two floors are packed with all huge amounts of men's clothing. Bear in mind that much of it is destined for the domestic market, a fact that is clear in the styles available. It also becomes very repetitive very quickly. There are entrances on both Xianlie Dong Lu and on Lianquan Lu. The Lianquan Lu entrance is signposted as 长运童装城 and is also sometimes referred to as the Chang Yun Merchandise Wholesale Market (长运小商品批发市场)/

Address: Lianquan Road, Shahe 广州市沙河濂泉路

Chang Cheng Underwear Market 长城服装

Yet another underwear market on the eastern side of Lianquan Lu. More grandma's shame than Victoria's Secret in terms of style.

Address: Lianquan Road, Shahe 广州市沙河濂泉路

Beicheng Men's Fashion Business District 北城时尚男装商务区

This is the very forefront part of the Beicheng complex, that is directly accessible from Lianquan Lu, where there is a China Construction Bank at the main entrance. There are five floors of men's fashion, most of it aimed clearly at the domestic market, but it is still possible to make some good finds in here. The third floor is mostly T-shirts and casual wear, while the second floor has a slightly for formal range including regular shirts and waistcoats. The first floor has a vast selection that fills in most of the gaps, from ties and socks to slacks and hats.

There are two basements in this particular building, both brimming over with every possible kind of denim wear, not just jeans.

At the rear of the menswear building is a separate three story building which the directly translated signs describe as the 'North City Kids The World.' (北城童装世界) Filled with a vast assortment of children's wear the horrendous English continues inside with store names and printed slogans on the actual clothes suffering from the same awful spelling blunders. This alone makes it clear that most of the stock is destined for the Chinese internal market, where nobody would ever notice such English mistakes.

Address: Lianquan Road, Shahe 广州市沙河濂泉路

Yimin Clothes Market 广东益民服装城

Right next door to Beicheng is the Yimin complex, so large that it has its own shuttle bus service to take buyers from one end to the other. There are ATMs all over the place but it is interesting that the largest bank here is a branch of the Bank of Jiujiang (九江银行), which perhaps says something about the origin of many of the vendors here. The building itself is a very spacious three floors and houses literally thousands of vendors. The basement is given over to car parking as is the rooftop. Sweat shop clothing is clearly a very profitable business endeavour by all the space needed to house all the owner's luxury cars.

The font sections of A and B are mainly ladies wear, while D and E towards the rear is largely women's jeans and assorted denim wear. Men's jeans make up most of E section while other menswear straddles the letters in a seemingly disorganised fashion. Styles are very low end, with lots of blatant designer copies, most of them appallingly spelled. This is a place to find the 'Procshe' (sic) T-shirts that are so popular in the hinterland at the moment, but there is also a good selection of Armwni, Paradi and Versaci and other misspelled knock offs. Quality of the clothes is about at the same level as the English.

Address: Lianquan Road, Shahe 广州市沙河濂泉路

New Field Fashion Centre (Xintiandi Fashion Centre) 新天地服装城

Turn left out of Liquan Lu (濂泉路) onto Baibuti

(百步梯) and the New Field Centre is around two hundred metres along the road past the Paco Business Hotel, a surprising lacklustre brand of accommodation despite all the Cayennes and top end Benz's parked outside. Up on the top floor, it is more of the same fake designer T-shirts aimed at illiterate locals. There is even a shop up here that has chosen to have the name CHIRS emblazoned over its frontage. It is quite common for Chinese to misspell my name but this is the first time I have seen it in such large letters over a store front. Thankfully the place looked as though it had been closed for quite while. The fourth floor is more of the same polo-shirt type casual wear aimed squarely at Chinese males.

The third floor down to the first floor is about the best selection of sportswear that I have seen in Guangzhou. A better selection than available at Meibo Sports Centre (美博运动城), at least to my mind, but most of it undoubtedly unauthorised. The third floor has everything from beach shorts to sports jackets with a couple of stores specialising is the decals used for team names and jersey numbers. The second floor is mainly basketball, football and badminton shirts with a good selection of socks and track suits thrown in for good measure. The first floor includes all of the above as well as large numbers of shell suits and other assorted recreational wear.

Down in the basement, the stock changes completely to non-sports related children-swear, similar to the clothes found at the rear of Beicheng and over on Zhongshan Ba Lu.

Address: 1858, Guangyuan Dong Lu 广园东路1858号

Guangzhou Guowei Clothing City 广州国伟服装城

Three floors of one of the oldest buildings on Lianquan Lu. The top floor is mostly jeans and denim wear, while the second and first floors are a mix of

children's wear and swimwear.
Address: Lianquan Road, Shahe 广州市沙河濂泉路

Tianbao Market 天宝装城
A single storied market of children's clothing suppliers, many of which seem to be in the process of moving out to more attractive locations.
Address: Lianquan Road, Shahe 广州市沙河濂泉路

Shahe East Children's Garments Wholesale Centre 沙河东童装批发市场
The eastern side of Lianquan Lu has so far resisted the corporate developers and houses a collection of run down markets that focus mainly on children's wear and underwear.
Address: Lianquan Road, Shahe 广州市沙河濂泉路

Shahe Second Children's Garments Wholesale Centre 沙河第二童装批发市场
More of the same cheap sweatshop tack destined for the cities of the hinterland.
Address: Lianquan Road, Shahe 广州市沙河濂泉路

The Shahe Third Clothing Market 第三服装市场
Directly opposite Yimin Clothing City, this looks to be an old school building that has be converted into a wholesale market. Along with The Second Clothing Market, both of these locations are devoted mainly to children's wear.
Address: Lianquan Road, Shahe 广州市沙河濂泉路

The Shahe Fourth Clothing Market 沙河第四服装市场
Plenty of children's wear here but with a much greater emphasis on cheap underwear than its first, second and third counterparts.

Address: Lianquan Road, Shahe 广州市沙河濂泉路

Jinma Clothing Centre 金马服装交易城

Guangzhou Golden Horse International Garment City is probably the busiest female fashion market in all of Guangzhou, if not the known universe. The crowds here are so intense that they make Baima look like like a ghost town. Even Shisanhang does not get this busy or this crowded. The conditions are a fire inspector's nightmare. Six floors are mostly broken down escalators, discarded packaging everywhere and an absolute multitude pushing and shoving to get past each other. Chungking Mansions in Hong Kong undeservedly has the reputation for being the worlds worst fire trap, but this place easy snags that title. I would feel safer in a Dhaka garment factory than I do here. To describe the clothing as fashion is charitable at best. A better description would be a selection of bargain-basement rags printed with horribly mangled English slogans that make little sense to an English speaker but which can be seen all over the country. Even so, it is worth a visit such to experience the throbbing mass of humanity that can fit into one building. If this is the market, then I would hate to think what the workshops are like.

There is a shuttle bus down to the Zhongda Fabric Markets every ninety minutes.

Jinma is spread over three buildings, the busiest being the six floors that are on the eastern corner of Lianquan Lu and Xianlie Dong Lu. The other two buildings are on the western corner directly opposite. The market on the western corner of the road is mainly ladies fashion, but the adjacent buildings such as Jin Ma Childrenswear Wholesale Market (金马网络服装城) have a strong children's focus Address: 149, Xianlie Dong Lu 广州市先烈东路149号

Woman's' World 女人街网络批发

Apart from Jinma, much of the northern side of

Xianlie Dong Lu is currently in the process of being demolished and rebuilt. The greater part of the street is currently home to a large number of delivery companies that are housed for the moment in temporary tents on sites that until recently used to be shops and department stores. Opposite these, the far end of Xianlie Dong Lu is home to the original slum area of Shahe that remains a Dickensian rabbit warren of back alleys, wet markets and hole in the wall eateries. These serve the staff the work in the huge buildings at the eastern end of the street such as Woman's World. Six cramped stories of ladies wear, very similar to the Jinma set up but aimed at a slightly old customer.

Address: 312, Xianlie Dong Lu 广州市先烈东路312号

Guoda On-line Clothing Wholesale City

Seven more floors of low end ladies fashions, churned out from hinterland sweat shops for a bottomless domestic market. Expect the same crush of people as in Jinma. Located next to the China Post Office, there are seven floors here, all filled well beyond capacity and attracting crowds that would have made even Moses uncomfortable.

Address: 306, Xianlie Dong Lu 广州市先烈东路306号

Dashi Dai Wanguo Pifa Cheng 大时代王国批发城

Located inside Shahe Hotel, the second and third floor are now filled with ladies underwear wholesalers aimed at foreign buyers. The brands here are head and shoulders above anything found on Lianquan Lu.

Address: 296,   Xianlie   Dong   Lu
广州市先烈东路296号沙河宾馆

Fuli   On-line   Clothing   Wholesale   Centre
富丽网络服装批发城

It is little surprise that the huge Fuli company has a property here in Shahe. Another five floors of mixed fashions, mainly low-end garments aimed at second and third tier Chinese cities. Prepare for the same kind of customer crush that is experienced in Jinma and Woman's World.

Address: 302, Xianlie Dong Lu 广州市先烈东路302号

Tailai Clothing Foreign Trade Wholesale 泰来服饰中心

Directly above the Bank of China and McDonald's, this is now largely empty and only the frontage signs remain. Also signposted as the Network Clothing Street (服装批发一条街).

Jinhuadi Commodities Market 金花地

Just past the Shahe Hotel is the entrance to the Jinhuadi Commodities Market. There is no English sign at the entrance but look for the Okuma advertisement with the polar bear logo directly above. This is NOT a clothing market but a selection of dry goods for locals. I have included it here so that will not waste you time in the wrong location.

Guangzhou Shisanhang Clothing Market Area 十三行服装批发城

The roads that make up the Shisanhang clothing area have been lined with markets since the 17th century and have long been a central import and export centre. Shisanhang refers to the thirteen factories that played such an important part in Guangzhou's history. It is ironic that one of the oldest trading districts in the city now focusses on the very latest fashions in clothing.

Shi San Hang refers to a number of markets including Xinzhongguo Clothes Wholesale Market, Hongbiantian Garment Wholesale Market, Guyi Street, Doulan Shang Jie, Heping East Road Clothes Wholesale Market and Da Shi Dai Clothes Wholesale Market. Most stores open around five to six o'clock in the morning and close at about half past twelve.

Subway Access: Exit Wenhua Park Subway Station from exit D out onto the main road and follow the crowds of young females through a shabby public park, where Shisanhang Lu is off to the right.

Alternatively, exit Yide Road subway Station and head east along Yide Lu past the Children's Park at the junction of Renmin Nan Lu. Shisanhang is on the opposite side of the road just to the south east.

New China Building (Xinzhongguo Dasha) 新中国大厦服装城

Constructed in 1996 and opened in 1998, this is the number one location for young ladies fashion. This used to be mainly name brand replicas but this is now changing to become just about any items with English slogans splashed across the front. Bear in mind that most of the stock here is aimed at an uneducated hinterland market and so you can expect to see all kinds of illiterate garbage on the front of baggy, oversized Tshirts. 'Pervert,' 'Acne' and 'Fuck What You Are' were some of the most popular printings during my most recent visit (spring 2015)

There are twelve sprawling floors of low-end sweatshop output trying to pass itself off as fashion but many of the rags here purchased straight from the markets at Shahe and resold. Out of three banks of lifts, only a single elevator was in working order. The best part about these stores is that it is possible to buy two or three pieces of clothes at wholesale prices. The 4th floor is mainly showrooms with offices. Many of the stores will not exhibit their latest styles of clothes there, fearing that they would be copied. One boss that I used to buy clothes from told me that usually the new styles would only be sent to their regular customers and they would be put on exhibition after a trial sale of one or two weeks. The minimum purchase quantity of clothes on the 4th floor is usually five or ten pieces,sometimes 20 or 30 pieces for latest styles.

Address: New China Plaza, 1, Shisanhang Lu 荔湾区十三行路1号, 新中国大厦

Opening hours: Daily, 06:00-13:00 for markets; 09:30-1:00 for retail stores

Hong Bian Tian Garment Wholesale Market 红遍天西门

Located directly behind the New China Market, this is almost an extension featuring more of the same. Crowded with pushy, ill mannered buyers, the phrase 'kan yi xia' is repeated ad nauseum by every single vendor and there are around a hundred stores on every floor. The only redeeming feature is that every store has three or four good looking girls modelling the latest offerings. By 9am it is all over bar the shouting and the main aisles are filled with huge quantities of oversized green woven sacks filled with stock headed for Hefei, Zhengzhou and other hinterland hell-holes. Hong Bian Tian used to have slightly cheaper products but these days the differences are minimal at best.

The second floor basement was being refurbished on my last visit. The first floor basement and the first four floors are packed to the gills with cramped little booths, knocking out low end ladies wear as fast as the sweatshop workers can produce it. The ground floor has around 140 shops but this drops to about ninety by the fourth floor.The fifth floor has around sixty shops, most of them curtained off to prevent casual onlookers from spying the latest creations. Needless to say, there is garbage everywhere. I do not mean the low-end products but visitors find themselves almost knee deep in discarded packaging and plastic wrappers.

Address: New China Plaza, 1, Shisanhang Lu, Liwan District 广州市荔湾区十三行路1号, 新中国大厦

Yao Sheng Clothing Wholesale Market

耀生服装批发市场

Yet more fashion items are crammed into the basement of the New China Building which for some strange reason has a separate side entrance and goes by a different name to the rest of the building.

Address: Below New China Plaza, 1, Shisanhang Lu 广州市荔湾区十三行路1号, 新中国大厦下面

Thanks to the success of Shisanhang, many stores have sprung up near the Xin Zhong Guo building, selling shoes, hats, scarves, etc. at discount rates. Guyi Lu for example is a narrow street between Hepingdong and Shisanhang. People have been doing business here for at least 300 years, selling everything from used clothes to fine silks. Modern retail and wholesale activity restarted in the 1980s. Doulanshang and Hepingdong Roads house even more clothing stores that stretch as far north as Guangfu Lu and east as far as the Culture Park. This is also a good area to find wholesalers dealing in fashion related items such as umbrellas, shop fittings and costume accessories.

Thirteen Factories International Fashion City
十三行国际时装城

A mere shadow of a market compared to the local competition. The second floor is largely empty and the ground floor houses about fifty stores of low end clothing stores. There is also a basement area with many dealers focussing on poor quality denim items.

Address: Renmin Nan Lu, to the left of the New China Building 人民南路新中国大厦左边

Children's Clothes

The largest concentration of children's clothing wholesale markets is centred around the busy thoroughfare of Zhongshan Ba Lu.

Zhong   Ba   Children's   Garment   Plaza
中八童装妇婴用品广场

Directly across the road from the subway station and the Guangzhou-Foshan Bus Station terminal. (95 Zhong Shan Ba Road 广州中山八路95号). Also known locally as 'Lihu Children's Clothing Wholesale Market' (荔湖童装批发市场), a huge red sign over the main entrance has the words Lihu Building (荔湖大厦) in big gold letters. For some reason there is a white sail boat logo and then below this is the Chinese name, the English name 'Zhong Ba Children's Garment Plaza' and the translation into Arabic. Lihu children's clothes wholesale market is one of the earliest wholesale markets in this area and is truly vast. In total it boasts 12 floors, and the corridor in the middle separates the wholesale market into Lihu Da Sha A Building and Lihu Da Sha B Building. The first to third floors are wholesale markets while the floors above the fourth are offices and showrooms.
Address: 97-101, Zhongshanba Road, Liwan District
广州市中山八路97-101号
Contact: 020 8181-1466

Fuli Kids World 富力 儿童世界 （大型童装批发商场）

Also known as R & F Children's World (广州富力儿童世界). Somewhat confusingly, there is no sign in English identifying this as Fuli Square.Instead the huge English sign at the front door says 'Kids City' in huge bubble letters with the words 'Super Children's Wear Wholesale Market' directly below. Inside there are more than 500 stores on three floors covering children's clothes, infant supplies, maternity goods, etc. More than 80% of the stores are manufacturers from Guangzhou or neighbouring cities with children's clothes covering different ages and different styles for different seasons. The underground floor covers a general mix of children's clothes while the first floor is mainly for branded

children's clothes. The second floor is more oriented towards infant wear, which continues up to the third floor
Address: 61, Zhongshanba Road, Liwan District
广州市荔湾区中山八路61号
Contact: 020 8119-5031
Website: http://www.kids-china.com/main.asp
Metro: Line 5 to Zhongshanba station. Exit A, turn left and walk about 200 metres. Fuli Kids World is on the corner across the street.

Zykids Clothing Wholesale Market 中易童装世界

Further east towards the Shiliju bus stop (石路基站), look out for the bright red LED signs in English, Chinese and Arabic. A pair a escalators at the main entrance leads directly to the upper floors where the range of baby, infant and children's clothes continues.
Address: 43, Zhongsha Ba Lu 中山八路43号
Contact: 020 8135-5111

Hoping to jump on the bandwagon, a number of smaller children's wholesale markets have opened up further along the Zhongshan Ba Lu. The product lines are very similar to the larger markets and they are in various states of occupancy. They include the following.
Zhongshan Nantian Children Clothing Wholesale Square 中山八路南天童装广场
Zhuo Rong Children's Clothes Wholesale Market 卓荣外贸儿童百货批发城.
Guang Hong Tong Zhuang Cheng 广鸿童装城
Hui Fu Children's Wear Centre 汇幅童装总汇
HBF Children's' Clothing Trade Centre 红八方童装交易中心
Song Yuan Children's Clothing Wholesale Market 松源儿童百货批发市场

NB: Under Chinese law, there is a difference in standards for infant clothes and clothes for children aged three or more. These standards on infant clothing are stricter in order to protect the health of small babies with regard to levels of chemicals such as formaldehyde, PH values and colour fastness. For babies under age 3, all the clothes should meet A standard. Darker colours tend to contain larger quantities of chemicals to maintain colour fastness which can be dangerous to children's health. Some manufacturers also use fluorescent whitening to brighten colours.

Other Areas

Jinsheng Baby Infants Wear Discount Store (Life Baby)

Just around the corner from the Zhongshan Ba Lu Markets, but closer to the Chen Clan Temple Subway Station on line one. Look for big-name brands at wholesale prices.

Address: 59-2, Liwan Road, Liwan District 荔湾区荔湾路59-2号

Li He Children's Clothes Wholesale Market 荔河韩国童装城

Sometimes also translated as the Lihe Korean Children's Market 荔河韩国童装精品广场), this market is located some distance away from from Zhong Shan Ba Lu wholesale markets on Huangsha Road. On my last visit, there were very few stores open here and whole place had a ghost town feel to it. Probably worth avoiding.

Address: Lihe Trade Plaza, 25, Yuenan Street, Huangsha Dadao 广州市黄沙大道粤南大街25号荔河商贸中心

Dongbao Women and Baby Clothing Wholesale Market 东宝妇婴用品童装批发城

Just opposite the Bank of America Plaza, this market is smaller that those on Zhongshan Ba Lu but has a lot of

variety crammed into a smaller space. It is possible to find maternity dresses, shoes, hats, scarves, bath tubs, pads, baby carriers, cribs and all kinds of baby toys here.
Address: 917, Renmin Beilu 广州市人民北路917号

Meng Jia Bai Yun Kids World 盟佳白云童装世界
Right next door to Guangda is the 'Meng Jia Bai Yun Kids World' a large children's clothing market, set back on two floors that has a huge selection of baby, toddlers, infants and children's' clothing outlets. There are even some maternity wear shops here.
Address: Fenggang Lu 凤岗路

There are also a number of children's clothing wholesale markets in the Shahe district. See above.

Beyond Guangzhou

Children's Clothing Wholesale Markets in Foshan
Foshan Jiancun Children's Garments Wholesale Center佛山简村童装批发市场
(Close to Tongji Road Metro Station on the Guang-Fo line, some people claim that this largest children's clothes market in southern China with the lowest prices.)
Address: Tangyun Street, Fenjiang South Road, Foshan 佛山汾江南路唐园街
Nanhai Huaping Children's Garments Wholesale Center南海华平童装批发市场
Address: Huaping Village, Shixi, Shishan, Nanhai District, Foshan 佛山南海区狮山狮西华平村
Foshan Huanshi Children's Garments Wholesale Center佛山环市童装批发市场
Address: Huanshi, Chaoan Road, Chancheng District, Foshan 佛山禅城区朝安路环市

Children's Clothing Wholesale Markets in Dongguan
Humen Children's Garments Wholesale Centre
虎门童装批发市场

Underwear
Jinxiang Lyla Underwear Market Place
站前内衣袜业批发市场 or 金象服装批发市场

The is the most professional underwear and socks wholesale market in China and consists of two large floors of socks, knickers, bras, underpants etc. It is clearly visible with English and Arabic signs as well as Chinese above the main entrance. The left side of the second floor has a large selection of shops that focus of glamour wear. Lots of sexy nurses' outfits and peekaboo play-sets but with quality that reflects the low prices. When buying for export, remember that much of the stock on display is destined for the domestic market. Much of this would be considered children's' only sizes in many western countries, so be very specific about the sizes that you need for your particular market.
Address: Jinxiang Building, 193, Zhanqian Lu Road
站前路193号金祥大厦

Gaodijie Wholesale Market 高第街批发市场

Twenty or thirty years ago, Gaodijie Market was one of the largest markets in Guangzhou. Once the government decided to relocate most of the large wholesale clothing markets out to the Train Station, Gaodijie was left out on a limb. It used to bring in 200,000 people every day in its heyday, but now that the surrounding area is mostly branded retail, it has become stuck in a little bit of a rut. The street is nearly half a mile long and connects the southern end of Beijing Road all the way through to Renmin Nan Lu. Most of the goods are underwear related although this changes to belts, purses and small leather goods as it reaches the Renmin Road end. Plenty of choice in socks, underwear, pyjamas, towels and swimwear. I know of an expat English teacher that stops of here every summer to buy a whole load of water wings, pool floats, goggles and pool floats. He then spends the hot season up in places like Guilin and Yangshuo. Every day he seems to attract a bevvy of good looking local tourists for some impromptu swimming lessons and seems to revel in the fact that even fewer Chinese can swim than can speak English. Some shops are wholesale only but the only way to find out which is to ask. In addition, there are sarongs, bras and lots of unflattering hosiery of the kind that Nora Batty would probably prefer. For more sophisticated lingerie and boudoir playwear, try the Jinxiang Lyla Underwear Market Place underwear market up near Bai Ma.

Address: Gaodijie Lu, Yuexiu District
广州市越秀区高第街路

Directions: From Haizhu Square Subway Station (海珠广场) take exit B3 onto Qiyi Lu and walk 200 metres north. Gaodijie is marked by a large stone archway on the right.

From Beijing Lu Subway Station (北京路站) take the main exit out onto Beijing Lu and walk 200 metres north.Gaodijie is marked by a large stone archway on the left.

Kota Plaza 雅凤针织城

A smaller underwear wholesale centre, popular mainly with domestic buyers. On the opposite side of Jichang Road to the cosmetics market, just north of the calendar market. Underwear in a variety of styles for both men and women, including a great deal of big brand copies. In addition, these stores stock large quantities of the kinds of pyjamas and longjohns that are popular with Chinese customers.

Address: Jichang Interchange North 机场立交北站

Jiahe Accessories City 广州加和城

What was once the Overseas Chinese Hotel was first reincarnated as a large home accessories wholesale market, but has now changed its focus to underwear, especially bras. The fifth and fourth floors are still populated by hat and scarf suppliers. But the first three floors are starting to fill up with underwear manufacturers' outlets. The second floor is home to one of the least busy McDonald's in the city, which stretches out over the bridge across the road across Zhanqian Lu.

Address: 90, Zhanqian Lu 广州市荔湾区站前路90号

Tianfu Housewear and Underwear Market 天富家居服内衣城

The third and fourth floor are mainly small offices. The second floor has a good selection of sexy underwear and playwear, not quite up to Victoria's Secret standards of quality but quite close in looks. There are at least six stores here than specialise only in basques. The first floor is dedicated mainly to house dresses, pyjamas and dressing gowns.

Address: 100, Zhanqian Lu Road 站前路100 号

Guangzhou Wufu Underwear Market 伍福内衣批发市场

This was once the largest underwear wholesale market in Guangzhou with more than 1000 shops featuring bras, underpants, nightwear, socks, all-in-ones, swimsuits etc. These days there is much more of a focus on beauty products but this market is still well worth a visit.

Address: 499, Sanyuanli Road. 广州市三元里大道499号
Guangzhou Metro: Line 2, Get off at Sanyuan Li Station, Exit C1, and About 10 minutes along Sanyuanli Road.

Gang   Dong   Sex   Toys   Market
广州港东(国际)成人用品城

Hidden away among the clothing markets that surround the Railway Station, this market is rather disappointing in that most of the stock is cheap tack that would impress very few people. Lots of dubious looking sex dolls, monster dildos low and quality playwear. Very little in the way of high-end bondage gear or even lingerie that matches up to the likes of Victoria's Secret, but this is China, so I do not suppose we should expect to much.

Address: 39, Liuhua Road, Liwan District
广东省广州市荔湾区流花路39号

Sportswear

Meibo Sports Centre 美博运动城

Five floors of sportswear, with a strong focus on soccer strips from just about every country on earth. A good selection of clothing aimed at other popular mainstream sports such as basketball but do not expect cricket whites, kendo armour or other minority sports gear here.

Address: 133, Huan Shi Lu 环市西路133

New Field Fashion Centre (Xintiandi Fashion Centre) 新天地服装城

Six floors in total but the sportswear begins in earnest on the third floor. The third floor has everything from beach shorts to sports jackets with a couple of stores specialising is the decals used for team names and jersey numbers. The second floor is mainly basketball, football and badminton shirts with a good selection of socks and track suits thrown in for good measure. The first floor includes all of the above as well as large numbers of shell suits and other assorted recreational wear.

Address: 1858, Guangyuan Dong Lu, Shahe

广园东路1858号

Guangzhou Shuiyin Street Sports Goods Market
广州市水阴街体育用品综合批零市场

This is mainly retail for local athletes and so there are many stores here that are focussed on local favourites such as badminton and table tennis, but is worth a browse although it is quite a long way from the city centre.
Address: 458, Guangzhou Dadao Bei Lu (near the entrance of Guangzhou Sport University) 广州大道北458号（广州体育学院门口）

Xingzhiguang Sports Goods Market
广州星之光体育用品批发市场

This is more oriented towards sports equipment (and also stationery) but there are also large numbers of manufacturers of sportswear here.
Address: Nan'an Lu, Liwan district. 荔湾区南岸路

Wedding Dress Street 婚纱一条街

Wedding Dress Street stretches from the northern part of Jiang Nan Da Dao, south of of the iconic Haizhu Bridge, down to the subway station at the Second Workers' Palace (Shi Er Gong.)

Dating back to the early 1980s, this was one of two overseas Chinese areas in Guangzhou at that time. At first this was mainly a pottery area, often with a shop in the front and a small workshop in the back.

Nowadays, this is one of the most colourful streets in Guangzhou and businesses here have benefited enormously from the rapid growth of Guangzhou as an export hub. The main drag is lined with fancy showrooms showing off the kind of ball gowns that would have put Audrey Hepburn in the shade at the Ambassadors' Ball. The side streets are also filled with shops, some having large two storey buildings that stretch far enough back to accommodate more than a hundred more stores. Everything associated with weddings can be found here from simple shoes and dresses to cosmetics and flower arrangements. Millineries sit alongside page-boy and bridesmaid specialists, where locals can dress up their toddlers to look like anything from a fairy princess or a Kuomintang Generalissimo. Tiaras, fur stoles, honeymoon bedding, even the chemists here have special bridal displays of celebratory tonics and cure-alls.

The range of goods here stretches all the way from naff tack to uber-glam, and even a confirmed bachelor like myself, begins dreaming of transforming a Cantonese Eliza Dolittle into an Ascot jaw dropper. Many of the ball-gown dresses especially, are works of art that would hold their own in New York, Milan or Tokyo. The immense Chinese wealth gap flaunts itself with a flagrancy that manifests in gaudy red gowns decorated with hundreds of cabochon crystals, ending up more caricature than item of beauty. Some shops really push the envelope, loading up their fashions with enough bling to make even Liberace gag. For more discerning buyers, there are islands of elegance and style here that are well worth a look even if you are not in the wedding business. On this last visit, one particular dress stood out in particular, its traditional Ming blue design giving it the look of a priceless imperial Jingdezhen vase. Men's suits are less enticing, many of the elaborate dress suits looking more like toy-soldier outfits to be worn at a fancy dress rather than a wedding ceremony.

Shops start just below the bridge at Haizhu Wedding Plaza (海珠婚纱城), two floors of everything from invitations to cake toppers, from photo albums to parasols. Directly under the pedestrian footbridge on the main avenue is the Times Wedding Plaza (二楼时代婚纱广场), and shops of all kinds continue all the way down to the Good Century Plaza (好百年（国际）婚纱婚庆摄影), situated under McDonald's, directly above the subway. In between, there are literally hundreds if not thousands of individual shops, often with bizarre Chinglish names such as the extraordinary "Nuptial Dress Fitting Confluence." In between, be sure to explore all of the side alleys, if only to see some excellent examples of Lingnan residential architecture before it is all bulldozed in the name of development. This part of the city is experiencing such a building boom that the parallel Xiaogang Lu is now almost entirely building materials shops and skyscrapers are spring up all over the place. Back alley malls include places such as the Jiangnan Wedding Articles Plaza International (江南婚庆用品广场)

Apart from wedding outfits, there are also many photographic studios here as well as a large selection of stores that sell all kinds of historical outfits from the dreary olives of red army fatigues to the blazing robes of a Tokugawa princess. Even these pale in comparison to the minority costumes that are found in Kunming and Yunnan, but that is another book entirely.

To order a dress takes about two weeks. Prices are generally halved for those simply wanting to rent a dress. For ball gowns and wedding dresses, the prices start at a level that would suit even Cinderella and go right up to stratospheric for items that fancy themselves as Chinese couture. Menswear shies away from such absurd heights. A standard two piece tuxedo starts at about 450 RMB deep in the side-streets but jumps up to two or three thousand on the main road, especially if you want a non-standard design that will make you look more like the emcee than the groom. The Boss at Mr Honey (汇美婚纱批发广场) (who is actually a friendly Mr. Chen) speaks reasonable English and has a well stocked outlet for his factory on the East side of the main avenue. Unfortunately no English at Shang Ping Jiayi (尚品嫁依), but the owner is friendly and has some of the better menswear selections in the area.
Address: Jiangnan Da Dao Bei, Haizhu District

江南大道北)
Metro: Shi Er Gong station, Line 2, Exit D

Haizhu Bridge

If you find yourself at Haizhu Square, then the easiest way to reach the weeding dress street is simply to walk across Haizhu Bridge. Originally constructed by the American Markton Company in 1933, using second hand steel imported from Britain to cut costs, this rivets and truss monolith is an icon of Old Guangzhou. It was recently undergoing restoration work and was closed to motorised traffic for around six months. Allegedly, these are safety inspections but a flurry of suicide attempts that have made the bridge notorious in the last few years may actually have more to do with the closure. Most revealing of all is the story of vigilante Lian Jiansheng, a 66 year-old, retired soldier who broke through a police cordon to push a suicide jumper off the bridge. Chen Fuchao had bought city centre traffic to a complete standstill and was threatening to launch himself off the bridge when Lian Jiansheng walked up to him, reached out to shake his hand and gave him a good hefty shove. Luckily, Chen fell only ten metres yards before landing on a partially inflated emergency air cushion. He was taken to hospital with minor wrist and back injuries. Lian Jiansheng railed at the endless stream of jumpers like Chen, calling them selfish and attention seeking: "They do not really dare to kill themselves. Instead, they just want to raise the relevant government authorities' attention to their appeals." Chen, who said he had debts of two million yuan because of his involvement in yet another failed building project, was at least the twelfth person in two months to threaten suicide at the very same spot.

At one time the bridge incorporated a central lifting mechanism similar to Tower Bridge in London. Back in the thirties, crowds would gather along the banks of the river and cheer as the sirens roared and steamers passed underneath. For many residents the bridge was a colossus the likes of which many had never seen before. When I lived south of the river back in the nineties, I would cram onto the trolley bus across Haizhu Bridge every morning to go to work, and always be amazed by the never-ending torrents of bicycles that flooded across the bridge beside me. Unfortunately those days are long gone and now the bridge has to deal with an endless flow of dangerously overloaded trucks. No wonder the authorities are concerned about its strength and integrity.

Beyond Guangzhou
Nanhai/Foshan has a number of large clothing wholesale markets:
Nanhai Clothes Wholesale Centre 南海市
Foshan Jiancun Clothes Wholesale Centre 佛山禅城区
Foshan Clothes Huanshi Wholesale Centre 佛山

Dongguan City is host to to the vast Humen Clothes Wholesale Centre which in turn features many small markets including the following:
Humen Huanghe Garment Wholesale Market 虎门黄河服装批发城（黄河时装城）
Address: Zhenhumen Dadao 东莞市虎门镇虎门大道
Fumin Garment Wholesale Market 富民服装批发城（富民商业大厦）
Address: 24, Yinlong Rd, 广东省东莞市虎门镇银龙路24号

6 DRIED MARINE PRODUCTS

Yide   Road   Dried   Seafood   Wholesale   Market
一德路海味批发市场

Yide Lu, where dozens of wholesale markets are concentrated, (also collectively known as 广州国际一德文具玩具精品广场 or simply Hai Wei Lu) has existed for over a century and is the largest retail area for dried seafood and shellfish in the country. More than two thousand booths line the road, selling items such as dried scallops, cuttlefish, abalone, fish maw, shark's fin, dried oysters, clams, dried fish skins, dried anchovies and sea cucumber. These dried marine products come from all over the world, from places as near as Shandong province to countries as remote as Argentina and Russia. Many of these products are now considered to be an environmentalist's nightmare

Five percent of the goods are used locally, and 95% are sold to markets and restaurants in other parts of the country; annual turnover has reached four billion RMB. Mass local migration has popularized Cantonese food and the demand for dried marine materials increased exponentially. Other products include dehydrated dried black moss, dried snakeskins, candied jujubes, dried mushrooms and Chinese sausages. I personally shop here for the finest quality nuts and dried fruits, including cashews from Myanmar and sultanas from Xinjiang. The market starts from Haizhu Square and continues to the west of Haizhu South Road, covering an area of more than a kilometre. Two of the largest markets are Shan Hai Cheng (山海城) and Hai Zhong Bao (海中宝海味干货交易中心) both close by to Yide Lu subway station.

Metro Line 2 and get off at Haizhu Square station.
Address: Yide Lu 广州市一德路
Contact: 020 8106-0150

A quick guide to unusual Cantonese ingredients

Dried abalone

The star of most Chinese banquets, dried abalone is valued for its resemblance to the ancient Chinese ingots that were once used as currency. The texture is like a meaty, chewy mushroom, and it is often cooked in a rich soy-based broth. Home cooks should soak the abalone in water for two to three days in the fridge, then dunk it in boiling water for an hour, and leave it to cool in the pot. After rinsing the abalone under running water for two hours, it is ready to be stewed with red meat such as ham and roasted goose.

Fish maw

Fish maw, with its silken texture and abundant collagen, is much loved by Chinese ladies. The best examples have a deep yellow hue, and the richer colour means the fish maw will maintain its texture even with prolonged cooking. The older the fish maw, the better. Older fish maws have less oil and thus less of the unpleasant fishy taste. It is especially popular in Chinese New Year banquets.

Black moss and dried oysters

These two delicacies are popular during Chinese New Year because of their auspicious Cantonese names. Dried oysters are called 'ho see' which sounds like good deeds, good fortune, or prosperity, while black moss is a pun on 'faat choi' which means 'to become rich.' The briny dried oyster is the perfect compliment to black moss, which is bland by itself but soaks up flavours like a sponge. The best dried oysters are plump ones from Japan and Korea. They should be soaked in water for half an hour before cooking. As for black moss, keep an eye out for fakes. The best way to tell is to soak a small section in water - fake black moss turns the water murky.

Conpoy

The brackish conpoy, or dried scallop, is a versatile ingredient that can either be served whole, or shredded in vegetable, meat and rice dishes. The best quality conpoys are from Japan and should have sharp, clean edges. They are the ones with strong aroma and flavour. The ones with rounded edges are from Mainland China and are generally less fragrant with more impurities. Conpoys should be soaked for half an hour in water before cooking.

Chinese Sausages

Preserved sausages, which are mildly sweet and have tiny pockets of fragrant fat, are usually steamed, sliced and served with rice. Do not buy preserved sausages that are too red in colour as this indicates a lot of artificial colouring. A good quality preserved sausage should also be free of stale smells and feel bouncy to the touch. As for cured pork belly, good ones should have alternating layers of fat and thin pork, giving it the moniker 'five-storey meat. Try boiling preserved meats for fifteen minutes to remove the surface layer of fat before cooking or frying them

7 ELECTRONICS

When it comes to electronics, there are three popular areas that dominate a large part of the business. The area around Dashatou is geared more towards second-hand phones than anything else, while the area around Ganding is focussed mainly on PCs. The area down by the river around the Nanfang Building is mainly orientated towards the brand new mobiles and accessories. I will start with the Dashatou Area.

Transportation: The Dashatou area is served by the Donghu subway station. Exit C emerges right outside the Haiyin Electrical Appliances City Market.

Shengxian Dashatou Second Hand Trade Market 盛贤大沙头旧货市场

Four floors of second hand goods, refurbished electronics and spare parts. Nearly ten years ago, Guangzhou's main flea market area was relocated from the riverside below Haiyin Bridge where it used to go under the name Dashatou Libei electrical appliances market (大沙头沥北电器市场), just 500 metres up the road to the Second Hand Market Building on the corner of Dashatou Lu and Lvyin Lu.

The first floor is filled mainly with second-hand phone dealers and is popular with buyers from the developing world, buying cheap, out-of-date phones for use in Africa and the Middle East. Here you will see Nigerians in long flowing djellabas negotiating hard over first-generation Motorolas and Nokias. Of course, the glass counter tops are now filling up with all kinds of smart phones and tablets. Perhaps not the best place to pick up the best deal on the very latest edition iPhone, but certainly a good starting place for earlier incarnations.

The basement is dedicated to accessories. All kinds of phone and tablet cases but plenty of spares and repair shops for fixing those orphaned phones that the big names forgot about long ago.

Up on the first floor the selection of second-hand goods diversifies extensively. Electronics of all sizes from walkie-talkies to full-sized office photocopiers. There is a good smattering of army-surplus type stores here serving mainly the local cosplay community but I did meet some English mercenaries that had come up on a shopping trip on their way home to Chiang Mai. Although they served in a number of current trouble spots they said that this was one of the best places that knew for buying quality military at great prices. So if you are in the market for a sniper's ghillie suit, some new desert fatigues or combat boots then this might be a good place to look. It is easy to see how shops such as Jungle Military (从林军品 4097) could be popular with third world dictators on Chinese spending sprees.

Up on the third floor the inventory continues to expand and you will find dozens of shops each with their little niche speciality. One dealer stocks only air-conditioning units while his neighbour focusses only on chest freezers. Others stock used PA and DJ equipment, while there are at least a half a dozen shops with large selections of musical instruments, ranging all the way from Gene Simmons axe-shaped bases to cornets and clarinets. One shop keeps all kinds of domestic kitchen appliances while just opposite petrol-powered generators are stacked up next to Yamaha outboard motors. At the east end of the floor, there is a large cluster of small electronics repair shops. Some shops specialise only on digital overhead projector bulbs while others refurbish older model digital cameras. Special mention goes to my old friend Summer who works out of a tiny booth at D111. I always stop off here for a cheap Canon Ixus digital camera, one of the few digital cameras that has a decent viewfinder, essential for long-sighted gentlemen like myself. As I travel, I meet many people that feel the same way and lament how difficult it is to find a camera with a decent eyepiece of any kind these days, and so I often end up selling mine (sometimes even giving them away) and coming back to Summer on my next trip for a cheap replacement. The third floor is more like an electronics abattoir then an gadget cemetery. Shops up here specialise in one particular type of innards such as camera circuit boards, autofocus lenses or winding mechanisms. Mainly digital camera parts but a few surprises thrown in such as microwaves and speaker spares.

If you have any kind of broken electronics lying around at home then this is the place to have them repaired or refurbished. With all the original factories, this is a huge sink hole of extinct technology and it is possible to find all kinds of obsolete and discontinued spares here.

Sprinkled among the electronics there are smaller stalls that deal in collectible technology such as Rollei cameras or Super 8 projectors. The last remnants of the worlds largest CD graveyards also cluster here, refusing to die despite the growing digital onslaught. Boxes of surplus CDs sit along side vinyl LPs which will certainly give away your age if you are tempted to have flick through.

Shengxian Hong Yun Photographic Equipment City
盛贤鸿运摄影器材城

Located directly behind the Second Hand Trade Market, this is a large concentration of high end photography outlets. All of the big names are represented here and is ideal if you are a National Geographic photographer off to the Serengeti and looking for a zoom lens the size of a suzephone. The shops are spread out over a number of buildings that lead up onto Dashatou Er

Ma Lu. This is also a good area to look for professional film and movie equipment. While there are plenty of second hand shops in the market selling big clunky video cameras, there are also a few outlets that deal in studio equipment from dollies and gantries to booms and spotlights.

Address: 24,   Dashatou   Er   Ma   Lu
广州市越秀区大沙头二马路24号
Contact: 020 8388-9580 8388-4418

Awesome Second Hand Mobile Phones Town Centre
澳讯数码手机城

Awesome was known as Aoxun Market until 2015 when all the signs were changed to reflect its popularity with overseas traders. While much of the ground floor is run of the mill iPhones and their knock offs, the first floor is much more interesting. Vendors sit behind glass cases filled with every kind of second hand phone that you could possibly imagine. Behind them, piled two and three high, each shop has a dozen steel reinforced safes, making a very bizarre sight indeed. Trade varies from brisk to absolutely manic and while there are some very knowledgeable engineers here, most are well protected by rows of ignorant country girls barely out of their teens.

Address: 36, Dashatou San Road, Yuexiu District
越秀区大沙头路36号
Contact: 020 8379-4101

Jinhon International Digital Plaza 精鸿（国际）数码城

Directly opposite the Shengxian Dashatou Second Hand Trade Market, this small market focusses mainly on smart phone accessories but fills the gaps with an assortment of other digital knick knacks. The ground floor has around forty or fifty small vendors, ranging from phone repair shops to LED factory outlets. As yet the basement is still unoccupied.

Address: 36, Dashatou San Road, Yuexiu District
越秀区大沙头路36号

Contact: 020 8379-4101.

Highsun Plaza or Haiyin Square
铁三角古拉专卖店(海印广场)

The ground floor is filled mainly with very high-end audiophile equipment, extremely expensive and very costly. Mostly for the domestic one percent who have more money than they know what to do with, but interesting for a wander. One day, when I have more time, I would like to go down there and pose as a buyer just to try out some there listening rooms. Take a few flacs with me and spend the afternoon sampling what Koyaanisqatsi, Jeff Wayne's War of the Worlds and Oliver Klitzing sound like on 100,000 thousand dollar plus stereo systems. The first floor is devoted to smart phones and DVDs. Mostly domestic issued material but plenty of copy stuff in the back rooms for those who ask. All the latest western movies and more porn than you can shake deluxe ultra-thruster rabbit at. I wonder if these guys know that their days are seriously numbered in the age of peer2peer file sharing and torrent trackers? There is also a good selection of gaming stores, all with the latest versions of PSPs, Kinects etc. This is a good place to find special Japanese release only titles that can be hard to find back in the West.

The second floor is a veritable orchard of suspicious looking Apple Stores selling all kinds of iPhone add-ons, attachments and accessories. Even so, do not expect to find any really exciting new products. As is usually the case with Chinese markets, products are very mainstream and decidedly mass market. This is a far cry from Akihabara and if you are looking for really original products, then Kickstarter and the newly emerging field 3D printing is a far better source of cutting edge products. Do not expect to find Occuli, Symphony Shells or even Soundcloud cases here. China specialises in mass production at very cheap prices. For innovation and creative you are best advised to look elsewhere.

Address: 21, Dashatou Road, Yuexiu District 越秀区大沙头路21号

Contact: 020 8379-4101

Haiyin Computer City 海印电脑城

When I first came to Guangzhou in the early nineties, this was one of my favourite places to come looking for the very latest computer add-ons. Since then it has slowly sunk into obscurity among all the other computer markets that have sprung up around the city. The good news is that at the time of writing, there is a major refurbishment program going on here, and so maybe this place will have a new lease of life. At the moment there are still a few stores open, including one that specialises in all kinds and sizes of till rolls and cash machines, which is something that I do not often see elsewhere. Check out the mezzanine floor for a large shop that I have previously recommended to friends for phone unlocking. Haiyin is worth a browse for the latest electronic gadgets, but as I have said this is not Akihabara by a long shot.

Address: 14, Dashatou Si Ma Lu 大沙头四马路14号

Contact: 020 8379-5897

Highsun Electrical Appliances Market 海印电器城

Yet another part of the sprawling Haiyin Electronics Market. More of the same mix of gadgets, appliances and phone accessories.

Address: 56-58, Donghu Lu 东湖路56-58号

Contact: 020 8379-2930

Xinhe Haiyin Electronics Market 信和海印电器商场

Two long alley ways stretch back from Dashatou San Ma Lu, that are filled with almost every electrical appliance imaginable. Lots of Arabs and well-heeled Russians here checking out the latest in pen cameras and other James Bond type gadgetry. Dozens of shops selling everything from RC helicopters to high-end digital projectors. This area is already very popular with overseas buyers so do not expect any real bargains, but it is still fun to have a browse. I picked up a nice little phone jammer here that I am sure is probably illegal in most countries, but this is a market that will only suffer as the maker movement matures and technology convergences mean ever less gadgets for us to carry about.

Address: 9, Dashatou Four Road 大沙头四马路9号
Contact: 020 8385-9825

Golden Haiyin Electrical Square 金海印电器广场

This place has everything electrical, from DVDs to air conditioners, anything you ever want with electrical wires and electronics is there including all accessories. This is the market the customers first encounter as they emerge from the Donghu Subway Station, with multiple entrances all along Donghu Road. The northern part of the market focusses on kitchen and home appliances while the southern part is mainly large audio. In between are all kinds of gizmo's and gadgetry.

Address: 166, Haiyin Donghu Road 广州海印东湖路166号
Contact: 02 8379-2853

Starlight Electrical Appliances Market 星之光电器市场

Located opposite the Shengxian Hong Yun Photographic Equipment City, the fact that customers have to cross over the Donghua South Road which runs directly under the inner ring road means that this particular building has been left out on a limb somewhat. There are a couple of floors of electronics dealers here but the place seems undergo refurbishment and reorganisation every year or two, not really allowing any of the vendors to

become properly established.
Address: Donghua Nan Lu 东华南路
Contact: 020 8380-5960

Sheng Xian Digital Appliance City 盛贤数码电器城

Described elsewhere on the internet as "the largest and most professional, the latest and most complete digital audio and professional audio-visual products market", this area is devoted mainly to the kind of kit necessary to start up a Chinese disco. Out in the countryside, small town development follows a very predictable pattern. Before anything else, the Party stamps it mark on even the smallest hamlets with a large police station. This is usually followed by a school building so that the party line can be firmly indoctrinated rather than having to be enforced by residents of the first building. Third on the list in what the Chinese call 'fa da' or 'development' is a thinly disguised brothel, posing as either a disco night club or karaoke. Which is where Sheng Xian Market comes in. A couple of rows of big bass speakers, a few spinning disco lights and the village leader is your xu-xu. Old-China-hands will have seen this situation repeat itself over and over again as one-donkey villages grown into small towns, often with the help of a nearby slave-run brick-yard or a few illegal mines.
Address: 31, Dashatou Four Road 大沙头四马路31号

Ganding Area

Gangding Computer Market is part of the Tianhe Business Zone in Guangzhou, also known as the Guangzhou Computer Shopping Circle, located along the Tianhe Road near Gangding Metro Station. Thousand of shops covers all kinds of latest model and top notch brand-name information technology products. Appliances and various digital products including computers, laptops, tablets, digital cameras, accessories, and software are widely sold here.

There are several computer shopping malls in this circle, the main ones being Tianhe Computer Mall (天河电脑城), Buynow Computer Mall (百脑汇), Pacific Digital Plaza (太平洋电脑城), Guangzhou Computer Mall (广州电脑城), and EGO Digital Plaza (颐高数码广场).

How to get there: Gangding Computer and Digital Shopping Circle is located in Tianhe District. Take subway line 3 and get off at Gangding Station (岗顶站). Exit D emerges outside the hospital, while exit A comes right up in the middle of Buy It Now. Exits B and C come out on the opposite side of the street.

Buynow Computer Mall 百脑汇商贸广场

Buynow is the newest and probably the largest of the computer centres. There are now 22 Chinese franchises of the Buynow PC Mall but this is the largest so far. It is generally more geared to the domestic office market and general retail but there are still interesting deals to be had here. In such a high volume market, it can be difficult for a newcomer to find a niche but there is plenty of variety and so you should not be put off from trying.

The whole building is built directly over Ganding subway station, and the basement is home to a selection of non-computer shops including a Mannings, a 7/11, a very dark Starbucks and a KFC. Down here, it is mainly copy smart phones that can usually be bought cheaper across the border in Hong Kong.

The ground floor is home to one of China's comparatively few authentic Apple stores as well as small army of sales, selling every brand of laptop and desktop that you have ever heard of. Well, nearly. There are definitely some names that are missing from this particular party. For example, Alienware has only just arrived, but perhaps this is not surprising considering that most of their custom work to Dell machines is done in the US. There is also a distinct lack of modded boxes and customised top-end gaming rigs. I always expected that a computer mega-centre of this scale would have some awe-inspiring semi-super computers to thrill and excite all the hard core gamers, but this is nearly all run of the mill production line models, not even a steampunk souped-up Beowulf cluster on display here.

First floor is more of the same, along with an ice cream parlour and a Pizza Hut. Looking around it quickly becomes clear that in many ways the Chinese consumer electronics market is quite different from its western counterparts. Many things are hard to find or missing altogether despite the fact that they are undoubtedly made here. I struggled to find a Kindle Fire, one of my local friends claiming that lower literacy levels and touchier publishing and censorship regulations meant that ebook readers were just not that popular. I also had problems finding PVRs and and digital video recorders, but have been subjected to the appalling quality of Chinese broadcast TV, I can hardly say that this is a big surprise.

Second and third floors are all kinds of accessories and peripherals, with so much choice that it quickly becomes a blur. Fourth floor is mainly showroom areas where potential customers from the lower floors are bought to inspect the merchandise and hammer out the final price.

Fifth floor is a very popular food court, with great food at very reasonable prices. All of the youngsters that work for a pittance in the rest of this building come here for cheap eats and I also like to grab lunch here when I am in the area. There are more than a dozen places doing rice, noodles and other Chinese fast food dishes. Good if you are by yourself and feel uncomfortable in regular Chinese restaurants where the smallest table is for a family group of ten or more. Look out for the unusual regulation signs posted everywhere that forbid such activities as sleeping on the tables and playing cards.

Address: 598, Tianhe Road 广州市天河区天河路598号

Contact: 020 8526-4249

Guangzhou President Digital City 广州总统数码港

Located in the front part of the the President Hotel, this is mainly retail outlets but can be interesting to gauge prices and gather price information about the very latest models. The ground floor was very recently refurbished (Fall 2012) is taken up mainly with laptop and digital camera vendors. Up on the first floor, dozens of smart phone and tablet dealers vie for customer attention, but prices here are nothing special. There are more phones on the third floor and tucked away at the back is one of my favourite little gadget stores that reminds me much more of Akihabara in Tokyo the Southern China. Although the owner does not speak any English, he does stock an interesting array of electronica that is more usually found in Taiwan and Japan. These include lots of snazzy little gewgaws such as power point pointers with built in lasers, electronic thermometers and personal hygiene tools. Each little device usually comes in two or three different brandings. The most recognisable big name Japanese brands such as Omron, Sony and Panasonic command the highest prices while local domestic brands are usually a fraction of the price.I picked up a small hair trimmer (a little gift for an uncle whose hairs seems to migrating from the top of his head to his ears and his nose as he gets older) The Panasonic version was a whopping 150 RMB while an almost identical version produced for the domestic market was just 35 RMB. The third floor is almost entirely devoted to CCTV equipment that is destined mainly for the domestic market.

Address: President Hotel, 586, Tianhe Road 总统数码港, 天河北路586号

Contact: 020 6286-8888

Pacific Computer City 太平洋电脑城

Also known as Pacific Digital Plaza (太平洋数码广场) or Taipingyang to locals. At the weekend this is one of the most popular markets in towns, with seemingly more people than Times Square on New Years Eve. This whole area gets so busy that I am sometimes amazed that the footbridge out front does not collapse under the weight of all the pedestrians. The first two floors are filled to bursting with the most popular electronic gadgets with which most of us are now familiar. Prices here are at the Chinese retail market level (but still significantly lower then the West). It is up on the third floor that things start to get interesting. Here in tiny spaces barely a metre or so across a frantic trade is done in chips, DDR Ram and hard disks. As a big documentary fan, I shop here for my own storage needs and find prices (Western Digital for example) comparable with the cheapest hard disks that I can find on the internet. Some of my ever so cynical Chinese friends claim that the products here are fake or even second hand but I have not had any complaints and have purchased at least twenty or thirty terabytes here for myself, family and friends. Only one disk ever gave up on me and the was replaced immediately without any questions asked.

Connected by a small door at the back are a myriad of smaller peripherals stores stock all kinds of add-ons and accessories for PCs. These are also accessible from five main entrances on Shipai Lu that are located directly below Chinese apartment buildings. Each is subdivided into narrow corridors that stretch away down low ceilinged corridors and contain all kinds of specialist dealers from PC speakers to gaming devices. There is also a good sprinkling of repair shops and data recovery guys thrown in for good measure.

One product line that I have have found particularly difficult to source here is that of PVRs. This is perhaps because the market leaders like Hauppage and other German brands are all based in Europe. That said there are plenty of services here that will digitally rip VHS, 16mm and other formats into PC readable standards, if that is a service that you are looking for.

Address: 560, Tianhe Road 广州市天河区天河路560号
Contact: 020 8758-8827

Tianhe Computer Mall 天河电脑城

Also known as Galaxy Computer Plaza, Tianhe Computer Mall has seven floors. B2 is mainly parking and warehousing while B1 is filled with stores that cater to the local DIY PC building community. The first and second floors are devoted to outlets pushing overpriced branded items, especially notebooks and desktops. This gradually peters out into accessories and peripherals on the third floor while the fourth and fifth floors are given over to offices and maintenance centres.
Address: 502, Tianhe Lu 广州市天河区天河路502号
Contact: 020 3849-9389
Transportation: Take metro line number 3 to Gangding.

Guangzhou Nanfang Science and Technology Plaza 广州南方科技广场

Located by the second pedestrian overpass, opposite Trustmart supermarket. This is another mix of mainly retail stores at lower levels with more factory outlets on the upper floors. The usual selection of computers, peripherals and accessories.
Address: 518, Tianhe Road, Tianhe District 广州天河区天河路518号
Contact: 020 8825-9646

EGO Digital Square 颐高数码广场

The last of the big computer malls before Tianhe Road intersects with Tianhe East Road. More of a focus here on portable devices such as laptops, tablets and mobiles. Four floors of more mainstream items rather than the more hardcore geekware that is sought out by the DIY guys and hobbyists up on Shipai Lu.

Address: Renfeng Plaza, 490, Tianhe Road
广州市天河路490号壬丰大厦

Away from the crush of the main Tianhe Road, it is down on Shipai Dong Lu, that things start to get really interesting. This is where the real wholesalers are located and then further down the road you will find all the second hand markets. Regular holiday makers with a local friend in the know can come here and pay for their entire Asian trip with a few carefully selected purchases.

Xin Gai Nian Computer Centre 新概念电脑城

Xin Gai Nian Computer Market is located at the back of Taipingyang Computer Market. The main products here are computer casings but there is also a wide range of other peripherals such as keyboards, mice etc. Be careful here as some of these items might in fact be second-hand computer accessories, repackaged and sold as new.

Adjacent to Xin Gai Nian Computer Centre are Jin Wang Computer Centre (金王电脑城) and Jin Gui Gu Computer Centre (金硅谷电脑城). These two computer markets in Guangzhou are of much smaller scale and they offer computer cases, computer power supplies, printers, printer consumables, etc.

Address: 560, Shi Pai Xi Lu, Tianhe District
广州市天河区石牌西路560号
Transportation: Get off at the metro station Gangding.

KB Electronics Plaza KB展望数码广场

If you are looking for computer accessories in wholesale quantities then this is the place to start. The first three floors and basement are packed to the absolute gunnels with almost every kind of home computer related device that you can imagine. Floors four and five are where the storerooms begin and by the queues at the elevators there must be hundred more offices and mini warehouses on the upper floors.

Starting in the basement, there are forests of skinny web cams, plagues of mice and possibly enough wires to lasso Voyager and bring it back to Earth. Wireless routers, Interruptible power supplies, USB connectors, splitters and gender bending joiners all have their specialist stores, although down here there are many shops that also stock a huge variety of different kinds of accessories.

On the ground floor, there are distinctly less of the jack-of-all-trades shops and many more factory outlets dealing in just one product, albeit a million and one variations on that particular item. For example, one mouse dealer stocks models in almost every major football clubs colours, although I am sure that the lawyers at Chelsea and Bayern would have something to say about this. The first floor is more of the same with a smattering of retail technology thrown into the mix. Here we can start to see shops that specialise in bar code scanners and supermarket anti-theft systems. Plenty of shops here selling refills and consumables for home printers, especially useful if you do not want to pay HP's eye-gouging prices for ink cartridges. Things become even more specialised on the third floor where dealers display all kinds of holographic stickers for every kind of electronic device, and there are large numbers of stores that deal exclusively in laptop power cables or notebook batteries. My experience yesterday at one of these stores should give you a taster of how business is done here. A teacher friend in Guangzhou had dropped his laptop (bought here at the second hand market under my instruction) in a late night drunken haze. Anyway, his laptop landed just on the point where the wire plugs into the side of the machine and it had a nasty habit of abruptly powering off without any warning whatsoever. Becoming tired of constantly trying to Jimmy it so that the power flowed through, I offered to buy him a replacement. On the ground floor, the first shop I went into stocked original branded items, but at a significantly higher cost. A wire and power pack for a Dell would have set me back 150 RMB and so I kept looking. Up on the third floor a little Cantonese girl called Vega explained that she had three different packs that would suit my needs. The authentic Dell version was slightly over 120 RMB, the fake Dell with the brand emblazoned clearly on the front was just under eighty and then there were two more Chinese branded examples priced at 50 and 25 respectively. Not wanting to look too cheap, I took the 50 kuai option knowing full well that I could have found a second-hand one further down the road for just ten or fifteen kuai. This should give you an idea of the bewildering choice that is available and how branding affects the final price. Plenty of choice is always available but only at the low to medium end of technology. If you are looking for haptic interfaces, stereolothographic 3D printers, or HD Oculus headsets, then I am afraid that you will be clean out of luck.

Address: Shipai Xi Lu 石牌西路

The Second hand Computer Markets

Across the road from the treasure house of the KB Building, the fun really begins with the first of the PC flea markets. This is just a taster of the delights that stretch all the way down to the end of the road. Back on the KB side of the road, there is a long stretch of shops selling unbranded ink refills for printers, right down to what was the old-second hand market in the now empty Zhong Yuan Building (广州市中原二手电脑市场). Just across the junction is the Anti-Smuggling Bureau Headquarters, with its gold lions and Greek columns, looking more like a Columbian cartel mansion than anything else, but maybe that is not a coincidence. There are just a handful of big name printer outlets e.g. Epson on this side of the road until it reaches Huangpu Da Dao where the new Beyond Asia Electronics Plaza is situated, but for the moment all the fun it to be had on the opposite side of the street.

The Go-old Computer Flea Market (金桥电脑), just

beside the ICBC bank, is a bargain hunter's paradise. Here you can buy everything from completely refurbished laptops right to the stickers that tell you which chip is on the inside. There is even a shop here that sells refurbished Apple machines on the first floor, but the fact they they make up only a fraction of one percent of all the other laptops here should tell you something about their relative popularity. Up on the second floor it is roughly divided by large format flat screen TVs to the left and desktop boxes with all their associated innards to the left. The third floor is a hardcore geeks heaven with motherboards, chips and almost expired hard drives, all available by the bucket-load. If you have even been to a scrapyard for cars, then just imagine what it would look like for PCs and you will have a pretty good picture of what this place is like.

Most people have a very poor image of these markets, thinking that they are dens of thieves that will rip anybody off at the first opportunity. For me, both Chinese and foreigners exaggerate the dangers, partly because they do not have any experience and partly because they are almost clueless when it comes to what goes on inside their PC. Just as anybody who does not understand the basic workings of a car engine runs a high risk of getting ripped off when they take their car in for a service, ignorant PC luddites are not going to be able to take full advantage of this electronic Aladdin's cave. I do not claim to be a computer expert but I do know to do all my research at the big retail outlets such as Taipingyang and President, and then come and look for refurbed bargains or end-of-line surplus in the second-hand markets. Despite the cries and horror and disbelief of other overly suspicious expats, my friends and I always do our upgrades here and have never had any problems. As a precaution, I usually take a small diagnostics program on a USB that I can plug into anything I fancy, and check that the internals match up to the vendors description. To give you an example of the savings that can be made here, let me tell you about the laptop that I used to write the words that you are now reading. Having worked as a travel writer for more than five years, I had all that time owned the same Fujitsu Lifebook, a diminutive but trusty little workhorse to which I was so attached, that tears were welling up when I finally traded her in. I was doing less writing and more relaxing, so I wanted something with a really big screen and a nice fast chip so that I could watch all the latest high-definition formats without the poor thing choking and dying. As usual I did my research in the expensive stores of Taipingyang. I spotted a svelte and lithe Dell Studio with an enormous seventeen-inch screen that dwarfed everything around it. The young sales guy told me that it was just a tad under thirteen thousand RMB and that I would need to act quickly as a new model was being released in the early new year. Armed with that valuable piece of information, I started looking for similar end-of-line models down in the Go-old market. It was not long before I found exactly the same model for just three thousand RMB, a saving of ten thousand RMB simply by walking just a few hundred yards down the road. I still miss my trusty little Fujitsu at times but this new monster with its i7 chip and cinema-like screen really makes up for the loss. And of course, this is not a one off story. A selection of friends have bought Toshibas, Acers, IBMs and now Lenovos without any problems whatsoever. Guangzhou is probably the best place on the planet to buy refurbished laptops .I have picked of dozens of top-end laptops at superb prices that make my friends back at home choke.

If you are still concerned about buying refurbished computers, then do a Google search for the Chinese cities of Guiyu or Taizhou. This is where the toxic electronic effluent of the affluent ends up when it goes to die. Unfortunately this harmful e waste is so deadly that it usually ends up killing those poor unfortunates that have to break it down into its basic component parts for a living. Buying second-hand or refurbished means one less box of industrial poison to pollute that Chinese (or Nigerian or some other third world) location.

At the other end of the supply chain, buying used means that there is less demand for blood minerals from countries such as the Congo. Everybody has heard of blood diamonds but few people even realise that their phones, their laptops and their PCs are all reliant of blood minerals such as tantalum and casserterite, which directly fund both rebel groups and the Congolese National Army. For more details look at the Wikipedia page on 'Conflict Minerals' or watch the amazing 'Blood in Your Mobile' documentary by Frank Piasecki Poulsen, one of the most amazing international exposes ever produced.

Continue south along the road and their are even more PC flea markets. The Last in line is the Hui Yuan Second Hand Market (汇源电脑城) which focusses mainly on used office equipment at the front but has an enormous selection of used screen dealers inside. The air reeks of methylated spirits as youngsters clean grime and labels off factory surplus and discarded screens of all kinds. For desktop users, the amount of bargains to be had here is amazing.

There are a number of second-hand computer markets but the area is in a constant state of flux as buildings close and everybody is forced to move just a few doors down the road. At the time of writing the following were open for business:

Yidong Computer City 怡东电脑城

Haizheng Second Hand Computer Market 海正电脑城

Shi Pai Xi Computer City Cheng 石牌西电脑城

Zhanwang Second Hand Mobile Phone Market 展望数码广场

The streets here are filled with middle-aged ladies selling baskets full of associated computer junk, and although there are bargains to be found, it will take a keen eye to spot them amongst all the junk. I know one Frenchmen that specialises in power cables, cherry picking the rarest and most sought after examples, usually paying pennies and selling them back in Europe for ten, twenty or even thirty Euros a piece.

At the very end of the road is a the brand new Asia Digital City Building (寰亚先达数码城), which is yet another example of Guangzhou's excessive overbuild and so far remains empty.

Hi-Tech Building Digital City 高科大厦数码城

While the first floor is devoted to the same kind of peripherals that can be found in Ganding, the second and third floors have a good selection of routers, CNC machines and large format printers. There are also specialist printing devices such as mug and T-shirt printing devices. Unfortunately, everything is marked up considerably from the factory prices that are available in the north of the country where much of this equipment is made. On my last visit in 2014, not one of these shops had a single 3D printer available for sale despite the media hype that was surrounding these machines. This market is good for buying sundries for local office but probably not suitable for international exports.

A better local option for CNC machines and routers is the Foshan Lun Jiao International Wood Machine Market (佛山伦教集约工业区国际木工机械城).

Address: Gaoke Building, 900, Tianhe Bei Lu 高科大厦, 天河北路900号

Metro: Line 3 to South China Normal University 华师科技大学. Exit C.

Office Printer Material Market 广州科贸园数码城

At Wushan Lu you will find the printer material market. A small market of just a few floors dedicated to printing supplies, ink, toner and other printing related products.

Address: Tian Li Da Sha, Wushan Road, 天立大厦 五山路

Metro: Line 3 to South China Normal University 华师科技大学. Exit C.

Nanfang Area

Xi Di Er Ma Lu electronic market zone is home to a large number of electronic markets that specialize mainly in mobile phone parts. The markets located around the Nanfang Building and the Cultural Park east of Shamian Island make up a business belt that extends from Liu Er San to Lu Renmin Nan Lu.

The markets begin at the junction of Kangwan Nan Lu where Gongye North Avenue crosses the river at the corner of Shamian Island. The nearest subway stop is Culture Park (文化公园). On the south side of Xi Di Er Ma Lu are a number of smaller markets including the following:

Guangzhou Lingnan International Digital Plaza 广州岭南国际数码广场

On the opposite corner to E exit of the Culture Park of Line 6, this is the western most of the markets on Xi Di Er Lu. On the third floor are many specialist shops selling professional equipment for the assembly and disassembly of mobile phones as well as a number of repair shops. The second floor is about half empty but does have a number of peripheral suppliers, alongside a selection of game controller and related accessories wholesalers. On the first floor are a large number of battery manufacturers along with shops selling adaptors, USBs and selfie sticks.

Address: 25, Xinji Road 新基路25号

Yuejing Electronic City 粤景电子城

Directly next door to Lingnan International Digital Plaza, the interior merges into Nantai Electronic Wholesale Market and Zhongbai Electronics City, which are all housed in the same building. In Yuejing, the four floors are given letters rather numbers and so A is the ground floor with D being the fourth floor. In this case the top floor is mainly spare parts and screen covers. The third floor has large numbers of covers, adaptors and power packs. The second floor features quite a few tools suppliers as well as masses of straps and covers. A floor at ground level is a maze of phone cover manufacturers.

Zhongbai Electronics City 中百电子城

Another mixed market with all kinds of phone accessories and components. Bluetooth headsets, card readers, memory cards, chargers, connectors and data cables.

Address: Dexing Road 德星路

Nantai Supplies Industrial Wholesale Market 南太日用工业批发市场

Focussing mainly on parts and components rather than finished items. Flex cables, LCD displays, micro SD cards and repair tools for mobile phones. Lower rents than the New Asia and Nanfang Buildings translate into slightly lower prices and lower minimum order quantities.

Address: Xidi Er Ma Lu 西堤二马路

Contact: 020 8184-3813

Kunpeng Digital Port 鲲鹏数码港

Located opposite the China Post Office on Jingyuan Lu, this is one of the smaller markets in the area. There are just two floors and the vendors focus mainly on parts and tools for mobile phone maintenance and refurbishment. Tall foreigners should watch out for the low ceilings on the second floor.

Address: 6, Jingyuan Lu 金园路6号

Xin Wen Yuan International Digital City 新文园国际数码城

Four floors of mobile phone accessories and mobile phone spare parts. Up on the fourth floor it is mainly showrooms and factory offices. Down on the third floor, it is chargers, components and assorted accessories. The first two floors are a vast selection of silicon phone cases, mobile protectors and tablet books. Be warned that the low prices hare often reflect the provenance of the products involved.

Guangzhou Xidi Electronics, Digital and Mobile Market 广州西堤电子数码手机城

What used to be the exhibition centre of the Cultural Park has now been converted into a vast personal electronics zone. More than 300 stores selling all kinds of batteries, buzzers, gaming consoles, headphones, LED lights, microphones, speakers, stylus pens and touch screens.

Address: 37, Xidi Er Ma Lu 广州市西堤二马路37号广州电子城

Nan Fang Building International Electronics and Digital City 南方大厦国际电子数码城

Located on the north bank of the Pearl River on the city, on Yanjiang Xi Lu, Guangzhou Nanfang Building (南方大厦) was built in 1922. It was the city's first tall building built with reinforced concrete. At first, it was home to the Xin Da Xin Department Store but has now become the biggest mobile phones accessory centre in Guangzhou. The façade is classical communist architecture and still has a large red star on the top. This is quite apt because this market is almost exclusively devoted to domestic products.

1st Floor: Mobile phones from name brands, cameras, MP3, maintenance equipment, phone card, pre-paid phone card, intercom, etc.

2nd and 3rd Floor: Mobile phone accessories and other electronic parts.

4th-8th Floor: Offices

Address: 28-32, Xi Di Er Ma Lu, Liwan District 广州市荔湾区西堤二马路28-32号

Contact: 020 8101-2133

The Canton Customs Mansion 粤海关大楼

Just behind all the mobile phone accessory markets is one of Guangzhou's most interesting classical buildings. The Customs Bureau was first established in the 24th year of the Kangxi Reign (1685). Designed by British architect David Dick in the style of European neo-classicism, and undertaken by the Huachang Engineering Company, the Canton Customs House finished construction in May, 1916. The four-storey high south-east façade of the mansion was masoned in granite. Both the inside layout and the overall structure of the building are very well-protected. On the roof of the façade is a four-sided, dome-roofed bell tower, decorated by thirteen-meter high twin Tuscan columns at each of the four corners and huge clocks on each of the four sides, which are 2.5 meters in diameter. At one time the bells would toll every hour, 24 hours a day but the Mansion is now the Guangzhou Branch of the China Customs Museum and this is no longer the case.

Address: 29, West Yanjiang Road 沿江西路29号

Opening time: 9:30 am - 04:00 pm (Only on Wednesday)

Ticket: free

New   Asia   Electronic   Wholesale   Market

新亚洲国际电子数码城

The largest electronic wholesale market in Guangzhou, specialising in phone accessories. At least eight floors filled with mobile phone accessories. More than a thousand stores stocking all kinds of mobile phone components and accessories along with cameras, console covers, intercoms, speakers, lanyards and just about any other small electronic device that you can think of.

Address: 37, Sai Er Road 广州市荔湾区西堤二马路37号

Contact: 020 8101-0028

LED lighting

The electrical wholesale markets of Jiefang Road and Yide Road (一德路) have large LED finished product selections. More can be found in the Taigu Lighting Centre (太古灯饰城) located nearby on Danan Road (大南路) but expect the kind of prices that are aimed at interior designers rather than budget exporters.

For individual LEDs start out at Huifu Xi Jinxu Electronic Wholesale Market, (惠福西今旭电子城) the oldest wholesale market engaging in electronic components. The market houses over 100 stores and its product lines cover a long list including diodes, transistors, LED backlights, ICs, electrolytic capacitors, resistors, plug-in connectors, electronic tools, electronic switches, computer cables, ribbon cables, AV caps, etc.

Address: 240, Hui Fu Xi Lu, Yuexiu District, 广州市越秀区惠福西路240号惠福电子广场

Huifu Lu has large numbers of electrical component stores including Yuexiu Henghe Electronic City, (越秀恒和电子城), Guangzhou Electronic Equipment Market (广州电子配套市场) and Asahi Electronic City (惠福西今旭电子城).

The extensive blocks along Jiefang Zhong Lu, Zhongshan Liu Lu and nearby Huifu Xi Lu are a world of electronic equipment and components. The business belt extends south to Liu Er San Lu and the Nanfang area of electronics markets. Expect lots 'localised' products in these markets, many with attractively low prices.

For those interested in buying unfinished LEDs for the maker or DIY market, the most important markets are on Mishi Road. These include the Guangzhou Yuexiu Jingxin (广州市越秀今旭电子城) at 40 Mishi Road (米市路40号), the Guangzhou Linghai Electronic Store (广州凌海电子商场) at 60 Mishi Road(米市路60号), the Haian Electronic Plaza (海安电子商场) and the Mishi Electronics Plaza (米市电器). Each of these are older but dedicated market places for buyers interested in single LED bulbs, all the way up to container quantities.

The area to the west of Jiefang Lu from the Gongyuanqian subway station is abuzz with all kinds of electronics markets which double as flea markets at the weekend. Those to the south of Zhongshan road are less orientated towards electronics and more general in their nature. Animal lovers should watch out for the second-hand TV dealers who constantly show dog fighting on large TV screens in the area. Here are a few of the larger markets.

Jiangjun Dong Electric City (General Electric City East) 将军东电器城

On the north side of Zhongshan Si Road, the main entrance (number 16) features a ballroom style double curved staircase. The ground floor is filled with all kind of miscellanea from washing machine parts to high-end audio cables. The second floor is half phones and half PCs, mostly refurbished. Up here there are specialist scavengers for chips, boards, screens and just about every other kind of component. There is even a collector's store up here that deals in vintage valves, some of them at well over a thousand RMB a piece.

The three roads that boundary Jiangjun are filled with small markets. Jiangjun Dong Lu (将军东路), Liurong Lu (六榕路) and Ruinan Lu (瑞南路) back onto the main road at Xingda Wujing Electronics Plaza (新达五金电器商场) which has large number of vendors selling minimalist ceiling fans to thrifty locals among other things. Up on the second floor is a large used tool market where the wares (often of dubious provenance, often stolen) are laid out on the floors for all to inspect. Lots of power tools and accessories such as Bosch and Makita.

At the junction of Liurong Lu and Zhongshan Si Lu is the relative newcomer, the Taojie Electronics City (陶街电器城). More finished appliances than components on this side of the road, especially items such as radios and mp3 players for the older demographic that still live in the district. Mixed in there are tobacconists, vinyl LP dealers and outdoor equipment specialists.

Out on Jiefang Road (解放路), the small markets continue to proliferate. At number 421, the New Tao Street Electronics City (新陶街电子电器城) features all kinds of small motors and internal parts, as does the Yulong Electronics Trade Centre (玉龙数码中心) which is just along the road. Also here is the Junhang Computer City (骏航电脑城). From Gongyuanqian subway station, take exit i2 up to the Jiefang Beilu intersection. Look for the New Poly Building on the other side of the road and the second hand markets begin behind here.

Further along Zhongshan Liu Lu near the Ximenkou Subway Station, the section of Haizhu Bei Lu that goes north behind Jie Tai Plaza is filled with air conditioners parts suppliers. Up almost until Liurong Temple, the street is lined with shops selling compressors, refrigerant gauges, hoses and miles of copper tubing.

Zhong Liu Computer Market 中六电脑城

Compared to the vast markets in Ganding, this is a relatively small market, probably used more by locals than large scale exporters. The first and second floor are dedicated mostly PCs and related components.Going up to the third and fourth floors there are more peripherals stores

Address: 192, Zhongshan Liu Road, Yuexiu District 广州市越秀区中山六路１９２号

Directions: Line 1 Ximen Kou Subway station, directly opposite the Tesco Lotus Supermarket

Contact: 020 8132-1818

Yulong Electronic Digital City誉隆电子数码城

The area of Lingyuan Xi Lu (陵园西路) between the concentration of military bases and the China Plaza Shopping Mall (中华广场) has large numbers of mobile phone vendors but most of the business here is retail for local consumers. While there are large numbers of street sellers offering very suspicious second hand models, the markets in Dashatou are probably better if you are looking to buy large quantities.

The two main markets here are the The Zhanwang second-hand mobile phone market (陵园西展望二手手机通讯市场) and the Lingyuan Xi communication City (陵园西通迅城)

There are other areas of the city that house large electrical wholesale markets but they might not suitable in terms of up to date products destined for the export markets. These include the following.

241

Ruyi Fang Electric City Square 如意坊电器城

From the outside, this looks like a huge, modern electronics market, but looks can be very deceptive. Both LG and Samsung have large showrooms at the front, filled with their very latest high tech offerings, from smart fridges to wall sized LED cinema screens, but this is where it ends. Inside is a collection of low rise factory outlets are filled with electronics that would only sell in the poorest regions of the Chinese hinterland. Most shops here sell very low-end stereo systems, with more focus on bells, whistles and flashing lights than sound quality or reliability. If Bang and Olufson represents the upper end of audio appliances then these unheard of Chinese brands are the very bottom of the barrel. Lots of large, but single speaker karaoke systems here with built in trolleys and gaudy graphic equalisers that would not look out of place on the very first Starship Enterprise. At least one shop here specializes in only radio cassette recorders, which should give you a clear idea of the kind of time warp in which this market is permanently stuck. Filled out with stores selling CRT TVs, air-con remotes and shoddy looking hair dryers that would have only a very slim chance of passing European safety regulations. If you are exporting to recently discovered head-hunters in Papua New Guinea or primitive Amazonian Indians, then there might be some bargains here but for every other market, these products are better consigned to yesteryear. Consequently, there are very few overseas buyers hear and barely any English spoken. This is one market where a local guide would definitely be useful.

Address: 155, Huangsha Da Dao
广东省广州市荔湾区黄沙大道155号

Contact: 020 8183-4386, 8181-8601
Directions: South of Zhongshan Ba Lu Subway Station

Fengning   Electrical   Wholesale   Market

丰宁电器批发市场

This is one of the oldest electrical appliance markets in the city and is definitely showing its age. Great if you are looking for rice cookers and twin tubs but not so great for items that are generally more popular in the west.

Address: 433, Zengcha Road 增槎路433号

Contact: 020 8198-4937

Lingnan International Electronic Commerce Industry Park 岭南国际电子商务产业园

Located directly behind the Xinji Shaxi Hospitality, this site initially held a great deal of potential as a new hi-tech hub for the city. Unfortunately most of the lots are still vacant and the management have not been able to attract a sufficiently diverse range of tenants.

Address: Shaxi Xia 番禺区沙溪厦滘岭南鞋城十一街40号

Xichang Electric City 西场电器城 and Xichang Commercial Electric City 西场商业电器城

Xicheng Commercial Electric Appliances Centre (西场电器城) was previously located on Dongfeng Road has now relocated. High-end audio has moved to Highsun Plaza, many with inbuilt Acoustic Display Rooms.There is still a small computer market operating on the corner of Dong Feng and Renmin Bei Lu but this is mainly small scale supplies for the local Arab traders.

Address: 23-45, Dongfeng Xi Road 广州市荔湾区东风西路23-45号

Contact: 8102-8427

Beyond Guangzhou

The Hua Qiang Bei electronics markets in Shenzhen are well known for a huge diversity of mobile phone accessories. Even so, in terms of price, the products made in Guangzhou are generally more competitive as the labour costs in Shenzhen tend to be higher than those in Guangzhou.

8 FABRICS

Zhongda Fabric Market 中大布料市场

So called, because the main street is located directly opposite the South Gate of Zhongshan University, abbreviated in Chinese from Zhongshan Da Xue (Sun Yat Sen University) to Zhongda. This is one of the biggest, busiest and most chaotic of all the wholesale markets in Guangzhou, and simply has to be seen to be believed. The range of fabrics includes silk, cotton, coloured fabric, fabric for men's garments, satin, synthetics, fabrics for wedding dress, denims, linings, flockings and much, much more

Directions: Take line 8 of the Guangzhou Metro to Sun Yat Sen University (Zhong Da 中大), Exit D. Push past the dozens of aggressive bicycle taxis that crowd around the entrance and walk east for another 200 metres past a number of sewing machine shop outlets down to the junction of Ruikang Lu. From the moment you step out the metro, at Exit D, you are faced with fabric sellers and accessories sellers of all kinds. If you go past the McDonald's' then you have gone too far. Actually, there are a few stores beyond McDonald's' but they are so few and out on limb that you will not be missing very much. If you keep walking until you can see the South China Institute of Oceanography, then you have gone way too far. Stay close to Ruikang Lu. This is where the madness begins in earnest. I can say without exaggeration that Zhongda fabric wholesale market is the most dangerous wholesale market in Guangzhou. Vehicles come from every corner and every direction.

Ruikang Lu is the main road for this fabric market area. This road is full of large and small markets. Immediately on the corner you will find a large accessories market on several floors. Walk a little further and you have an old two storey high fabric market on your right side. On the opposite side of the street is the main market right now. It is modern, with broad walkways, and hundreds of shops on each floor. In the basement you have accessories, and on the other floors fabrics. Walk further down the street from this market, and you will see a small street with laces and glitter fabrics, then the old original Zhongda Fabric Market Building, and soon after that – at the end of the street – you have a brand new fabrics market. This market is huge and consists of two buildings on each side of the street interconnected through a bridge.

Changjiang Garment Accessories Plaza
长江服装辅料广场

Known on Google as the Yangtze River Costume Accessories Centre. With your back towards the main entrance of Sun Yat-Sen University, Ruikang Lu is lined on both sides with wholesale markets on a such a scale that actually finding the product that you are looking for can be a really daunting task. Directly to your right, are the crumbling remnants of the earliest fabric markets but much of this is being slowly demolished and the tenants are moving into new premises further down the road. For the moment there are still two storey accessories markets on either side of the road with hundreds of small shops crammed into these old buildings. Products include all kinds of lace, ribbons, embroidery, braids, elastics, bra cups, buttons, labels and rhinestones. Changjiang begins at the large yellow sign that is almost as high as the glass elevator beside it but stretches away down the road and it is difficult to see where it actually finishes, as construction seems to be continuous despite and obvious over saturation. Fabrics include silk, cotton, satin, denim, linens, furs, flocking, glitter, lame, in fact just about any material you would care to imagine.

Address: Ruikang Road, Xingang Xi Road, Haizhu District
广州市海珠区新港西瑞康路
Contact: 020 8888-6666

Yinling Kuanda Accessories Market 银岭宽大辅料城

The market directly facing Changjiang fabric wholesale market is Yin Ling Kuan Da Accessories City, also specializes in different kinds of lace, along with zippers, buttons, transfers and just about every other kind of accessory you can imagine.

Address: Ruikang Road, Haizhu District, Zhongshan University, opposite the south gate
海珠区瑞康路，中山大学南门对面
Contact: 020 2237-7018

China Fabric and Accessories Centre 广州国际轻纺城

This is followed by the truly enormous China Fabrics and Accessories Centre .Just the basement alone is large enough to make a grown buyer weep and has almost bought me to tears on a number of occasions. The selection of accessories down here will make your head spin, and this is where a good local guide familiar with the layout is worth their weight in gold. Perhaps I am a little biased, as my last trip to this underground labyrinth was a complete wild goose chase. I was searching for micro-zippers and micro-buttons that are used on collectible miniature figures, and spent many hours getting the same negative responses over and over. The smallest buttons that I could find were 5mm, while I was looking for 3mm at the very largest. Combine with this with the fact that western style customer service is almost non existent, this can be a very trying episode.

The basement is a vast expanse of just about everything and anything than can be used to jazz up a piece of clothing. Billions of buttons and hundreds of thousands of hot fix stones. Bows, ribbons, patches and lace of all kinds. Zippers, laces, D-rings, collar pieces, metal pieces for jewellery and corners of handbags. With so much choice, it is a relief that this building has good air-conditioning.

Floors one, two and three A are filled with almost every kind of fabric in existence, with the distinct exception of Interface type upcycled materials. With there being almost no regulations enforced, there is little need to think beyond the next dollar here and so the waste is wanton and excessive. Countless swatches/headers displaying fabrics are manufactured. Some fabrics need to be ordered while others are available immediately from stock. In some cases it might take an hour or so while the fabric is collected from a warehouse nearby. The second floor and floors above are not as busy as the underground and first floor. Floor four is dedicated to home textiles.
Address: 114, Xingang Road
海珠区新港路144号(近中山大学)

Another 200 metres south on Ruikang Lu are located two enormous new wholesale market buildings and this is where the madness begins. Bicycles loaded up with huge rolls of fabric loaded horizontally across the rear zip around at breakneck speeds, barely avoiding the hordes of domestic buyers with their overladen trolleys in tow. This is not a place for the faint hearted.

As you can probably tell, the Zhongda fabric markets

are one of my favourite locations in Guangzhou. For many years I was a major dealer in woven patches and insignia. At first, I was just buying surplus, all the leftovers of international buyers from all over the world. At the time this is included official patches from the FBI, the Secret Service and the DEA as well as shoulder patches from just about every state police force on the continent. I spent many happy hours sifting through huge boxes of army, navy and air force insignia, cherry picking the very best examples which I soon found out could sell for in excess of a hundred dollars a piece to hardcore collectors. At the time I was paying less than five dollars a kilo and so the margins were fantastic. The range of patches was so wide and eclectic that I learned a great deal about the huge variety of international collectors markets and the items that they are looking for. I also learned how ridiculously protective and litigious some organisations are about their brands. My eBay partners were receiving threatening letters from lawyers on behalf of all kinds of companies ranging from Ferrari to Harley Davidson. We even had a cease and desist order from the office of the New York City Government, claiming that anything to do with '9/11' (we had a few Fallen Heroes Biker back patches) was their exclusive copyright. I would visit at least three or four times a year and buy at least a hundred kilos per trip. Even to this day, I still have partners in the US and Europe who still make a good-part time living from the stock that I sent to them. Eventually I gained such a good understanding of the product, all the way from design and manufacturing right down to the whims of the final customers that I began commissioning my own patches that were extremely successful. In recent years Chinese factories have really improved their quality control and there are far less discards than before. In addition, we had such good business selling very hard-to-find rarities to collectors that the commissioning organisations came down hard on the agents, angered that their unique designs were creeping out into the public market place. 501st Imperial Stormtrooper battalions for example expressly forbid members to trade their insignia on eBay. Obviously demand for these in particular was very high. I still have a small collection of unusual SWAT unit patches but with the decline of the US economy, the market for patches has shrunk considerably and I have since moved onto more profitable lines. These days the only patches that I regularly buy are hard-to-find Chinese People's Liberation Army Patches. Supposedly these are prohibited from being sold to non-army personnel (especially foreigners) but occasionally on my travels, I find a dealer who will look the other way and help me add to my collection. Chinese army patches are not yet hugely collectible but I see them as a long term investment and I am keeping them stashed away for when patches command the same prices as stamps, antique porcelain and contemporary Chinese art.

At meal times, street vendors appear from nowhere and fill the streets with local favourites. Lots of soups and noodles along with some delicious Cantonese style pizzas. This area is also popular with immigrant Uighurs from the distant Xinjiang province selling raisins, almonds, cashews and kiwis off the back of tricycles, all delicious and well priced. Occasionally you will see a Muslim vendor with a huge slab of fruit and nut cake. While this too is delicious, be warned that it has an unpleasant tendency to pull out loose fillings faster than a Mossad agent with pair of pliers.Quite a high level of tension exists between the Uighurs and the local authorities. One day while I was buying at Zhongda, I saw a battalion of twenty seven police, all fully armed in clad head to toe full riot gear proceed to evict a single Uighur fruit seller.

Zhongda Jiuzhou Textile Trade Plaza 中大九州轻纺广场

Directly opposite Changjiang International Fur City, this is yet another vast array of prints, satin, denim, cotton, zippers and hardware accessories. A hodge podge of smaller stores and mini malls on the left hand side of the road is followed by the tough to pronounce Jiu Zhou Plaza, yet another white-tiled mega-mall filled with even more merchants, opportunists and outright crooks. I try not be so cynical but with the Wenzhou Chamber of Commerce being located up on the top floor, I think I have a right to be suspicious. Despite this bias, I did great business for years with a local Cantonese embroiderer, up on the second floor, with a factory just over the river in Fangcun District. Without a doubt the best police and military insignia manufacturer on the planet, and a niche collector's market that is still very close to my heart. First floor is another bazillion yards of cloth, second floor is accessories of all kinds, and the third floor reverts back to cloth again.

Address: Ruikang Road, Xingang Xi Road, Haizhu District
广州市海珠区新港西瑞康路
Contact: 020 8888-6666

Changjiang International Fur City 长江国际皮草城

Mostly synthetics rather than genuine furs, this is perhaps a good place to wear a mask. If you are not overwhelmed by the glittering array of products, then the smell will certainly knock you sideways. Most of these vendors have recently moved here from a much smaller, dedicated fur market up near the subway which is about to be demolished.

Yinling Lace Market 银岭广场花边专业市场

The first market on the left side of the road heading south is the two storey Yinling Lace Market (银岭广场花边专业市场) which stocks even more of the same. Look out for both A and B entrances. This is followed by the Jiahe Textile Exhibition centre (广州嘉禾纺织品展示中心), where the first and second floors also specialise in lace.

From here, a number of new market buildings have sprung up like mushrooms after the rain. These include the following, and range from completely packed to almost empty. Wholesale markets stretch away to the south until they are replaced by sweat shop type factories and small workshops. Markets also continue across to the west behind Zhongda subway station.

Zhongfan Huali Buping Shichang 中纺华丽布匹市场

Inleader Textile City 广州轻纺交易园导购中心

Zhongda Jiujiang Qing Feng Guang Chang 中大九洲轻纺广场

Pearl River International Textile City 珠江国际纺织城

Kang Sheng Fabric and Textiles City 康盛轻纺城

Zhongda Ruikang Garment City 广州中大瑞康服装配料城

One thing of which to be aware is that the light can be less than sufficient, especially inside some of the older buildings. Therefore it is very important to pay very close attention to subtle colour differences before placing any orders.

To the west of Zhongda subway station a number of new wholesale markets have opened up.

Guangzhou International Textile Exchange Park 广州国际轻纺城

Touted as having more than 4,000 shops, and millions of fabrics, this new development only opened in October 2012 and is still half empty at the time of writing. This is one of the few fabric markets that are located to the west of Zhongda subway station, and can easily be spotted by the giant sewing machine statue, positioned out front. Unfortunately, despite the interesting collection of fabric wholesalers and the attractive buildings, there is just not the momentum yet to drive large numbers into this particular market. In fact, it seems almost like a ghost town compared to the manic activity that takes place down of Ruikang Lu.

Address: 144, Xingang Road, Haizhu District, 新港西路 144

Contact: 020 8900-0000

Other Wholesale Fabric Areas

Guangfu South Road Fabric and Textile Supplies 光复南路布料市场

Guangfu South Road in Liwan District has the longest history in fabric and textile supplies distribution in Guangzhou but cannot compare in size to the massive Zhongda markets. Many of these small dealers used to be located on Shang Xia Jiu Pedestrian Shopping Street, until clothing retailers pushed up the rental rates and the fabric dealers began to move away. Guangfu fabric sellers now stretch all the way down to Zhuang Yuan Fang and beyond. Plenty of shops here that specialise in everything from quality shirt cottons to psychedelic camouflage prints. Mix in a good selection of uniform manufacturers for good measure.

Address: Guangfu Lu 光复南路

Haiyin String and Cloth Market 海印布料市场

Haiyin is a centre for tailors and seamstresses rather than the large factory outlets of Zhongda. While on a much smaller scale, each of the four floors of this building have at least a hundred stores. Popular with expat 'tai tais' (well-to-do wives), a number of stores have English speaking staff on hand. There are three main buildings with a surplus of shops spilling out onto Yangjiang East

Road. The main building has four floors and is by far the busiest of the three.

Most customers here are retail, having items specially made but wholesale prices are also available. If buying in bulk expect to pay about 60% of the retail prices.

The ground floor is mainly fabric shops with all kinds of silk, velvet, cashmere and linen available. Shops that sell clothing fabrics will not sell furnishing fabrics, while tailors will not sell upholstery fabrics. Each line of business is specialised. There are two or three custom shirt specialists here, but it is up on the first floor where most of the tailors are situated. Silk comes in all varieties and price ranges, including plenty of fakes and blends. Expect to pay 50 - 500 RMB per metre depending on quality. Cottons start at 30 RMB per metre. The second floor is more of same with lots of haberdashery thrown in for good measure. All the usual buttons, bows and zippers to make that new dress look absolutely fabulous. Plenty of foam and knitting supplies and lots of bedding supplies.

With some gorgeously exotic dragon and phoenix pattered silk, this is a great place to have a qipao or a cheongsam custom made. I have had numerous 'zhongshan zhuangs' (what we westerners erroneously call Mao jackets) made here for the New Years celebrations and they always knock the socks of both my Chinese and overseas friends alike. If a jacket like this can make even George Bush good, then they will make the rest of us look like Tony Stark in full oriental splendour. I have had numerous bespoke outfits created here, from regular business three piece suits to traditional Zhongshan style suits. We have also had a few outrageous outfits made here for locally held costume parties. Perhaps the most memorable the zebra and leopard ensembles that we had made for a Pimps and Hos party that was being held in one of the bars near the Garden Hotel. We kitted ourselves out with lots of crazy accessories from the various wholesale markets until we were literally covered in bling. After an evening of partying like top level politicos (as well as winning the first prize for best outfits), we immediately sold the outfits on eBay for three times the price that we had paid for them.

Another very successful line was a simple three-piece Japanese schoolgirl outfit that I originally had custom-made for my own girlfriend. At the time eBay was not as swamped as it is now with Chinese sellers and we found a very profitable little niche that was expanded into a selection of sexy bedroom type outfits, all of which I personally tested and approved before releasing on the market. I even made a number of Japanese-style boyfriend pillows that went surprisingly well in the US. It is surprising the level of success that can be achieved with just a little imagination and creativity.

Up on the fourth floor is mainly suit fabric wholesalers. Dozens of shops with huge rolls of houndstooth, herringbone, nail-head, bird's eye window pane, pin stripe and just about everything in between.

Address: 429-431, Yanjiang Dong Road
广州市沿江东路429-431号
Contact: 020 8379-6572

New Haiyin Wool and Cloth Exchange Square
新海印毛线布匹交易广场

Also known as the Haiyin String and Cloth Market Annex, with a large sign on the front door describing it as the 海印布艺总汇. Stretching away almost to Donghu Lu, the fabric market has spread out into a second building directly to the east on the same road. More of the same as found in the original market.

Address: 418, Yan Jiang Dong Road, Yuexiu District
广州市沿江东路418号
Contact: 020 8381-5883

Yingxuan Textile Market 盛贤布艺城

Across the road and to the north, tucked away behind the Gong Yin Building that houses the Industrial and Commercial Bank is the Yingxuan textile market, an offshoot of the cloth and string market, that focuses more on on curtains, bedsheets and soft furnishings than clothing. Customers can order complete sets of custom-made bedding, curtains, upholstery for sitting and dining rooms and other accessories for the home.

On the ground floor are a selection of soft furnishings specialists, doing upholstery, curtains and every kind of cushion that you can imagine. The most popular styles at the moment are garish nouveau and heavily quilted jacquards, guaranteed to make any house look like a mafia-run brothel. I personally prefer shops like South Cloth Art up on the second floor that specialise in distinctly oriental styles rather than the crushed gold velvet chaise lounges and ridiculously high upholstered leather Chesterfield wing backs that seem to appeal to China's easily impressed arrivistes. Unless you reside full time at Versailles or Le Château de Chenonceau with the Sun King and his courtiers as regular house guests, then you probably agree. At the String and cloth market annex be sure to check in at Royal Cloth Arts to see how badly this kind of textile bling can come out. What is meant to look like the Baccarat room at Baden Baden or the private quarters of a Burgundian Prince ends up looking cheap and tacky. The staff here have never seen a château in their lives.

Prices have risen considerably in the last few years and I no longer use this particular market, preferring tailors out in the western provinces that still operate at bargain prices. So many foreigners come in and pay full price that shopkeepers here are no longer are so willing to bargain. Even so, you can still have suits and dresses made here at a fraction of what it would cost in the west. Firstly find a tailor or dressmaker and discuss the practicalities of the project. If you want to copy existing items, make sure that you bring them along as examples. Copying from magazines is no problem so feel free to bring along back issues of GQ and Cosmopolitan. The tailor will then take you to another store to select the actual fabrics.

Address: 429-431,   Yanjiang   East   Road
广州市沿江东路429-431号，即海印桥西北引桥侧
By metro: Take line 6 to Donghu subway station, take exit B and and walk south past the digital markets. Take the first main road on the right under Haiyin Bridge and walk west for 200 meters

The Second Largest Fabric Market in Guangdong

A large number of the suppliers in Zhongda Fabric Markets order goods from Pingdi Fabric Markets and then resell in Guangzhou fabric wholesale market. There are several large fabric wholesale markets in Pingdi Fabric Market area. The following are some of the major markets.
Pingdi Fabric Wholesale Markets in Foshan
Pingdi Business Square 平地商业广场
Pingdi Jeans City 平地布匹市场牛仔城
Pingdi Zhong Xin Jeans City 平地中心牛仔城
Pingdi New Jeans City 平地新牛仔城
Pingdi Fabric Market 平地布匹市场
Pingdi Number One Jeans City 平地第一牛仔城
Note: There are also shuttle buses from Pingdi Fabric Market to Zhongda Fabric Market.

9 FLOWERS

The south western part of Guangzhou has long been a celebrated business and botanical centre of flowers and domestic plants for years, thanks to its warm and humid subtropical climate, which is good for plants, and a local flourishing tradition of cultivating domestic plants for pleasure. Fangcun Area of Liwan District has a flower growing history of 1700 years and is the cradle of Lingnan bonsai. Numerous scholars and poets have left a great number of poems to praise Fangcun. Kang Youwei wrote "The flowers are still in bloom in their thousand year home, former vagabonds can now return" in Visit to a Place of Flower.

Lingnan Flower Market 岭南花卉市场

Located in Wuyanqiao Village, the market is regarded by many as the largest of its kind in China, with only maybe Dounan Flower Market in Kunming being a close competitor. The flower centre covers 22,000 square meters with 19,000 stalls and 8 specialized zones selling all kinds of flowers, both real and artificial. The market is divided into different sections for easier navigation, and includes a rose area, a chrysanthemum area and a gladiolus area among others. A great place to browse for bargains, even if this is not your usual area of business.

Address: 57, Fangxing Lu (near the bus station), Liwan District 广州市荔湾区芳兴路57号(近窖口汽车客运站)

Contact: 020 8167-2516

Getting there: Take metro line 5 to Jiaokou Station, walk 100 metres from the north entrance

Yuehe Flower and Bird Market 越和花鸟鱼艺大世界

Opened in 2011, Yuehe Flower and Bird Market also known as Huadiwan (花地湾花鸟鱼虫批发市场) is not strictly a fresh flower market in the same sense as Lingnan Market. There are some plants in the gardening section but this place is better for bonsai and rare viewing stones rather than freshly cut blooms. Plenty of ornamental water equipment and gardening tools. This first section of the market also features high-end furniture, marine life, dry flowers, as well as an arts and crafts area.

Address: 271, Huadiwan Xique Lu, Liwan District 广州市荔湾区花地湾喜鹊路271号

Contact: 020 8152-9230

Getting there: Take metro line 1 to Huadiwan Station, use exit D

There are a number of smaller flower markets in Guangzhou including the following:

Huangcheng Flower Wholesale Market 花城花卉批发市场

Fresh flowers for retail as well as wholesale, along with artificial flowers, dried flowers, gardening goods and tools, root carving goods, handicrafts, fish, shade plants, fertilizer, and gardening equipment.

Address: Huangcheng Flower Wholesale Market, Yuexiu District 广州市越秀区花城花卉批发市场

Danan Flower Market 大南花卉街市

Very similar to Huangcheng with similar products and a similar size.

Address: Danan Lu, Yuexiu District

Huangsha Flower Trading Market
广东黄沙花卉精品交易市场

This market was the first indoor market in Guangzhou open 24 hours a day with a fully lit night market. At the beginning there were also expert demonstrations and industry seminars.

Address: 185, Huangpu Dadao, Liwan District
黄埔大道185

Guangzhou Flower Expo Park 广州花卉博览园

Located in the south-western part of the Fangcun area, this large expo park is divided into three main sections: the flower exhibition area, the research area and the ecological tourist area. Open since 2003, this is Asia's largest flower park with an area of nearly 30,000 square meters and over 500 flower stalls. In addition to the countless different species of flower on offer, you can also pick up various handy gardening tools.

Address: Longxi Zhong Lu, Liwan District
广州市荔湾区龙溪中路

Contact: 020 8141-8245

Getting there: Take bus to Guangzhou Flower Expo Park Station

In addition, there are two more wholesale markets worth looking at if your business involves artificial flower and ornamental arrangements.

The New Five Line Crafts Wholesale City
新五线工艺品批发城

Just outside the main subway station, on the other side from the adjoining bus station, this market has a good selection of artificial plants and flowers suitable for home and shop decoration.

Address: Jiaokou Subway 滘口站 on line 5

Contact: 020 8111-4528

Hua Hai Jin Ping Shi Chang 花卉精品市场

A smaller market of maybe a hundred or so stores close by to Sheng Di New World Decorations Wholesale Market (圣地新天地装饰材料城)

Address: Nanan Road 南岸路

Contact: 020 8651-8765

Getting there: Take metro line 5 to Zhongshanba station. Exit D, walk along traffic to the large intersection and turn right there. Hua Hai market is immediately on the right.

Beyond Guangzhou

Huadu Flower Market 花都花卉市场

One of the largest flower trading centres in Southern China, Huadu flower market opened in 2011 and includes a seedling section as well as an exhibition hall selling a diverse selection of flower that are carefully cultivated in greenhouses. Also known as the Huadu Nanfang Flowers Trading Centre (花都南方花卉交易中心) this large modern trading centre handles flower exhibition, wholesale, retail, storage, transportation, quarantine, and business affairs. The centre has four sections: a plant wholesale market, a flower market, a flower auction centre, and a floriculture art park.

Address: 137, Huahui Shichang, Huadu District 广州市花都区花卉市场137号

10 FOODSTUFFS

Jiangnan Fruit and Vegetable Market 江南果菜市场

The Jiangnan Fruit and Vegetables Market is the largest of its kind in Guangzhou and is located here in Chatou (槎头) on the Zengcha Lu on the north western outskirts of the city. It has grown much larger than the Tianping Jia Fruit Market (天平架水果市场) which is located in the north-east of Guangzhou in the Shahe area near Tianhe (沙河天平架). Thanks to its proximity to the north-bound Guangzhou-Qingyuan Expressway and Guangzhou's largest logistics area, Chatou is the biggest wholesale food market in the province. A torrent of food and goods arrive and leave this area at every hour of the day, often descending from the north of the province before being dispatched across the city.

Address: Chatou, Zengcha Lu, Baiyun District 白云区增槎路槎头

Clustered around Jiangnan on the same main road are a number of small food related markets, including the following.

San Yi International Food Market 五一国际食品城

Stores here carry a good range of imported products and is a good location who want to set up their own bar or coffee shop.

Address: 210-211 Zengcha Lu, Baiyun District

白云区增槎路210-211 号 槎头
A Liu Frozen Products 阿六冻品

A small market of only a couple of dozen stores, with more live animals such as goats and chickens at first sight than frozen foods.

Other markets on this main drag include the following:
Zhijing Commercial Market 志金商贸中心
Nuan Ren Pi Jiu Cheng 暖润皮具城
Dong Heng Market 东宏装饰材料城
Hai Wei Gan Huo Pi Fa Cheng 海味干货批发城
International Liquor Market 国家洋酒贡检中心
Guangzhou Xing Yuan Foodstuffs Market 广州新源粮油副食品批发市场
Dong Wang Market 东旺食品市场

Qingping Frozen Food Market
While most people are familiar with Qingping Herbs Market, fewer know about all of the frozen food wholesalers that are clustered around Heping Xi Lu, Zhuji Lu and Tiyun Lu. Nearly every store in this district has a large freezer room at the rear taking up most of the first floor. These store rooms are filled with all kinds of meats and seafood. Apart from frozen crabs and eels it is possible to find just about every kind of meat all the way up to marbled wagyu beef. There are also large numbers of shops here selling air dried hams from Yunnan and elsewhere from the west of the country.
Directions: Exit Huangsha Subway station into Mopark Shopping Plaza and look for the rear door on Heping Xi Lu. Turn left onto Heping Xi Lu.

Changjiang General Commodities Market 长江百货交易城
One of the older markets that sits on the fringes of

Guangzhou down near Luoxi Bridge towards Panyu District. This is frequented mostly by domestic buyers who are purchasing household items. This is the place to buy everything from toothpaste to kitchen housewares including ceramics and small electrical appliances. If the average housewife is going to buy something for the house, it can probably be found here. The market is divided into the North and South sections with the North part focussing mainly on towels, bedding and linens. This market is a world away from places like One Link. Here the surroundings are gritty and the what most of us would describe as slums. There is a great deal of new construction in this area but the market and it environs reflect the wafer-thin margins of the products sold here.

Address: Nan Hang Si Jie 南场四街

Directions: Sanjiaocun bus stop 三滘村站. Take the 188 bus from Nantian International Hotel Supplies Wholesale Market (南天国际酒店用品批发市场) at the Guangxuan Hotel terminus (广轩大厦 （南天商业城） 总站)

By metro: Take line 3 to Lijiao.Motorbikes cluster around exit C2 and will ferry you the five minutes across the river for around 10 RMB.

Haiying Jiangyuan Liang Yu Shihai Pifa Shang Chang 海印江南粮油食品批发市场

A relatively small market selling mainly food items in bulk quantities including staples such as rice, sugar and alcoholic drinks. Only domestic items are available and there are very few imports that you would find at locations such as Nantai and Yide markets.

Address: Nanzhou Mingyuan (Ruibao Garden) Nanzhou Lu 南洲名苑 （瑞宝花园） 站

By metro: Take line 3 to Lijiao. Motorbikes cluster around exit C2 and will ferry you here for around 10 RMB.

Yide Lu Groceries Market 一德路市场

As well as toys, stationary and dried seafood, the markets that stretch along Yide Lu also carry on a wide range of candies, fruits, peanuts, beans, nuts, and other agricultural products. The stores are mostly found in traditional local Qilou buildings on the narrow old-town streets. Cargo goes to and fro all day long and parking here is a struggle due to the limited space, crowds of people and chaotic traffic. But with such diversity of aromas, colours and people, it's very hard to not get pulled-in to the excitement.

Address: Eastern Section of Yide Lu, Yuexiu District (west of Haizhu Square) 越秀区一德路东段

11 FURNITURE

Furniture wholesale markets in Guangzhou are located in Fangcun, Guangzhou Da Dao South, Huangpu Da Dao, and Dashi in Panyu.

Fangcun Huadi Furniture Centre
Huge showrooms are devoted to replica Chinese furniture that make the Forbidden City look spartan in comparison. This is where locals come to furnish their most opulent tea houses and residential buyers can find everything from Qing-style four posters to floor-to-ceiling apothecary drawer cabinets. New additions to tempt your credit card might include the beautifully ornate jewellery boxes and the octagonal temple abaci. Passing through the life-size mythic figures of the woodcarving section.
Address: 271, Huadiwan Xique Lu, Liwan District
广州市荔湾区花地湾喜鹊路271号
Huadiwan Subway Station on line number 1. Look for exit C and head straight into the market complex directly ahead.

Panyu Dashi Furniture City 广州番禺大石家私城
Dashi Furniture City encompasses and area of more

than a million square metres, divided into blocks A, B, C, D, E, F, and G.

Address: Panyu Dashi Furniture City
广州番禺大石祺瑞国际家具博览中心

Contact: 020 8479-6079

Directions: Take metro (Line 3) first and then take a taxi to the Dashi Furniture City (Da Shi Jia Si Cheng, 大石家私城).

Guangzhou has a number of large furniture markets but many of these are focussed towards retail rather than wholesale and they pale into insignificance compared to the Lecong Market in Shunde. These include the following:

Zhujiang New City Furniture Mall 维家思广场

Hong Shu Wan Jia 红树湾家具博览中心

Weijia Best International Furniture Exhibition Centre
广州维家思广场

Address: 188, Huangpu Avenue West
广州市天河区黄埔大道西188号珠江新城广场

Mangrove Bay Furniture Expo Centre
红树湾家具博览中心

Address: 201, Dongxiao Haiyin Bridge Road, (opposite Vanguard) Haizhu District
广州海珠区海印桥南东晓路201号 （华润万家对面）

Lecong International Furniture Exhibition Centre (LFC)
广东省顺德市乐从镇广湛公路段团亿国际家具城

First opened in 2003, LFC is located in China's furniture capital – Shunde. Not only is Lecong the largest furniture market in China, it is the largest in the world at present. LFC covers an area of about 3 million square meters with well over 200 furniture sales buildings including Lecong International Furniture Exhibition Centre, Shunde Empire Group, Sunlink Group, Taunyi

International Furniture City, etc. The complex stretches for more than 5 km and has attracted 3,300 furniture dealers as well as 1,500 furniture manufacturers. There is a vast array of products including bedroom furniture, living room furniture, dining room furniture, bathroom furniture, kitchen furniture, hotel furniture, restaurant furniture, café chairs, bar stools and sanitary ware. Especially spectacular (or garishly crass depending on your taste) is the Splendid Palace of the Renaissance, which has to be seen to be believed.

Address: Foshan City, Shunde, Lecong Town, 佛山市乐从镇

By Bus: Guangzhou Liu Hua Bus Station (流花汽车站) has one bus to Lecong every twenty minutes from 7:30am - 6:30pm

Subway: Their is a free shuttle bus at Kengkou metro station (Exit C), on Saturday and Sunday.

Guangzhou Kengkou metro station to Louver depart times are: 10:00 10:30, 14:00

Louver to Guangzhou Kengkou metro station depart times are: 12:30, 17:00, 18:15

The Louvre EurAmerican Furniture Plaza
罗浮宫家具博览中心

Right beside LFC, there is even more furniture here, with office furniture located on the first floor. The website claims that the customer service centre offers a free translation service.

website: http://www.louvre-group.cn/en/index.aspx

Address: Lecong Town, Shunde, Foshan City 佛山市乐从镇

By Taxi: 150 RMB to 300 RMB from the airport or train station

Subway: Kuiqi Lu Station (魁奇路站) is the terminus on the Guangfo Line (FMetro Line 1) and takes about thirty minutes from the Xilang terminus station on Line One.

For Louver take Exit C at Kuiqi Lu metro station. From here take bus 255A bus to the Louver Furniture Market. The ticket is 3 RMB, taking eight stops from Kuiqi Lu to Ji Ju Bo Lan Zhong Xing (家具博览中心)

More furniture markets are located on both sides of the highway. These include Foshan International Furniture Expo Mall, only three stops from Kuiqi Lu metro station by bus, the Redstar Macalline Brand Furniture Exhibition and Wholesale Centre 红星美凯龙品牌家具博览中心 (http://www.lcredstar.com/EN/Main/Index.aspx), the Sunlink Lighting and Kitchen Cabinet City 顺联橱柜灯饰城, and the Tuan Yi International Furniture City (广东省顺德市乐从镇广湛公路段团亿国际家具城) on Guangzhan Road.

12 GLASSES AND OPTICAL

The wholesale spectacles markets consists of at least six different buildings along the eastern side of Renmin Zhong Lu, south of the Children's Hospital, just above Dade Lu, close by to Shangxiajiu Shopping Street. In addition, there are showrooms all along this stretch of the road.

Guangzhou Glasses City 广州眼镜城

The first four floors are devoted to every possible kind of frame and lens. Up on the fifth floor is all the equipment required for professional optometrists, from processing machinery to eye testing equipment. I picked up a very nice ultrasonic cleansing device here last year for less than twenty bucks. I have always craved one of these since I first saw them in the optician's and now my whole family uses it on a regular basis.

Even if your market is for other products, this is a great place to make some incredible savings on glasses and contact lenses. I usually have a pair of glasses and a pair of sunglasses made when I am in the area. Frames and lenses made in just a couple of hours never comes to more than 500 RMB for a pair. Of course if you are buying frames wholesale, then you can get them at far lower prices. Frames come in all shapes and sizes and all price ranges, from a few kuai up to a few thousand for designer brands. Choose from all kinds of materials, plastic metal, even wood and bamboo. There are also plenty of places where you can do a quick eye test just to make sure that your prescription is up to date. While you wait, take a stroll down the main Shangxiajiu shopping street which is very nearby, or maybe explore some of the alleyways that snake out from here and visit some of the other smaller glasses wholesalers. How to get there: Metro line 1 to Ximenkou. Exit B, turn left and walk 150 meters towards Renmin Zhong Lu (Renmin Elevated Rd on Google maps). Turn left again and walk a few hundred meters past the hospital, and you will see the glasses shops on your left.

Address: 260, Renmin Zhong Lu 广州市人民中路260号
Contact: 020 8188-2626

Wider Lenses 现達光学

In the far left hand corner of the second floor of Guangzhou Glasses City is a small booth called Wider Lenses that sells lenses to go with all the frames. Their main workshop is just a few doors up the road on a small side street. This is my own personal choice for lens grinding, with a huge range including polycarbonates, trivex, high index plastic, aspheric, photochromic and polarized.

Address: Renmin   Zhong   Lu
广州市越秀区人民中观绿路34号首层
Contact: 020 8188-9563
www.founderoptical.com.

Guangzhou Xinjiang Yanjing City 广州信江眼镜城

Opened in 2003, many of the storekeepers hail from Chaozhou where there is a large concentration of frame manufacturers, but there are also representatives from Jiangsu and Zhejiang provinces here. Not only frames but contact lenses and glasses cases in every colour and design that you can think of.

Address:250, Renmin Zhong Lu 广州市人民中路250号
Directions: Directly beside the access road to the Guangzhou Daily Newspaper office. Some ten minutes walk south from Ximen Kou subway station.

Guangdong International Eyeglasses Centre 广东（国际）眼镜中心

From the most serious looking librarian style lunettes to the wildest party designs, it is possible to find just about any spectacle design imaginable here. There are always design improvements available in the latest styles from frameless frames to flexi arms and screwless bridges.

Address: Fen Ning Building, 313, Guangfu Zhong Lu, West of Renmin Zhong Lu 人民中路丰宁大厦

Spread along the east side of Renmin Road are at least half a dozen wholesale markets devoted to optical products. Apart from those mentioned above, there are also the following:

Fuming Glasses Market 富名国际眼镜城
Yue He International 越和仰忠精品批发商城
Nanfang Glasses Professional Market 南方眼镜专业市场
International Glasses City 越和国际眼镜批发市场

13 HOME DECORATION AND BUILDING MATERIALS

Chebei   Decorative   Materials   Market
广州车陂装饰材料城

Chebei can be divided roughly into three areas. The southern portion is mainly heavy building materials including large lumber stores and metal fixture shops. The remainder is a large central two-storey building with an elongated annexe on the east side specialising mainly in interior decoration materials. Prices are on the low to medium side but most of the stock is from local brands that are almost unheard of outside of China, and therefore suitable more for the domestic market than international exports.

Chebei is now conveniently accessible at Chebei Nan subway station. Chebei City is where the urban area merges into the industrial area, as can clearly be seen by the names of the bus stops approaching the centre, such as 'chemical factory' and 'paper mill.' This is actually quite a common situation in Guangzhou. I recently paid a visit to an old friend who had moved into a huge apartment complex just south of the river. Only when I arrived did I realise that his new home had been directly on top of the old site of the Guangzhou Sulphuric Acid Factory. No wonder he was suffering from previously unexplained bouts of severe depression.

Address: The Junction of Chebei Road 车陂路 and Huangpu Avenue East 黄埔大道东

Contact: 020 8232-1676

Directions: Take the metro to Chebei South Station 车陂南站,the interchange station of Guangzhou Metro Line 4 and Line 5. The market is directly opposite the Fusheng Hotel, on the north side of the first bus company parking lot Jubei Road East.

Chebei Road Yuexing Steel Market 车陂路粤兴钢材市场

Representatives from all the major steel mills, Baosteel, Anshan Iron and Steel, Shougang, Shaoguan Steel and other manufacturers of steel can be found here. In addition, distributors from Taiwan, Zhejiang, Shantou, Shenzhen, Jiangmen wholesale all kinds of stainless steel pipes, plates and accessories, plumbing equipment, valves and aluminium, metal parts etc. The Chebei Stone Market is an annexe to the steel market that focusses on more natural materials.

Address: 233, Jubei Road, Jubei Road and the junction of Guangyuan Expressway

Contact: 020 8523-8460

Yuehe International Building Materials Centre 越和国际建材中心

Despite its grand sounding name, this smaller market located on the ground floor, directly underneath a Carrefour supermarket is mainly for domestic buyers. That said, there are still some interesting options among the eighty or hundred stores located here, including the fascinating Mr Mosaic store at B051A.

Outside the east entrance is the much smaller Yuen

Chong Kang Hu Wholesale Market (员村康湖装饰材料商业街), with just twenty of so wholesalers, focussing on building materials for the local area.

Address: Huangpu Da Dao Zhong 黄埔大道中

Yibao Decoration Material City 亿宝装饰材料城

Further along Huangpu Da Dao, another market specialising in all kinds of building materials as well as kitchen and bathroom fittings. Most of the products are domestic, but could conceivably be used for export.

Address: Huangpu Dadao East 黄埔大道东

Contact: 020 3820-0270

There are a succession of decoration markets along Huangpu Avenue that are now starting to show their age and may not last much longer. Some of these are now much more retail based for local city dwellers. At the moment these include the following.

Xinyang Decoration Material City 新羊装饰材料城

Address: 413, Huangpu Road 广州市黄埔大道中413号

Qianjin Decoration Materials Market 前进装饰材料市场

Address: Huangpu Da Dao Dong 黄埔大道东圃前进石溪村AEC汽车城东侧

Home Expo 广州家居世博园

Address: 663, Huangpu Road East, Yuzhu Station 广东省广州市天河区黄埔大道东663号

Meiling Home Deco 美林家居

Address: 663, Huangpu Da Dao 广州市天河区黄埔大道东663号美林饰品中心

Meiju Centre Area D 美居中心D座

Address: 68, Huangpu Avenue, Tianhe District 天河区黄埔大道68号

Taikang Decoration Material Street 泰康装饰材料专业街

This street includes the Guangzhou New Taikang Decoration Mall (广州市新泰康装饰城) and the Taikang-Haizhu Deco Market (泰康满意一百精品广场). Directly across the road from the Taikang Jewellery Market, what used to be the city's prime location for hardware, sanitary ware and other decorative materials is now well past its prime. There are now so many dedicated markets on the outskirts of Guangzhou that this area has lost much of its original significance and will probably soon be demolished to make way for more spillover shopping malls from Beijing Road. Even so, in the meantime, there is still a useful collection of outlets here with a special focus on bathroom fittings and shop outfitters as well as a few more specialist stores.

At one time, this market extended one block north onto Danan Road Decoration Material Street (大南路装饰材料专业街). This used to be the home of many decoration markets including the Huagan Décor Market, Guangzhou Textile Decoration Store and the nearby nearby Huifu Dong Deco Market. Of these only the Taigu and Jiaming Lighting Markets have yet to be pushed out by the ever increasing downtown rental prices.

Address: 25-109, Taikang Road 广州市泰康路25-109号
Contact: 020 8332-4462, 8332-4463

Nanan Road Building Materials Market 南岸装饰材料专业街

At Nanan Road in Liwan district you will find a large wholesale market for building materials, sanitary ware, wallpaper, ceramics, handles, doors, windows, gypsum board, plywood, windows, doors, balustrades, tiles, floors, counter tops, kitchens, wardrobes etc.

Address: Nanan Road 越秀区南岸路
Directions: Take metro line 5 to Zhongshanba station.

Exit D, walk along traffic to the large intersection and turn right there. Within one hundred meters start to see the markets and stores on both sides of the inner ring road.

Sheng Di New World Decorations Wholesale Market 圣地新天地装饰材料城

A very popular market with Middle Eastern buyers located on the first two floors of a large new apartment building. Despite its small size, there is a great deal of choice of higher end products here. As well doors, lighting and carpets, there are a number of impressive sanitary ware stores, stocking everything from urinals to jacuzzis. This is the first time that I have seen bath tubs with built in TVs, but maybe that says more about my ascetic lifestyle than their general availability. A huge choice of attractive glass shower doors that I would happily have in my home along with at least fifty different styles of glass blocks. At least half a dozen shops specialise in cladding materials of all kinds, for adding that luxury feeling to any refurb. Ornate gypsum ceilings in Islamic designs that would look good in even the most upmarket Muslim restaurant and enormous 3D carved murals. It would not surprise me if the interior decorators of the Burj did a fair amount of their shopping here.

Address: Nanan Road 南岸路

Yuntai Decoration Material Market 运泰装饰城

Just around the corner from Xichang Subway Station, this sad looking collection of empty units has been all but completely abandoned, perhaps due to the intense competition further south on Nan'an Lu.

Address: 84, Nanan Road 南岸路 84号

South China International Decoration Material Trading Centre 华南国际装饰材料交易市场

Located just to the south of the Hua Nan Sports and

276

Stationery Market (华南国际文体用品交易市场), the South China Market is much more suited to provincial buyers than international professionals. Much of the stock here is the kind of over the top décor seen in Chinese-owned hotels and karaoke parlours. If you are in the market for wall sized LCD video screens and chandeliers suited to Saddam-type palaces, then this might be place for you.

On the southern edge is a long row of stores specialising in the kind of reinforced steel doors that are so popular in countries where law enforcement is an ideal rather than and everyday occurrence. The rest of the market is quite disorganised but covers a huge variety of goods, from fully fitted kitchens to vinyl and PVC floor coverings. Plenty of shops selling door handles, hinges, drawer slides and other miscellaneous fittings.

Address: Nanan Road 南岸路

South And North Decoration Market 南北装饰市场

One of a number of small markets in this area, all focussed on building and decoration materials. They are all clustered in the same section of Nanan Road and include the following:

Guangzhou Construction Decoration Material Plaza 广州装饰材料市场

Xinzhiguang Construction Decoration Material Market 星之光装饰材料市场

Guangdong Construction Decoration Material Market 广东装饰材料市场

Nanan Construction Decoration Material Market 南岸装饰材料市场

Address: 17, Nanan Lu, Liwan District南岸路17号
Contact: 020 3848-1239

Cai Hong Ceramics Market 彩虹建筑陶瓷市场

The area bordering up to the railway lines around Xinhua Lu has a large number of dealers selling ceramic tiles for use in bathrooms and kitchens.
Address: Xinhua Lu 西华路

Doors

There is a large concentration of Chinese style door stores on Yuexiu Zhong Lu, just off Zhongshan Fourth Road, near the Peasant Movement Institute (Nong Jiang Suo 农讲所). These are mostly retail outfits concentrating on the kind of heavy metal security doors that are favoured by domestic Chinese customers (and yet they say that China is such a safe country!!) but many outlets have strong factory connections if you wish to buy in wholesale amounts. Many African and Arabian traders buy these doors from middle men on Guangyuan Road, but this is probably a better place to obtain them direct from the source.
Address: Yuexiu Zhong Lu 越秀中路

Shihan Dasan Building Materials Market 石汉大森林装饰材料城

Another wholesale market focussing on mainly domestic buyers, also known as Shixi Decoration Material City (石溪装饰材料城). Approximately two hundred stores on two floors selling all kinds of interior decoration supplies from doors to fully fitted kitchens. There are even some basic materials suppliers including merchants specialising in timber, marble etc.
Address: 656, Gongye Avenue
广东省广州海珠区工业大道南656号
Contact: 020 8436-2985

Nanyu International Home Building Material City
南域建材装饰城

The first floor is devoted to building materials such as

ceramic tiles and even a shoe cabinet specialist. Unfortunately about 80% of the shops are closed, perhaps signifying that the China housing bubble is reaching its peak. Upstairs on the second floor, the entire building is devoted to the Xuping Jewellery Company, where there facility is so large that a golf cart is made available for buyers to get from one end of the shelving-based warehouse to the other.

Address: Tanwei Nan Lu 坦尾南路

Contact: 020 8198-8188

Directions: From exit A of the Tanwei subway station head directly under the highway flyover and out onto Tanwei Nan Lu.

Deco - Wuzhou (Five Continents) Decoration Materials Shopping Centre 五洲装饰世界

Previously known as the Continental Decorated World, this huge mall has now adopted to new and much simpler name of 'Deco.' Much more luxury orientated than other markets, there are representatives of famous western brand names here including Siemens, Vohringer and Kohler. Products are divided in eight different category areas: bathroom, lighting, kitchen and electrical, wood flooring and stairs, ceramics and stone, textiles, wallpapers and paint, doors/windows and wardrobes and something that is described as 'syntheticals'.

Address: Yingbin Road, Panyu District 广州市番禺区迎宾路

Contact: 020 8450-8877

Tianpingjia Building Material Market 天平架装饰材料城

While Shahe clothing market has exploded in recent years, Tianpingjia has lost much of its early significance. This might be because recent subway access has pushed up property prices, making it difficult for businesses that require a large amount of floor space, such as those involving building and construction materials. Even so, there are still large numbers of suppliers in this area supplying raw materials such as plywood, wpc, pvc flooring, osb and finished products such as paint, windows, doors, plywood, floor boards, ceilings, lighting, curtains, gypsum board, counter tops, etc.

Address:512, Guangzhou North Avenue, Shahe District
广州大道北512

Beyond Guangzhou

The largest building material markets are situated well outside of the city centre, often in suburban areas that are experiencing building booms themselves. At the same time, as the property bubble expands, some of the markets suffer from over development and empty out even faster than they have grown.

Hongxin Decoration Plaza (宏信装饰城) is more than 100 acres of commercial construction market that was fuelled by the massive urban growth that has concreted the Panyu District and beyond with examples such as Lijiang, Clifford and Country Garden, which are very close by.

The satellite towns around Foshan have a large number of building material markets including the following:

Foshan Huayi Decoration Material Market
佛山华艺装饰材料市场

Address: Jihua Xilu He 325 Guadao
佛山市季华西路和325国道交汇处

Foshan Dazhuangwan Building Materials Market
佛山大转弯装饰材料市场

Badatong Home Decoration Market 八达通家居市场

Address: Foshan Nanhai Lishui
广佛高速盐步里水收费站旁

Shiwan Zhiye Ceramic Market 石湾置业陶瓷批发市场

Address : Shagang Section, Lanshi, Shiwan Town Middle Road, Chancheng District, Foshan
广东省佛山市禅城区置业陶瓷批发市场

Huaxia Ceramics Expo City, Nanzhuang
佛山市南庄华夏陶瓷城陶博一路九座金地带大楼

China Ceramic City 中国陶瓷城

China Mosaic City 中国马赛克城

Address: 2, Jiangwan San Lu 江湾三路2号

Huadu Building Decoration Plaza 花都建筑装饰城
        Divided into four main areas.
Block A: kitchenware, ceramics, doors and windows
Block B: hardware, plumbing, chemical coatings
Block C: lighting, fabrics
Block D: wrought ironware and other decorative materials
Address: At the crossroads of Jianshe Bei Rd. and Yongfa Blvd. Huadu District 广州市花都建设北路永发大道口

Many of these markets are supplied by factories situated in Guangdong, including towns such as Jieyang and Gaoyao city which churn out huge amounts of construction hardware each year.

14 HOTEL AND RESTAURANT SUPPLIES

Guangzhou Nantai Kitchen Accessories Wholesale Market
南泰百货批发中心

The main entrance is on Nantian Lu, behind the new Yen Hui Guang Chang Shopping Mall. The market itself is divided into three main sections. D area is mainly foodstuffs, both imported and domestic. Expats in the know come here for decent coffee, European spirits and cream cheese. I often stock up with Malaysian Old Town, Jagermeister and Philadelphia down here. Centre section is more kitchen supplies and utensils and there are interesting stores here filled with everything from baking equipment to cleaning fluid. The southern edge of the market is known as the SP section and focuses mainly on appliances and fixtures and fittings. There are plenty of crockery shops and a couple of very good Tupperware type plastic container wholesalers. Larger fixtures and fittings such as tables and chairs and clustered on the opposite side of Nantian Lu.

For bargain basement shoppers, the second hand appliance market is just opposite the rear entrance at 109

Jiangyan Lu. This is like a restaurant and bakery scrapyard with all kinds of used ovens, hobs, freezers etc.

Address: 168, Nantai Lu, Haizhu District南泰路168号

Contact: 020 3423-4082, 020-8435-5370

Transportation: Exit D from Jiangtai Lu Subway Station, will bring you out at the very bottom of Jiangnan Da Dao. Walk fifty metres to the first corner and turn right. This small connecting road will take you 200 metres up to the main intersection with Jiangyan Lu. Turn Right again and the rear entrance of the market is about fifty metres across the road.

Nantai Second Hand Kitchen Market 南燕厨具

Just across the road from the Jiangyuan Lu entrance to the Nantai Kitchen Accessories Wholesale Market mentioned above is a small second hand market filled with all kinds of industrial kitchen equipment from freezers to ovens. Inside is disorganised and is more like a scrapyard than a wholesale market. It is only a fraction the size of the second-hand kitchen market at Tanwei but it is worth a browse if you are looking for cheap kitchen hardware.

Address: 109, Jiangyuan Lu 江燕路109号

Contact: 020 8431-5775

Daxing Second Hand Kitchen Market 大型厨具

Almost directly under the stretch of subway line from Tanwei to Jiaokou sits Guangzhou's largest second-hand catering market. There are around thirty large enterprises here that deal in all kinds of used kitchen equipment. A lot of it has been subject to elements being stored out in the open and is rather the worse for wear but there are still bargains to be had, especially if you are planning to set up your own restaurant.

Address: Tanwei Subway Station 坦尾站

Directions: Exit B from Tanwei Subway Station on line 5,

down the stairs, across the small bus station and look for the large archway.

Shaxi International Hotel Supplies Market
广州沙溪国际酒店用品城

Guangzhou Shaxi International Hotel Articles City is the largest hotel article wholesale market in China at present. It occupies an area of 120,000 square meters, now with more than 1000 shops. You can find just about anything that is related to the catering and restaurant industry and hotel industry, from linen through to cookware. Uniforms, tableware, kitchenware, kitchen appliances, signs, dish ware, glassware, stainless steel, guest-room articles, food packing, There is an especially large range of ceramics, including many companies that will custom make cups, plates etc. with the customer's own design.

Across from the market is the Continental International Decoration Centre and directly behind the market is Lingnan International Footwear City. Also nearby is the Guangzhou Xinsha Hardware and Plastics Market (广州新沙五金塑料城).

I was disappointed to find that on my last visit (April 2015) that much of this vast complex is now closed and vacant. I would estimate that some 60% of the ground floor and almost 90% of the second floor is now empty, with many of the tenants having gone out of business. Part of this can be attributed to the fact that 'Peak China' was at least five years ago and a great deal of business has moved away from the increasing expensive Guangdong province and out into the hinterlands. The hotel industry especially is experience a massive glut in this part of the world. The other problem is that rents here in the new building are simply too expensive. Fortunately there are still plenty of active suppliers in the main covered area directly behind the main building.

Address: Shaxi Road, Lopu, Panyu (Shaxi exit, Panyu

bridge,   Hua'nan   Highway)
广东省广州市番禺区洛浦街沙溪大道
Contact: 020 3452-1098
Metro: Take metro line 3 to Xiajiao station, exit B

Nantian International Hotel Supplies Wholesale Market
南天国际酒店用品批发市场

Just to confuse things, there is a second Nantian Market down by the river that dwarves the Jiangyan Lu version. Also known as Guangzhou Nantian International Hotel Facility Trading Centre and Nantian Trading City, opened in 1999, this vast complex stretches out over more than 20 million square meters, 1500 outlets supply all kinds of hospitality equipment. Just about anything related to hotels and restaurants can be found under the corrugated tin roofs of this massive market. From kitchen utensils and buffet equipment, all the way up to the full size freezers and cold room/storage. From janitorial supplies, all the way up to control panels and even elevators. Lots of local specialist equipment such as soup tureens big enough to hide Ali Baba and giant duck roasters. I counted more than fifty individual buildings. The right side begins with furniture (look out for the bamboo mats stacked three or four metres high) and finished on the far left with a selection of health and safety supply stores, especially ironic in Mainland China.

Address: Guangzhou Road South and the north-west corner of Luo Xi Bridge 广州大道南

By Bus: The Guangxuan Hotel terminus (广轩大厦（南天商业城）总站) of bus number 188 is located right next to the main entrance.

By metro: Take line 3 to Lijiao. Motorbikes cluster around exit C2 and will ferry you the five minutes across the river for around 10 RMB.

15 JADE

For over three thousand years, jade (Chinese: yù; 玉) has been treasured by the Chinese. One of the earliest domestic sources of the stone was the White Jade (Yurungkash) and Black Jade (Karakash) Rivers near the town of town of Hotan (aka Yutian, Khotan; Chinese: Hetian; 和田) in western China's Xinjiang Province (Chinese Turkestan). From these deposits comes a creamy white to greenish stone, with the most valuable being pure white.

Jade carving has been practised in Guangzhou for more than a thousand years. Many of these businesses stretch back to the Qing Dynasty when locations such as Waring Street and King's Gate and Daihe Lu (now Kangwang Lu) had long been famous for skilled artisans. From 1873 to 1878, an average of 200 tons of jadeite was imported yearly through Guangzhou. Another important entry point lies along the border between China and Myanmar in Yunnan province, China's earliest jadeite import locale. There were about 6,000 jadeite companies in Yunnan in 2007; five years later, this number had increased to 21,000. The main markets there are concentrated in

Tengchong, Yingjiang, and Ruili. Most traders sell products they process themselves. They generally buy roughs from Yunnan province for processing in the suburbs of Guangzhou and sell the processed items in the jade market. It is claimed that many were formerly master craftsmen working at the Guangzhou Jade Factory and Nanfang Jade Carving Factory, who resigned and set up their own businesses. The jade handicraft industry in Guangzhou reached its peak between 1929 - 1936. Shengxiang Jade Market on Changshou Lu and Chongde Jade Market on Dai He Road were the two giants in the field in South China, having world-wide fame at that time. The Pingzhou region of Guangdong is China's largest jadeite rough market, is referred to as the hometown of the jadeite bracelets which are drilled from pre-cut circles. More than twenty auctions are held here each year, attracting dealers and retailers from all over the country. The Sihui area draws carvers from Putian and Nanyang, who apply skills and concepts from wood and stone carving to jadeite.

Since the early Qing Dynasty, large quantities of a white-to-bright green jade has been appearing in China, sourced from mines in Upper Burma. The Chinese understood this material was different from the Hotan jade, and named the vivid green variety feicui (翡翠) or kingfisher jade, due to its resemblance to the colour of the feathers of the kingfisher bird. By the mid-16th century, the Spanish had spread across much of the New World. In the process, they discovered a stone treasured throughout Mesoamerica. Noticing that it was used for pains of the side and lower back, they named it piedra de ijade (stone of the flank of the lower back). In French this became ijade and then jade, in Italian giade and jade in English. In Dog Latin it was lapis nephriticus (stone good for the kidneys). Mesoamerican jade was the mineral now called jadeite. Axel von Cronstedt (the geologist who named nickel) renamed lapis nephriticus nephritein Swedish in

1758. That became the German scientific name when he was translated, 1780. It entered A.G. Werner's classic system (1791).

Jadeite is a relatively recent entry to the jade family. While some traditionalists feel that it lacks the rich history of nephrite, nevertheless the "emerald" green colour of Imperial jadeite is the standard by which all jades – including nephrite – are judged by most Chinese enthusiasts today. Due to the fact that translucent gems such jadeite and nephrite (and materials that resemble them) generally consist of mineral aggregates rather than single crystals, identification by traditional gemmological tests is very difficult. While it is relatively straightforward to determine what they are not (nephrite or jadeite), it was maddeningly difficult to learn exactly what they are. Watch out for clever glass imitations with a composition corresponding to canasite. Try looking for gas bubbles as an indicator or obvious secondary iron-oxide staining that had been applied manually. Some stones are artificially stained so as to give a russet coloured surface skin which enhances their value. According to the 'experts' this process takes about a month and the colour is fixed indelibly in the jade matrix.

In Hong Kong, jewellery stores are filled almost entirely with jadeite. But if one journeys to mainland China, one can rediscover the ancient Chinese appreciation of jade in the form of nephrite from Xinjiang. This is a stone that does not display the intense colour and glossy lustre of its jadeite cousin. Instead, its beauty is more sublime. Chinese nephrite has a creamy texture that coaxes, rather than shouts. Picking up a piece, as you caress it, you will quickly understand why this stone was so revered. It truly is the stone of heaven.

In the later years of the Qing Dynasty, the Xi Guan area of Guangzhou was heavily inhabited by a group of celebrities, politicians and merchants from high society, who became the first owners of the famous Xiguan houses. Yuansheng

Xijie Street, famous for its porcelains and jades, is encircled by four pathways, namely, Kangwang Lu, Changshou Xi Lu, Wenchang Bei Lu and Longjin Zhong Lu. The Hualin Temple here has been especially influential. Founded by a prominent Buddhist monk from India, Monk Zongfu collected funds and built the Mahavira Hall in 1655 and later other structures in the temple. Abbot Zhiyuan later built a hall to house statues of 500 arhats (Buddhist saints) at the order of the emperor.

From 2000 to 2009, the price of jadeite rose by an average of 20% annually. For 2011 and 2012, this rate increased more than 30% annually and the Chinese demand for high-end jadeite continues to grow. Some jadeite dealers were forced to tap into their reserves to deal with the lack of rough. At the June 2013 Myanmar jadeite auction, rough prices sky rocketed. In total, fewer than 10,000 pieces were available for purchase (compared to 20,0000,000 pieces in previous auctions), while prices were three to ten times higher. High-end jadeite products are still in demand among Chinese collectors and investors in China and around the world even at significantly marked-up prices.

The Jade Market in Guangzhou has grown rapidly and is now centred around Yuansheng Xijie Antiques Market (源胜陶瓷玉石工艺街). To the south of Changshou Lu, all the way down to Shangxiajiu shopping street, the area surrounding Hualin Temple is a maze of ancient alleyways filled with small workshops. Changshou Lu itself is lined with equipment suppliers, gemmological tool sellers and packaging suppliers. To find where the market extends north of Changshou look for number 87, directly opposite one of the remaining Xi Guan houses at number 128, near the Bao Wan Hotel (宝湾酒店). Slip back into the rabbit warren of jade vendors here and get lost in the Yuansheng Xijie Antiques Market as it stretches all the way up to Longjin Zhong Lu.

On the Kangwang Lu side of this quadrangle, the authorities have built a large number of huge mall building to house the exploding jade trade. The oldest of these is the Huicheng Garden Complex at 181 Kangwang Lu, opposite the GZ Elizabeth Women's Hospital. Look out for the unusual carvings outside of stylised camels and rhinos, or the English sign for the Dong Hong Hotel. This is a run down mall that has seen much better days with as many porcelain dealers as there are jade carvers. Even so, at least 70% of the stores are now abandoned.

The Hualin International Jade Market (华林金镶玉珠宝广场) has now spread into at least three new buildings and is still growing. The most interesting of these is the C Building at the junction of Kangwang Lu and Changshou Lu. The top floor houses some of the most enormous gemstone superstores that I have ever seen, along with a branch of the Agricultural bank and the National Gemstone Testing Centre which stretches down to the fifth floor. Much of the fourth and third floors are dedicated to Buddhist temple decorations. (The Buddhist Cultural and Antique Jewellery Market 佛教文玩珠宝市场) As well as jade objets d'art, there are large amounts of agate, agar-wood oil, sandalwood oil and just about anything that you might need to establish a fully functioning temple. This ranges from incense all the way to monk's outfitters.

On the second floor expect to see large amounts of crystals and beads included in the mix while the ground floor includes pearl, emerald and white jade.

The Hualin layout is repeated twice-fold on the opposite side of Kangwang Lu and has now been added to in the form of the Liangang International Jewellery Centre. Just north of the C Building is a traditional Chinese memorial arch entrance in Yuansheng Xijie, an area filled with open stalls and booths, selling a wide range of ancient antiques and handicrafts as well as jade. Expect to see Yixing teapots, Fujian Shoushan stone, soapstone,

Myanmar jade and bamboo, wood carving, root carving, bronze and mammoth ivory.

Transportation: Guangzhou Metro Line 1 goes to Changshou Lu (长寿路), exit D2 which emerges into Hengbao Plaza (恒宝广场). Alternatively, line 6 goes to Culture Park. From exit D under walk ten minutes directly north on the main road up past Liwan Plaza to the main junction with Changshou Lu.

Hualin Jade Street 华林玉器街

Also adjacent to Shangxia Jiu, Hualin Jade Street (华林玉器街) encompasses an area of over 10,000 square meters and is home to over 80% of Guangzhou's jade products, making it the true hub for jade trading in the city. Prices vary dramatically; you can pick up a jade stone for as little as 10 RMB, or for the big spenders out there, over 10,000 RMB. In the middle of the street stands the Hualin Jade Plaza (华林玉器大楼), which is the largest indoor jade market in the area offering over 280 stands selling pendants, bracelets, and flowers made of jade. Jade hunters will not be disappointed with Hualin Street, and are sure to go home happy with a beautiful piece of China's most well-known precious stone in their hands.

Address: Hualin   Xinjie,   Xiajiu   Lu

广州市荔湾区下九路华林新街

Christian D. Taulkinghorn

16 JEWELLERY

Hong Kong's appetite for jewellery is well known around the world, as can be seen by the large number of jewellery trade shows that take place here every year. It therefore makes sense that just over the border, Guangdong should have become Hong Kong's largest jewellery manufacturing base in the mainland, as many Hong Kong jewellery makers have moved to the area in an effort to find low cost and skilful craftsmen. In the Panyu District of Guangzhou City, more than two hundred Hong Kong jewellery companies have set up manufacturing factories, employing more than 50,000 workers. The district processes more than 100 tons of gold and platinum every year, which now accounts for ninety-five percent of the jewellery on Hong Kong's market. In addition to Panyu, the Chonghua District of Guangzhou, Shenzhen and Dongguan have also witnessed the building of many jewellery manufacturing factories. Just to the north of Guangzhou, Huadu is also trying to become established in this profitable manufacturing sector. In addition, the establishment of mainland production bases makes it easier for Hong Kong jewellery to enter the mainland market.

Taikang Plaza Jewellery Market 泰康饰品城

Opened in 1997, Taikang Plaza (also known as Yangzhong Accessories Wholesale Market) is situated on the first five floors of the Taikang Plaza Building. On the sixth floor is a small cosmetics wholesale market while the seventh to tenth floors are given over to office space. There is a hotel on the eleventh floor and the rest of the building is private apartments

The first five floors are filled with small wholesale booths selling low to mid range costume jewellery, earrings, rings, necklaces, packaging and related items. Products include headgear, belts, necklaces, bracelets, hats, even leggings and phone accessories. The first floor has a large number of scarf specialists, while the lower floors have huge quantities of tiaras, purses, headbands and bows. Up the fifth floor, most of the stores specialise in stainless steel with a large concentration of body piecing jewellery suppliers. There are also a couple of interesting shops up here that make studded leather to order, lots of wristbands, chokers and post-holocaust style masks with distinctly Mad Max influences.

Address: 111, Taikang Road 泰康路111号
Contact: 020 8141-8245
Transportation: Taikang Road is served by the number 2 line at Haizhu Square as well as the number 6 line at Beijing Lu. Take Metro line 2 to Haizhu Square, exit B2, turn 180 degrees and cross the large interchange next to the statue. Walk straight for 150 meters and the Taikang Building is on the right. It is only a short walk from here to the Beijing Pedestrian Shopping Street.

Xijiao Jewellery Market 华南国际小商品城

Officially referred to as the South China International Commodities City, Xijiao Plaza opened in 2000 and is now the largest fashion accessories wholesale market in Guangzhou. It is divided into two interconnected 13 storey buildings: Building A and Building B. Xijiao jewellery market also covers many other kinds of fashion accessories, including hairpins, bracelets, scarves, hats and even mobile phone accessories.

The main products at the 1,800 stores that are located here are costume jewellery, including stainless steel, gold plated jewellery, glass beads, hair decoration, shell jewellery, jewellery packaging and much more. The selection is similar to Taikang jewellery market, with a focus on slightly higher quality at Xijiao.

Address: 2, Zhanqian Road 广州市站前路2号

Contact: 020 8107-1183

Transportation: Take Metro Line 2 or Line 5, get off at the Guangzhou Railway Station, take a taxi from there or walk along Zhan Qian Road to the end, you will find Xijiao wholesale jewellery market at the very end past all the Russian cargo shipping agents.

International Commodities Mall 广州站前国际小商品城

Just up the road from Xijiao Jewellery Market, this is a huge high rise building, but only the lower two floors are home to jewellery suppliers

Address: 19, Zhanqian Lu 广州市站前路19号

Contact: 020 8107-7183

Transportation: Take Metro Line 2 or Line 5, get off at the Guangzhou Railway Station, take a taxi from there or walk along Zhanqian Road to the end, you will find Xijiao wholesale jewellery market at the very end past all the Russian cargo shipping agents.

Xinghua Jewellery Market 兴华饰品城

The very last of the wholesale markets on Zhanqian Lu, opposite the junction of Liuhua Lu, across from the North East corner of Liuhua Park and the Xijiao Jewellery market. This area used to be the old West Railway Station but now most of it lies abandoned. As well as being the last wholesale outpost, this is also one of the newest and like most modern Chinese buildings is already starting to fall apart. The ground floor hosts a number of lacklustre costume jewellery stores, ranging from small individual stainless steel pieces to complete finished display sets. The second floor has more of the same, although at the moment only half a dozen of the showrooms are occupied.

Address: 1, Zhanqian Lu 广州市站前路1号

Contact: 020 8109-7876

Transportation: Take Metro Line 2 or Line 5, get off at the Guangzhou Railway Station, take a taxi from there or walk along Zhan Qian Road to the end, you will find Xijiao wholesale jewellery market at the very end past all the Russian cargo shipping agents.

Liwan Plaza Jewellery Market 荔湾广场

The twin towers of Liwan Plaza signify the centre of Liwan district and the Shangxiajiu shopping district. This was one the first skyscraper-type apartment complexes built in Guangzhou and soon gained notoriety due to its poor construction. The earliest bouts of property speculation took place here and for a long time it was infamous for suicides when residents who had over-paid for apartments finally realised their expensive follies. If you are looking for silver, coral, zirconia or semi precious stone then you should head for Liwan Plaza. The complex is divided into two towers, one in the north and one in the south. There is a circular open-air square between the North Tower and the South Tower. Also referred to as the China Crystal and Gems City (中国水晶宝石城), this has gradually become a national market since 2001, and is currently South-East Asia's largest crystal jewellery wholesale market with more than 3,000 individual operators. Some first time buyers claim that it is not so much a jewellery market but more of a city. But it cannot be a city because it is inside a mall, even though it takes up most of the mall. On seven floors, you will find all kinds of jewellery, stone, shells, corals, semi precious stone, silver, jade, zirconia, zircon, crystal, leather straps, plastic straps, fittings and packaging. Be careful here about taking photos here and take note that many stores have "No Photos" signs. The main shopping area ranges from underground floor to the fourth floor, where you can find a full range of 925 Silver Jewellery, crystals, etc. Usually for stores on underground, first and second floors, silver jewellery is sold by piece, not by gram. If you want to buy according to gram, it is better to go to the third and fourth floors, where many suppliers sell by gram, targeting overseas markets. The most confusing part of the centre is the basement directly under the plaza between the two buildings. The circular layout can be very disorientating for first time visitors.

If you are planning to buy pearls, you do need to know something about the subject, but there are good ones here to be found, for a fraction of the price jewellery stores charge in the USA. If you bargain hard, think in terms of paying about 10% of the retail price of what you would pay in the USA. There is a famous pearl market in Beijing but even this is dwarfed by Liwan Plaza. Many high quality freshwater pearls are coming out of the Shanghai vicinity. Freshwater pearls come from freshwater mussels, unlike salt-water or Akoya pearls which form in oysters in a salt-water environment. Liwan is fast becoming a one-stop-shop for even the pearl suppliers out of Zhejiang province who position themselves here for easy access to clasps, threads, corals, shells etc. Zhuji in Zhejiang is the biggest trade centre of FW pearls, not the biggest origins of FW pearls. The akoya pearl farms in China lie in Leizhou peninsula, Beihai in Guangxi and Sanya in Hainan. If you have done your research, it is still possible to sell pearls with a 300% mark-up - especially in the lower-end goods. A strand of 'ok' freshwater pearls in the 8mm range can still be garnered for about $10 per strand.
Address: Hualin New Street, Xiajiu Lu 下九路华林新街
Contact: 020 8132-5643

Metro: Take line 1 to Changshou Lu, exit A. Turn 180 degrees when you get out of the exit, then turn right on Changshou Xi Lu.Walk to the junction with Kangwang Zhong Lu. Liwan Plaza is located on the south east corner of this junction.

Liangang International Jewellery Centre 华林玉雕展览馆

The Guangdong Geology Department has its offices up on the fifth floor, while the Gem Association of Great Britain offers university courses on the fourth floor. There are also a few dealers up here but the majority supply packaging and display equipment rather than actual jewellery. On the third and second floor is a full selection of precious and semi-precious stones as well as wood carving and silver, with traders from countries such as Pakistan and Myanmar as well as China. The first floor is a similar selection of high end jewellery.

Address: Hualin New Street, Kanwang Zhong Lu 康王路华林新街

Contact: 020 8139-9988

Metro: Take line 1 to Changshou Lu, exit A. Turn 180 degrees when you get out of the exit, then turn right on Changshou Xi Lu. Walk to the junction with Kangwang Zhong Lu. Lianggang is located on the north east corner of this junction.

Hualin Market International 华林国际

Although this market is included in the jade section of this book, it offers much more for those willing to take the time to explore. The sixth floor is slowly being populated by jade dealers in a huge open plan area, while the fifth floor hosts a branch of the Agricultural Bank of China and the China National Gemstones Testing Centre. The fourth and third floors have enough specialist stores to equip even the largest Buddhist temple or monastery. Everything from enormous statues of exotic deities to Tibetan Thangkas and wall hangings can be found here.

Saffron robes, incense, agarwood and anything else a monk might need are on sale here. Look out for solar powered prayer wheels, which are very popular with Chinese car owners as dashboard decorations. The first two floors are filled with every kind of precious stone, from tiny pre-drilled beads to huge chunks of crystal that would give the Hope diamond a run for its money. Expect to see pearls, emeralds agate and white jade here. There are even Burmese pigeon blood rubies from across the border in Mogok and star sapphires from Chantaburi in Thailand.

Address: Hualin Jadeware Building, Kangwang Zhong Lu 康王路华林玉器大楼

Contact: 020 8139-6284

Metro: Take line 1 to Changshou Lu, exit A. Turn 180 degrees when you get out of the exit, then turn right on Changshou Xi Lu. The main Hualin Market is on the north west corner of the junction with Kangwang Zhong Lu.

Hualin Gold and Silver Market 华林金镶玉珠宝广场

A newly opened high-end jewellery market, located just to the north of Liangang Centre. A large concentration of gold and silver shops on the first and second floors but still filling up in the rest of the building.

Address: Hualin Jadeware Building, Kangwang Zhong Lu 康王路华林玉器大楼

Contact: 020 8139-8899

Metro: Take line 1 to Changshou Lu, exit A. Turn 180 degrees when you get out of the exit, then turn right on Changshou Xi Lu

Trendy Plaza Guangzhou 骏田批发广场

This is not solely a jewellery market, but there is plenty of fashion type jewellery included in the mix here. Do not expect to find lots of high quality 925 silver jewellery here. Instead this is going to be budget-priced copper jewellery, very lightly gold plated jewellery and plastic stuff. Consult the entry for Trendy Plaza in the Beauty Products section for full layout details.

Address: Beijing Nan Lu 北京南路

Contact: 020 8564-4724

By Metro: Line 6, get off at Beijing Road

Guangzhou Wanfu Exquisite Commodity Place 广州万福精品广场

Up on the third and second floors, there is a good selection of budget fashion jewellery, mainly for the domestic market, mixed in with lots of other products. These include cosmetics, accessories, and even packaging and display products. The first floor is almost exclusively hat wholesalers.

Address: 70, Wanfu Lu 万福路70号

Contact: 020 8658-3150

Transportation: Wanfu Exquisite Commodities Plaza is served by the number 6 line being located almost directly between Beijing Lu and Tuanyida Square 团一大广场站. Take Metro line 6 to Tuanyida Square, exit A, turn 180 degrees and walk back up the Yuexiu Nan Lu past the First National Congress Chinese Communist Youth League Memorial Hall (团一大纪念广场). Wanfu Lu is the first on the left and Wanfu Exquisite Commodities Plaza is about 50 metres along on the left. From Beijing Lu Subway Station take Exit A, turn right on to Wanfu Lu and walk about half a km until Wanfu Exquisite Commodities Plaza is on the right.

Asia Pacific Boutique Trading Centre 广州亚太精品交易中心

Situated directly opposite the 1916 Christian Savior Church on Wanfu Lu, this looks promising but only has a half a dozen open stores on the ground floor and an escalator that leads to a completely deserted second floor. It is best to keep moving East along Wanfu Lu until you reach the busier markets.

Address: 60, Wanfu Lu 万福路60号

Contact: 020 8657-7688

By Metro:Line 6, get off at Tuanyida Square Station 团一大广场站

Yue He Market 越和仰忠批发商城

A converted wet market in a very basic single story building. Expect lots of stores selling products aimed at young ladies. These include hair accessories, low end fashion jewellery, scarves etc. There are even a couple of specialist wig stores here. Small cosmetics and jewellery stores spread out into the nearby streets.

Rather than walking all the way from Beijing Lu, it is slightly easier to catch the metro to Tuanyida Square on line 6. Take exit A which will bring you out opposite the China Telecom Building. From here head west along Dong Yuan Heng Lu past the bus station until you reach the Police Station. Turn right here and it will bring you out directly between Yue He Market and Wanfu Market.

Address: At the junction of Dezheng Lu and Wanfu Lu 德政路和万福路交汇处

Contact: 020 8745-632

By Metro: Line 6, get off at Tuanyida Square Station 团一大广场站

Transportation: Take Metro line 6 to Tuanyida Square, exit A, turn right onto Dong Heng Lu opposite China Telecom. Walk past the public bus station to the police station and turn right. Yue He is on the left at the top of the road.

Nanyu International Home Building Material City 南域建材装饰城

While 80% of the building materials shops on the

ground floor are closed upstairs the entire building is devoted to the Xuping Jewellery Company, where there facility is so large that a golf cart is made available for buyers to get from one end of the shelving based warehouse to the other.

Address: Tanwei Nan Lu 坦尾南路
Contact: 020 8198-8188
Directions: From exit A of the Tanwei subway station head directly under the highway flyover and out onto Tanwei Nan Lu.

A Visit to Yakushi Pearl Factory

The Yakushi Pearl Factory is a privately owned, Japanese company with a Guangzhou branch has been operating since 1987. The factory sources its select freshwater pearls from farms along the Yangtze River in Jiangsu and Zhejiang. Yakushi is perhaps most famous and proud to supply its jewellery to the Tiffany's and Cartier brands.

During these regular factory tours, the President Mr. Yakushi, assisted by Mr. Li, fluent in both Japanese and English explains the entire life cycle of the company farmed pearls. At the end of this fascinating tour, Yakushi offers their visitors to purchase any of their strung and set pearls for a discounted warehouse price. Earrings, rings, and necklaces are on display, ranging anywhere from 1,000 RMB upwards of 15,000 RMB and even higher, are all at 50% off the tag prices.

Tours can be scheduled for small to medium-sized groups by contacting Yakushi company representatives. A maximum of twenty people are allowed on the group tour, but frankly, the fewer the better for each person on the group. A tour shuttle is provided by the company, which will pick your group up at a designated location anywhere in Guangzhou and take you to the factory. After the factory visit, the company treats its visitors to a Cantonese lunch at a nearby restaurant. There are no additional costs to schedule a tour.

To organise a tour, contact Simon Li from Yakushi Factory at stemalee@hotmail.com. The factory is located in the Taiping Industrial Zone, Xintang, Zengcheng, in Eastern Guangzhou at the border of GZ and Dongguan.

Huadu International Jewellery Market 花都国际珠宝城

Further out of town, Huadu District has become an important industrial base of jewellery. At first this area was noted for its automobile leather production base, another young sunrise industry but the rapid rise of the gold and silver jewellery industry has now eclipsed this sector. Huadu Jewellery City industrial park now exceeds more than 5,000 acres, housing more than 40 production companies, mainly in the export of gold and silver jewellery inlaid with precious stones and semi-production processing.

Address: 168, Xindu Dadao, Huadu District 花都区 新都大道168号

Contact: 020 3686-2888/3687-5123

17 LEATHER GOODS

The City Centre

Haopan Shoe Leather and Metals Market
濠畔皮革五金鞋材市场

Centred around Haopan Road and Xiaoxin Road (actually old style alleys rather than main thoroughfares), in between the main roads of Dade Lu and Huifu Lu, is what remains of the original city-centre leather wholesale market. Sellers here focus mainly on shoe leather and cobbling equipment. Here it is possible to buy everything you need to set up a shoe repair shop or even a shoe cleaning store, examples of which are appearing all over the country as the wealth gap continues to increase. Shops here sell everything from rivets, fasteners and glue to lasts, zippers and punches. Moving west, the focus is more and more upon fasteners until buyers reach the dedicated fastener centre known as Wan Hao Accessories Centre (广州市万濠五金皮料) on the corner of Haizhu Nan Lu.

San Yuan Li District 三元里

Much of the leather and associated components used for handbags and luggage have long since moved away from the city centre and up to the San Yuan Li District, directly to the north of the city, which is right on the the border of of the Yuexiu and Baiyun districts. This   has always been a turbulent area and there is even a large propaganda site, allegedly in remembrance of the Anti-British struggle. When I first arrived in Guangzhou in the early nineties, I asked some missionaries that were working at the the local Foreign Language University to show me this memorial, thinking that it might be quite poignant to a Brit like myself. As it turned out we were unable to find the site itself and became lost in a never-ending labyrinth of cheap brothels posing as beauty salons. At the time I was flabbergasted that such an enormous red light district, much bigger than say, Miari in Seoul or Nana in Bangkok could even exist in a communist country. I was soon to learn that China is all about appearances rather than truth. When we finally escaped this enormous den of iniquity, we were pounced on by Cantonese gangster-types wanting to peddle us all kinds of illicit pharmaceuticals. It turns out that at one time, this area was home to a large population of Muslim Uighurs, whose religion forbade alcohol, and so many of the older generation partook in a little medicinal/recreational herb instead. Once word of this got out, the local mafia moved in and started peddling all kinds of nasty stuff from ketamine to heroin.

In more recent years all the brothels and the their working girls have been relocated to Panyu and the Uighur population was decimated when the troubles in Urumqi spilled over into the rest of China, and Han populations extracted revenge attacks on the innocent local residents. The number of Uighur residents has since dwindled to a fraction of what it once was. What was once mainly Uighur homes and restaurants was quickly demolished to make way for just a handful of enormous leather wholesale markets. This is an area with lots of character and history. Some of that can be glimpsed in the documentary Disorder, but it is best experienced up close and personal.

Much of the leather district is clustered around the Guihuagang (桂花岗) area. This is the area that lies between the railway station and the Traditional Chinese Medicine University. In the five years following 1992, more than five thousand leather wholesaling companies located their stores in Guihuagang, and it has brought along fast development of neighbouring markets. Many of the markets are located on San Yuan Li Avenue, but there are lots more lesser known markets on Ziyuangang (梓元岗) which runs parallel to the railway line from Guihuagang to Guangyuan Xi Lu

Beginning at the Guihuagang (桂花岗) area of Jiefang Road, heading North West the northern side of San Yuan Li Avenue begins at the very corner with a brand new market that is built into the San Yuan Li Hotel, called the Wang Jiao Foreign Trade Leather Purchasing Centre (望角皮具商贸城). At the time of writing this is still unopened, with red cloth covering the Wang Jiao characters at the main entrance.

A few hundred metres to the east, just past the main entrance to San Yuan Li Village, is the four story Hongsheng Nations Leather Wholesale Market (广州市鸿昇国际皮料五金城). This is a strange building indeed with escalators jutting out at seemingly random points and a very tacky knight on horseback, fashioned in cheap gold plastic at the main entrance. Clearly the architect for this building was suffering from an incredibly bad hangover, as the layout is all over the place.

The ground floor here is devoted to tanned leather of every colour and design possible. Or at least that used to be the case. At one time large rolls of Louis Vuitton, Chanel and Gucci designs were clearly on display, and although these are not put on display any more, they are still available to regular customers from store rooms hidden away at the back of the site. At one time I used to buy a few metres of the classic LV leather now and again to make one off's for friends with pets, such as luxurious dog carriers or classy cat leashes. This was my one-stop shopping location where I could pick up designer leather that was almost indistinguishable from the original, with all the matching straps, clips and buckles to make a very authentic looking product. These days I restrict myself to an occasional few bookmarks.

Even though the LV patterns may not be as desirable as they were, there is now a much greater variety of colours and patterns available. Along with the most garish of colours, it is also possible to find emu, stingray, alligator and even anaconda, although I personally am still not sure how to verify whether these are genuine or not. What is real is the overpowering odour. On the day that I was conducting my research, I had the remnants of Guangzhou Urban Flu and the smell of all those hides was making me feel very nauseous as I walked around the first floor particularly. The second floor is more accessory parts such as buckles and fasteners, while the third floor is devoted to finished items, mainly belts in this case.

Beyond Hongsheng (鸿昇皮料五金城) is the even larger Gainhall International Leather Ware and Metals City (佳豪国际皮料五金城), and it practically is the size of a small city. Apart from tanned leather, you will find all kinds of belt buckles and bag accessories here. These include purse locks, chains, pin fasteners, snap hook, chains and even cases and boxes. If you are looking for any kind of part for making bags and luggage, this is the first place to begin your search. There are also a few smaller markets here selling a similar range of components. These include the Shenghao Leather and Metals Material City (盛豪皮革五金材料城).

Shichang   Leather   Global   Exchange   Square

时畅皮料全球采购中心

Just beyond the San Yuan Li subway entrance is the much newer Shichang Leather Global Exchange Square (previously called the Baizhuang Leather Exposition Centre 百壮国际皮具汇展). Built on a large paved square directly between the Gainhall and the now defunct Mingsheng Market (明圣商贸城), this is for finished items rather than individual parts. The first floor contains around a hundred shops, all selling different varieties of handbags. There are a few shops up on the second floor but for the time being most of the units remain vacant. One interesting store just outside Baizhuang concentrates solely on golf bags and related equipment. This is China, so expect to see some of the loudest and gaudiest golf bags on the planet. With bright Hello Kitty pinks and faux gold lame, you will probably need an automated-cart as even the most desperate third-world caddy would not be seen dead carrying one of these monstrosities.

Address: San Yuan Li Avenue 三元里大道

Mensa Leather Hardware No.1 Centre 名商天地皮料五金龙头市

Next to Tangqi Clothes Market is the vast new Mensa Leather Centre, although the relation to the high IQ society is distinctly unclear. There is a large Bank of China branch on the corner of the first floor. The fourteenth floor is given over to property management, while the thirteenth through seventh floors are offices for tenants. The sixth and fifth floors are mainly for related accessories, such as clasps and buckles. The fifth floor is still very sparsely populated. The fourth and third floor are for stores specialising in all kinds of artificial leather but both floors are still half empty at the time of writing. The first two floors are for real leather, mostly in its rawhide form. Crocodile hides in a full range of rainbow colours seem to be especially popular here at the moment.

Address: Directly above San Yuan Li Subway Station, Guangyuan Xi Lu 袋料鞋材皮革五金配件批发广场

Xin Hao Pan 新濠畔

Directly to the left of the Mensa Leather Centre is the original Xin Hao Pan Leather Wholesale Market. While the Mensa Market has a modern high tech feel, Xin Hao Pan is much more low end with corrugated tin roofs and dark interiors. Inside is a cluster of leather hide wholesalers but to be honest, the selection around the rear of the shoes district is far superior to anything found here. I would not be surprised if this market is bulldozed and redeveloped by the time that you read this. The Xin Hao Pan Yaotai Guangchang (新濠畔瑶台广场) market next door is clearly also on its last legs.

Address: Guangyuan Xi Lu 广园西路 袋料鞋材皮革五金配件批发广场

Take Metro subway Line 2 to Sanyuanli Station.Look for Shichang Leather Global Exchange Square and Mensa Leather Hardware No.1 Centre and walk straight past to see Xin Hao Pan.

Guihuagang 桂花岗

Guangzhou Baiyun World Leather Trading Centre 白云世界皮具贸易中心

Back at Guihuagang, Baiyun World is ground zero for the fake handbag industry and the ideal place to locate the latest information on the big designer brands. Handbags, wallets and all kinds of accessories. Also known as Baiyun Leather City, this is a very interesting shopping complex. Quite elegant, tiny, glass front shops. Only a few floors, but lots of shops. There is a large central escalator to help you to keep your bearings. There is also a restaurant which sells reasonable Chinese food. This is the most popular starting point hunters of replica handbags, replica belts and fashion accessories. Each shop has their handbags and accessories displayed. These items are only from the current collections. If you are looking for specific brands, make sure you know what you are looking for as each handbag is displayed without labels. Some shop assistants speak market English and know their brands. Remember again that they are wholesalers and are unlikely to bargain on smaller quantities.

Expect fake and replica everything here: briefcases, sunglasses, scarves, cuff-links, handkerchiefs, T-shirts, fashion, hair clip, lighters, pens, slippers, and shoes. So many labels are available here but LV, Gucci, Chanel, Burberry, Chloe, Christian Dior, Balenciaga, YSL, Hermes, Marc Jacobs, Hugo Boss, Fendi, Valentino, Playboy, Dunlop, Tucano, ST. Dupont, Polo, Kangaroo, Windsor, Prada, Miu Miu, D&G, Bottega, Veneta, Thomas Wylde, Jimmy Choo, Kooba, Versace, Barbara Bui, Celine, Guess, Juicy, Luella etc. are some of the more popular purchases. Expect to see unusual items with the designer logos applied to products that are never found on the Western markets such as LV waste paper bins or Burberry basketballs. Be warned that with so many fake products, the stench of synthetic plastics can be overpowering for some visitors.

The market is situated on the corner of Jiefang Bei Lu and Guihua Lu. Directly behind the market building on Guihua Lu, dozens of specialist packaging shops have sprung up. Every inch of floor and shelf space is packed with designer carrier bags and boxes. I am not talking about plastic supermarket bags that are good for little more than bin liners, but the nicely designed paper and card carriers that come from Louis Vuitton, Gucci and Prada. On my last visit there were about thirty different brands on display, in a wide range of different sizes. Every few minutes, a local will drop in and ask about the availability of shoe boxes or watch cases. After all there is no point in buying a nice pair of Louboutin high heels or the latest Jimmy Choos if they do not come in a suitably emblazoned box. These stores are now beginning to stretch all the way down Jiefang Bei Lu, interspersed with even more handbag shops.

Address: 1356 - 1358, Jie Fang Bei Road 解放北路1356-1358号

Transportation: Metro Line 2, Yuexiu Park Station. Walk north past the Huanshi Road intersection, under the train line underpass and onto the large pedestrian overpass.

Zhong'ao Leather Products Trade City 中澳皮具城

Built and opened in 1995, this is another one of the many markets here that focus on men's and women's bags, luggage, suitcases, wallets, leather belts and leather goods.

Address: 1107-1111, Jiefang North Road 解放北路1107-1111号

Contact: 020 8669-2052

How to get there: Metro Line 2, Yuexiu Park Station. Walk north past the Huanshi Road intersection, under the train line underpass and onto the large pedestrian overpass.

Jiahao International Leather Wholesale Market 佳豪国际皮具皮革城

Yet another market offering all kinds of leather bags, luggage, shoes, etc.

Address: 228, Sanyuanli Da Dao 三元里大道228

Zhonggang Leather Goods Wholesale Market 广州中港皮具商贸城

One of the newer but less crowded leather wholesale markets. A wide selection of wallets, handbags and purses, located on three separate floors. Many dealers here specialise in genuine leather and high end replicas of designer labels. At the time of writing, the basement was still not open for business.

Address: 11-21, Sanyuanli Da Dao 三元里 大道11-21

Directly behind Zhonggang on Xiangyuan Road is the annexe building of Zhonggang Xiang Tian Leather City 中港 祥天皮具城, which is devoted more to parts than to finished items.

Continuing along Xiangyuan Road, the stores become dominated by packaging vendors, selling cardboard boxes of all sizes, tape, bubble-wrap and even postal sacks. The road continues to a large new apartment complex but it is better to take a sharp left onto Xiangping Jie (祥平街), where you will see more cardboard vendors and another sharp left will take you to the back entrance of Jinye Leatherware Plaza.

Jinye Leatherware Plaza 金亿皮具广场

A good selection of cheaper items destined mainly for the domestic market. Lots of Chinese style manbags, school-bags and briefcases.

Dong Er Lou Leather Plaza 东二楼皮具

Facing directly opposite Jinye Leatherware Plaza this market is mainly low-end school-bags, backpack, rucksacks and satchels

Luan Ren Leather City 暖润皮具城

Back out on the main Jichang Lu, this market is on the other side of the tunnel that goes under the railway tracks, on the stretch of road near the Huan Shi Road roundabout. Two floors of handbags, satchels, wallets and purses. In my own personal experience, the vendors here are will to work that little bit harder, perhaps because they are just that little further away from the main markets such as Baiyun and Yisen
Address: Jichang Lu 机场路

Ziyuangang 梓元岗

Yisen Wholesale Leather Market 亿森皮具城

This is actually one of the smaller buildings with about three hundred vendors operating on three rather cramped floors. As with all the other buildings, touts loiter around the entrance offering in very limited and broken English copy watches and copy handbags. Despite regular crackdowns (that are usually announced well in advance) copies of all the very latest brands and styles are always available, even if they are no longer on open display. Yisen is mainly ladies handbags but expect to see lots of shoulder bags, travel cases, and wallets thrown into the mix. Up on the third floor is an exit that leads directly out on the the Jiefang Road central footbridge, saving you the trip back all the escalators to the front door.

Address: 1389, Jiefang Bei Lu 广州市解放北路1389号

Yisen is located at the very beginning of Ziyuangang, but market complexes stretch all the way up the Guangyuan Dong Lu. Those closest to the main road have the highest quality and the prices to match. As you travel west along this road, the products drop in quality and price accordingly. These markets include the following:

Yifa Wholesale Market 亿发皮具城

Shenjia Leather Trading Centre 圣嘉皮具商贸

Guihua Lou Leatherware Mall 桂花楼皮具城

Guangzhou Jin Yi Leather Wholesale Market 金亿皮具广场

Xin Dong Hao Leather City 新东豪商贸城

Huihao Wholesale Market 汇豪皮具城

Xin Hui Hao Leather Trade City 新汇豪皮具商贸城

Park Lane Leather City 栢丽皮具城

Qian Se Leather Plaza 广大外贸鞋业商贸城

Tian Hong Leather Mall 天泓皮具城

Xiang Mao Leather Mall 祥茂皮具城

Anxing Wholesale Market 安兴皮具城

Mingzhu Leather Centre 广州名驹皮具商务中心
Jiang Xiang Leather Market 金祥市场
Sen Mao Leather Centre 森茂皮具城
San Yi Leather Centre 三亿皮具城

Guangyuan Lu Leather Materials Markets

At the rear of the main shoe wholesaling district on Guangyuan Lu are located vast numbers of leather wholesalers all clustered into about a dozen large buildings. The westernmost stretch of Zhanxi Lu is filled with shoe material markets all the way down to the pedestrian railway crossing. Xin Hao Pan is the largest and busiest, while the others become older and quieter doing down the hill.

Xin Hao Pan Shoes Market Guangzhou 新濠畔鞋材批发市场

Built in 1998, this is the oldest shoe leather market in Guangzhou. It has five buildings, and more than 1300 factory outlets. Uppers, linings, soles, heels, accessories and lasts can all be found here on two massive floors directly behind Xingqi Lu. The upper floor is devoted mainly to raw leather wholesalers, each shop having an amazing selection of swatches with just about every colour and texture that a layperson like myself could imagine. The first floor has more material as well as related working equipment, especially for cobblers and shoe makers. This is the place to find lasts, soles, laces and just about everything else related to shoe manufacturing. The market extends out past the rear courtyard where a second section contains more of the same products. Xin Haopan section A is at the very rear. Although the second floor is half empty, the ground floor is filled to the brim with leather wholesalers. I personally find the advertising here to be hilarious. Lots of pictures of contented grazing animals, all clumsily photo-shopped into Himalayan pasture scenes.

Address: Nan Feng Building, 37, Zhan Xi Lu 广州站西路
37 号南方分场

Jin Ma Leather City 金马鞋材城

Yet another shoe leather market, this time directly behind Xin Hao Pan and decorated with the same corporate colours. A vast selecting of leather and shoe making equipment inside.

Address: 40, Zhan Xi Lu 广州站西路40号

Hong Yun Leather Market 宏运皮革市场

With its massive red entrance and escalators leading up to hundreds of leather stores, it is difficult to tell whether this is yet another extension of Xin Hao Pan which is next door or Da Feng Liao Jing which seems to be an extension of the first floor. Whatever the ownership situation, this market is well stocked, busy and well worth a visit.

Address: 44, Zhan Xi Lu 广州站西路44号

Da Feng Liao Jing 大洋皮料城

The rear entrance is adjacent to the Yuan Wang Leather and Shoes Materials City while the front entrance is on Zhanxi Lu next door to Xin Hao Pan. The first floor is filled with all kinds of shoe leathers, both genuine and synthetic, in almost every colour from casual brogue brown all the way up to Sigue Sigue Sputnik shocking pink. The second floor is almost half empty.

Address: 33, Zhan Xi Lu 广州站西路33号

Yuan Wang Leather and Shoes Materials City 源旺皮料鞋材城

Located next door to the rear Xin Hao Pan building, this market is quite confusing in that it connects directly to the second floor of Xin Hao Pan but is described as a separate entity. Very similar products to Xin Hao Pan with a wide range of shoe manufacturing materials and accessories. The second floor is currently about thirty percent empty.

Address: 22, Zhan Xi Lu 广州站西路22号

Talent Shoes Trading Centre 无伦鞋业交易中心

A new entrant to this area, it is certainly the nicest of the markets in terms of environment and decoration but as yet is not even close to being filled with dealers and manufacturers. The third floor is currently home to large numbers of shop outfitters and store designers. The second floor is about fifty percent full of leather dealers and some accessories, as is the first floor. The basement is still only about twenty percent full.

Address: 18, Zhanxi Road 广州市站西路18号

Yue Fu Footwear Materials Plaza 和富鞋材广场

One of the oldest buildings in the area. Situated on the north side of Zhanxi Road, there are only a handful of dealers here on the first and second floor.

Address: 12, Zhanxi Road 广州市站西路12号

Shang Feng Hardware and Leather Trade Plaza 广州尚峰五金皮料交易城

Up towards Guangyuan West Road, this is one of the newest buildings in the area, but perhaps the furthest from Guihuagang proper. Two floors of shoe leather and shoe accessories.

Address: 1, Zouma Gang, San Yuan Li 广州市越秀区三元里走马岗1号

Beyond Guangzhou

Shiling International Leather City 狮岭国际皮具城

Shiling lies just 20 km north of downtown Guangzhou in Huadu district. With more than 2,100 shops it is quickly becoming a centre for leather goods and leather materials for all of China. Today, Guangdong's leather trade makes up half of the national total. Leather goods from Shiling play a leading role in the Guangzhou market, which in turn accounts for 60% of the Guangdong market. Annual output tops 230 million leather products. More than 4,000 enterprises produce and trade leather goods, as well as wholesale raw and ancillary materials, employing an estimated 65,000 workers. For finished goods, accessories and raw materials. this is a cheaper market than places like Guihuagang or Zhanxi Road and well worth a visit if you are purchasing very large quantities Address: 71-74, He He Road, Shiling Town, Hua Du District 花都区狮岭镇岭南工业区合和路71-74号

Directions: Take subway line 3 to get off at Renhe. Then transfer to bus number 701a to Huadu Shiling Leather Market.

A taxi from the city centre to Shiling will cost you about 150RMB. You can also get a shuttle bus from the Baiyun Leather market to Shiling every 20 minutes between 6:30am and 7:00pm.

18 LIGHTING

Taigu Lighting And Decoration City 泰古灯饰城

Located on the the lower floors of what Google Maps describes as the Holdround Building (合润国际中心), just a couple of blocks north of the Haizhu Square subway station. This large round building is located at the junction on Danan Lu and Qiyi Lu and contains more than a hundred shops selling all kinds of light fittings and fixtures, from small bedside lamp stands to the most monstrously vulgar seven-tier chandeliers, big enough to give Del Boy and Rodney nightmares for the rest of their natural lives. A number of shops here focus on oriental style lighting that I find particularly attractive. Lighting shops continue west along Danan Lu, all the way up to the Beijing Road intersection. These include many stores specialising in LED fixtures and light boxes for retail outlets.

Address: Danan Lu 大南路

Jiaming Lighting Market 佳明灯饰城

What was once the largest lighting market in Guangzhou, is now just a small selection of vendors in the

middle of Danan Road.
Address: Danan Lu 大南路

Guangzhou Nantian International Lighting Centre
广州南天国际照明中心

With more than 30,000 square metres of floor space, this is one of China's largest lighting wholesale markets. Indoor lights, outdoor, classical, modern, high-tech or old fashioned, just about every style imaginable can be found here.

Address: Nantian International Business Centre, No 7, Huacheng   Avenue
广州市越秀区花城大道7号南天国际商务中心

Contact: 020 2222-3390 2222-3399

Directions: Just south of the crossroads of Huangpu Dadao Blvd. and Guangzhou Dadao Blvd. 广州大道南

Deco - Wuzhou (Five Continents) Decoration Materials Shopping Centre 五洲装饰世界

Although this is a home decoration market that covers almost all aspects of the various building trades, there are a good number of lighting specialists located here too. Bear in mind that this is the expensive end of the market, with large numbers of designer styles and Sino-baroque styles that are popular with the Chinese nouveau riche.

Address: Yingbin   Road,   Panyu   District
广州市番禺区迎宾路

Contact: 020 8450-8877

Anhua Lighting City 安华装饰材料城

First opened back in 1998 and sometimes spelled as Anwar, this is one of the city's older lighting markets but still worth a visit. This complex includes Anhua Lightwares Mall and Anhua Deco Mall in the east and Baifuwei Deco Market in the west.

Address: 488, East Huangshi Road
广州市新市黄石东路488号
Contact: 020 3631-2299

Christmas Lighting

At certain times of the year the pavements around One Link plaza are filled with Christmas trees all lit up like a Vegas casino. Directly across from One Link on Yide Lu are about a dozen stores that specialise in all kinds of rope lighting, fairy lights, party lights and outdoor lighting. These stores continue south around the corner onto Jiefang Nan Lu.

Address: Yide Lu 一德路

Beyond Guangzhou

Guzhen Lighting City, Zhongshan 古镇镇, 中山

Also known as the Lighting Era Centre (时代灯饰广场), Guzhen has recently earned the title of "China's LED Capital" and has played host to the China International Lighting Fair since 1999. There are over 5,000 lighting suppliers in Guzhen and even the main street is locally known as Lamp Street. Most of the stores are showrooms for factories in town or nearby Henglan. Together they supply more that 60% of the domestic market and include a vast array of lighting fittings. According to Wikipedia, the production of lighting fittings is the primary industry in Guzhen, accounting for nearly 88% of the town's industrial output.

A number of markets currently exist including the following:

Chuangzhan LED Wholesale Market
Dongfang LED Wholesale Market
Shihao LED Wholesale Market
Yongwei LED Wholesale Market

Address: 12, Dongxin Middle Road, Guzhen, Zhongshan中山市古镇镇东兴中路12号

Contact: 760 2238-6220

Transportation from Guangzhou:

By train. Take train to Guzhen, Zhongshan from Guangzhou South Railway Station. Ticket: about 40 RMB, 1 hour. Guzhen is about 20 km north west of Zhongshan City proper.

By bus: Buses leave for Guzhen, Zhongshan at Guangzhou City Coach Station, Provincial Coach Station or Liuhua Coach Station.

Taxis will run between 200 and 300 RMB to Guzhen from Guangzhou. There are also direct ferries to Zhongshan from Hong Kong International Airport.

Web: http://www.sddsgc.com/index.asp

19 MEDICAL PRODUCTS

The old part of the city around Huangsha is well known for Traditional Chinese Medicine markets and hospitals but is is also a large wholesale area for modern medical equipment.

Directly behind Mopark Plaza which is situated directly on top of Huangsha Subway Station are three or four blocks of some of the oldest buildings in the city. Concentrated on Conggui Lu and Datang Lu are large numbers of hospital equipment suppliers. Directly behind the rear entrance to Metropolitan Plaza 西城都荟 (8 Huangsha Avenue 荔湾区黄沙大道8号) is the Qihua Medical Equipment Showroom on Heping Xi Lu, which features a huge range of scalpels, clamps and related surgical operating tools. Nearby stores focus instead on products geared toward China's rapidly ageing population. Apart from walking sticks and wheelchairs, this is a good place to find the very latest in health related gadgets from big brand manufacturers such as Panasonic and Omron. Here you can find everything from mobile nebulisors to ultrasound scanners. This is the ideal location for anybody looking to open their own clinic or care home, as many

Chinese are now doing in other South East Asian countriesAddress: Congui Lu 从桂路 Enning Lu 恩宁路 Huangsha Da Dao 黄沙大道
Directions:Exit D from Huangsha subway station onto Heping Xi Lu
和平西路一带医疗器械公司（黄沙）广州市中医院附近（药材市场附近）

Further out of town are two more major areas focusing on medical equipment.

GZ International Medical Devices Exchange Centre广州国览医疗器械城
Also known as Guolan Medical Equipments City, slightly further out of town near the Huadiwan markets.
Address: 650, Huadiwan Road, Fangcun
芳村花地湾，花湾路 650号
Metro: Huadiwan Exit A, line 1

Luoxi Qiao Xia Yidai Medical Equipment
洛溪桥下一带医疗器械公司
Address: Ji Xiang Bei Dao, Luoxi New City
广州市番禺区大石镇洛溪新城吉祥北道

20 MOTORBIKE PARTS AND ACCESSORIES

Three of the largest motorcycle parts markets are located within easy walking distance of each other at the Songnan Lu intersection of Zengcha Lu, close by to the Luochongwei bus station. This area is only a few bus stops away from line five of the Guangzhou metro. The area is well served by public buses with many lines, including numbers 3 and 19 connecting with the subway stations and Xichang and Xicun. Alternatively a taxi from either station will only cost about 10 RMB.

Be aware that what we westerners consider motorbikes and motorbike parts might be considerably different to what Chinese think. Motorcycle culture has developed very differently here than in other parts of the world and brands that we grew up with such as Harley or Triumph barely even exist here. Even the ubiquitous Japanese brands like Yamaha, Suzuki and Kawasaki play a most definite second fiddle to locally produced knock-off brands. Few people even realise that China's motorcycle production surpassed that of Japan as far back as 1993, and there at least a hundred companies that simply copy their Japanese counterparts. Exports are increasing rapidly, although fifty percent of all bikes shipped out of the country go to neighbouring Vietnam and another twenty percent to Indonesia.

More than two hundred first and second tier cities have stopped issuing licences for new petrol motorbikes, with Xiamen for example issuing restrictions as far back as 1987.A long with increased affluence has come increased traffic, construction and pollution. This is obviously having an impact on domestic sales. Allegedly this has been for environmental reasons, although stories of chopper gangs persist in Guangzhou and Shenzhen particularly. Guangzhou has banned motorcycles and motorized bicycles in many parts of the city mainly as an anti-crime measure. The motorcycle thieves in Guangzhou are particularly brazen. In October 2005, a woman who tried to stop motorcycle thieves from stealing her purse had her hand chopped off. Thieves apparently worked for a gang that called itself the Hand Choppers. These and other crimes prompted the city to ban motorcycles from the downtown area of Guangzhou. Pickpocketing evolved into an appalling situation where two-man teams would use motorbikes for bag snatching, sometimes the pillion passenger accomplice using a machete to ensure that the handbag or briefcase came away easily.

Much of China's motorcycle industry is focussed more on Chongqing than in Guangzhou, but that does not mean that there is not a thriving parts market here.

For an interesting background read on the motorcycle market in China, I would highly recommend http://www.chinamotorcyclenews.com/ and the personal website of acclaimed motorcycle journalist, David McMullan: http://www.englishmaninchina.org/china-motorcycle-news

The following markets are clustered around the Luo Chong Wei Coach Station (罗冲围客运站), which is situated at the Songnan Junction (Songnan Lukou Zhan 松南路口站) on Zengcha Lu.

Guangzhou Baiyun Motorcycle Parts Market 广州白云摩

Baiyun Motorcycle Accessories Market is the largest of the parts markets in Luochongwei and contains almost seven hundred outlets, offering all kinds of motorcycle accessories and spare parts. In addition, many shops also offer other products that range from generators to chainsaws, clear evidence of how many manufacturers are having to diversify into different areas in order to stay in business. Motorbikes above 125cc are relatively uncommon in China so do not expect to find parts for Ninjas, Fatboys or Bonnevilles here. Far more common are those silent but deadly electric scooters that creep up behind us on the side-walk and then scare the living daylights out of us.

Luo Chong Wei, Zengcha Lu, Baiyun District
广州市增槎路罗冲围白云摩配市场

Luckystar Motorcycle Accessories Mart 福星摩配城

Sometimes referred to as Guangzhou Songnan Motorcycle Parts Market, located next door to the two huge gas tanks that serve as a major landmark in this part of town. Expect to find another hundred outlets here specialising in everything from clutch assemblies and mufflers to crank shafts and cam cases.

Address: Zengcha Dong Lu, Luochongwei
增槎路松南摩配市场

Zhonghua Motorcycle Parts and Foreign Trade Centre 中铧摩配外贸城

Located on the opposite side of Zengcha Road from the Luckystar and Baiyun markets, this smaller collection is much more suited to overseas buyers. Dealers here stock helmets and leathers with designs and brands far more recognisable to western customers. Expect lots of brightly anodised parts good for all kinds of off-roaders, street machines and pocket rockets.

A number of smaller markets fill in the gaps here. These include the Zhonghua Motorcycle Trade Exhibition (中铧摩配外贸展示), the Fuxing Motorcycle City (福星摩配城) and the Fuxing Wuo Pei Market (福星摩配市场).

New Great Wall Motorcycle Accessories Trading City

新长城摩托车配件交易城

Over on the other side of the city, out past Tian Ping Jia is an alternative motorcycle accessories market that is comparable in size and scope to the Luchongwei cluster of markets.

Address: 28, Yinli Street, Shatai Road, Yuexiu District

广州市越秀区沙太路银利街28号

Contact: 020 8750-3455

21 ONELINK

Onelink International Toy and Gifts Centre 万菱广场

Known as 'Wang Ling Guang Chang' in Chinese, Onelink International Plaza is situated on the corner of Yide Road and Jiefang South Rd. The forty-one storey building stands out as one of the tallest buildings on the northern bank of the river and with layered chocolate cake style appearance. What was once home to the Parkson department store was transformed in 2004 into the landmark wholesale shopping centre of Yide Lu with 40,000 square meters of factory, manufacturer and wholesale outlets. The first nine floors carry a huge variety of shops while the rest of the building is filled with offices and private showrooms. Many of the smaller shops spill over into nearby buildings where they keep larger storage spaces for extra stock. The centre attracts customers from all walks of life, from local day trippers to international purchasing managers, and it is quite easy to buy small amounts as well as container quantities.

The basement is well stocked with cuddly toys and children's gift items. The first three floors have a little bit of everything including jewellery, clothes and accessories and toys while beyond the fourth floor the focus moves towards furnishings and artsy home decorations.

The 4th underground to the 2nd underground: parking lots

The 1st underground to the 6th floor: toys and gifts wholesale markets with a market area of 40,000 square meters

The 7th and the 8th floors: dining areas

The 9th floor: business lounge

The 10th floor: gifts, toys and home deco exhibition centre

The 11th floor to the 17th floor: gifts, toys, home deco, etc, show rooms and offices

The 18th to the 24th floor: showrooms and offices

The 26th to the 37th floor: offices

There are no annoying touts nor high pressure sales tactics. If anything, it is just the opposite and some of the shop keepers are so laid back that you might wonder if they are even awake. Do not worry about being hassled by pushy salesmen. In general, goods that are available in Onelink are about a quarter of the price that you would have to pay in Hong Kong and about half of what is asked in Shenzhen. Even so, this is one of the most well-known markets and therefore one of more expensive wholesale centres in Guangzhou.

The layout is a simple L shape with escalators at each end and large glass elevators in the centre of the building. It is very easy for first time visitors to become lost so ask for business cards from shops in which you are seriously interested, so that you can find them again next time.

There is no problem in buying single pieces although you will be able to negotiate discounts if you buy in bulk. Even when purchasing single items, do not be afraid to bargain as it it usually possible to bring the price down anywhere from 5 to 30 percent. Most of the shops moved into this building around ten years ago when much of the old wholesale market complex at Haizhu Square was demolished. All that is left of the original site is the large 1920's power station, which is now used for discos and restaurants, along with a handful of wholesale remnants. Only a few stores remain in that location, but it is worth a look if you are interested in cross stitch, cosmetics, plastic flowers and festival decorations. By the time you read this, even those will probably have been bulldozed to make way for insatiable property developers.

There are plenty of eating options in the area, including a Kentucky Fried Chicken on the ground floor for the culturally challenged. Around the main entrances there are plenty of street vendors selling drinks and small snacks among the Xinjiang tribesmen trying to flog pelts and body parts of various endangered species. Over by river on Haizhu square is a western restaurant called 1920 run by Filipinos and popular with local expats. They do a number of set lunches in a very civilised atmosphere.

Security inside Onelink is fine but be vigilant on the stretch of Yide Road that extends back east to Bin Bin Plaza and Haizhu Square. This area is very crowded and attracts pickpockets who use the pushing and shoving to their distinct advantage. Onelink is open from 9am to 6pm, but our advice is to leave by 5pm if possible. Leave it any later than that and the traffic will become unbearable.

Address: 39, Jiefang Nan Lu
广州市越秀区解放南路39号
Metro: Take line 2 to Haizhu square. Exit B2, then walk straight ahead for about 300 metres. One Link Plaza is the large building directly across the road at the first main junction.
http://www.onelinkplaza.com/en/main.php

22 PET PRODUCTS

Dong Feng Xi Lu Bird Market

Located on the southern side of Luhu Park, this is definitely one of the most unusual markets in Guangzhou. Here the Chinese passion for songbirds is at its very clearest. Not only are there birds of all kinds for sale here but an enormous variety of spectacular looking cages and feeding accessories. Even if you are like me and feel that it is cruel to keep these tiny avians locked up, the quality of the cages is amazing and they make wonderfully exotic interior design pieces. There are dozens of different designs and sizes available from just a few inches square to at least six feet tall. I especially like the selection at 'Art Shop' at number 59 on the second floor, which has some of the most impressive designs, even including a cage in the shape of the Canton Tower. This and a few other shops are also the workshops where craftsman can be seen putting these incredible items together on their workbenches. Down on the ground floor, all kinds of seed and other bird food ranging from live grasshoppers to trays filled with wriggling maggots give off the most offensive odour. Faeces from thousands of birds add to the heady mix and yet above all of this, the public bathroom in the far corner easily manges to surpass all else with its foul stench. Only in China!

First time visitors to Asia might not appreciate seeing so many tightly caged animals, and it really does seem a shame that most of the country is almost devoid of a morning chorus just to please uneducated old men.

Cages here are a very distinct Chinese style, very

different to what you will find in Thailand for example where most of the cages resemble the Buddhist monasteries and temples that dot the entire kingdom. Prices start very low for single ceramic feeder pots.

Address: Dong Feng Xi Lu 东风西路

Chengnan Pet Market 沥新城南宠物市场

While there are decently sized pet markets in Guangzhou at Huadiwan and Shangxiajiu, these are aimed mainly at the retail markets. For true wholesale, buyers of larger operations will need to head out to the Nanhai District

At the rear of Metro Mall in the Dali Cheng Qu area there is a specialist concentration of pet product wholesalers. As always this is China, so do not expect to find a lot of hi-tech items such as collar-cams and electronic door flaps but there is plenty of choice when it comes to beds, toys and other accessories. I was especially impressed by Cat King (Maowang, coincidentally this is also the phrase that the Chinese use to translate Elvis) at the main entrance, with its huge range of leather dog collars, up to the largest sizes imaginable and even the kind of bite-suit sleeves that are used by police trainers. This market has grown in size over the past few years but unfortunately most of the growth has come from puppy farmers and dog breeders at the expense of accessory outfits. Dog lovers will undoubtedly be upset by the sight of so many dogs kept caged up in dirty cramped conditions. Until China does something about its animal protection policies, do not expect this situation to change.

Address: Gongye Da Dao 工业大道

Contact: 0757-85592510

Directions: Take the subway out to Xilang, the last stop on line one. From there change to the Guangfo Line and continue out to Guicheng. Take exit B out onto Nanhai Da Dao (**南海大道北**) The bus stops are opposite the large shopping mall (凯德广场) with a Walmart, all heading down to Dali Town. Otherwise you can take a taxi outside the appallingly named Starry Winking Development (越秀地产). Buses go all the way down to Pan Cun Industrial Area (潘村工业区站) which is right behind the pet market, while most taxis will go via the large T Plaza (中盈广场) at the very heart of Dali Town. From here walk along Gongye Da Dao (工业大道) past the Guangdong Finance and Economics School (广东省财经学校).

23 SEAFOOD

Huangsha Aquatic Products Wholesale Market
黄沙水产交易市场

Huangsha is one of the three largest wholesale seafood markets in China, where an average of 180,000 tons of product is traded each year. A visit to this wet and wild market will reveal more types of seafood than you could ever imagine, some disturbing images, and a glimpse into an ancient tradition within a rapidly evolving city.

Opened in July 1994, the market covers an area of 26,000 square meters, including nearly 10,000 square meters of parking. Apart from three or four hundred wholesale operators, there are a great many restaurants here where locals pick out a few delicacies and have them prepared and cooked on the spot. Even if you do not trade in fish products this is one of Guangzhou's liveliest markets and is well worth a visit as a tourist.

Address: Nanzhan Da Yuannei (next to Shamian Island), Haotie Lu, 15, Huangsha Avenue 黄沙大道15号铁路南站大院内(近沙面)

Directions: From the Huang Sha Subway Station, cross Huang Sha Avenue and the look for the Bank of Jiujiang and Golden Plaza (黄金广场). The Seafood Market is directly behind.

There are two separate fish markets located close by to the Country Garden Estate (广州市番禺华南碧桂园) on the way down towards Panyu. H&H International Seafood Trading Centre (五湖四海国际水产交易中心) and Kingda Sea Food and Special Local Product Market Plaza (金达海味 干货食品城) are both accessible from the Dashi subway station but they are mainly for diners who wish to eat at what has been described as the world's largest seafood restaurant, Fisherman's Wharf (渔人码头) on 559 Yingbin Lu in the Louxi District (洛溪), rather than professional corporate buyers. There is even a restaurant street here known as 洛溪食街 which means road full of many fantastic restaurants.

24 SHOES

The largest Guangzhou footwear wholesale markets are clustered in and around Zhanxi Road (站西路), just west of the Railway Station and the Provincial Bus Station. Zhanxi literally means 'station west' in Chinese and so the name is rather self-explanatory. Zhanxi Road Wholesale Street (站西路鞋业批发街) in Guangzhou hosts the biggest wholesale base in China for distribution of shoes and related materials for making shoes, accompanied by shoals of dealers and distributors specialized in shoe products. There are other shoe markets on Jiefang South Road, and along Guangzhou Da Dao South across the river but it is Zhanxi Lu that has the highest concentration. Walk from the Train Station west until you reach the main junction with Guangyuan Lu. The biggest markets begin in earnest on the far side of the road. The first is Xingqilu Shoes Plaza (新其路鞋业广场) which has a good preliminary assortment of men's styles, but this is only the beginning.

Guangzhou Xinqilu Shoes Plaza 广州新其路鞋业广场

Housed in the same building as MacDonald's, there are three floors of shoe wholesalers here but the multi-level floors make it seem like a lot more. The vast majority of the product on sale here are men's styles and is home to some of my favourite producers in the world. Expect everything from gold-studded loafers to desert boots and lots more. Many shoes are quite open to retail and I have picked up Oxfords, brogues, and even some slick looking Chelsea boots here. My favourite store is Hua Er Kang Shoes Industry Company (华尔康鞋业有限公司) Address:
(广州市环市西路133新其路鞋业广场二楼A205档) run by the boss, Sophie who has an amazing range of chrome-tipped creations that are favoured by high class Japanese gigolos and Mexican drug dealers.
Address: 30-32, Zhanxi Road 广州市站西路30-32号

Guangzhou Bu Yun Tian Di International Trade Centre 广州步云天地国际商贸中心

Also known by its English name, Global International Trade Centre is 100,000m with 12 floors, more than 1500 famous shoe manufacturers for export and domestic sale in China and consists of two different sections. The front of the building is for finished shoes while the rear is for shoes materials, such as leather, PU, buckles and more. The shoe materials segment is much larger than the finished shoes market.

The B/F to 10/F of phase 1 and 2, and the 8/F to 10/F of phase 3 are selling and exhibiting men's and women's genuine leather shoes, PU shoes, casual shoes, sports shoes and children's shoes. Above this is mainly office space.

B/F to 7/F of phase 3 are selling and exhibiting such shoe materials as genuine leather, PU, special shoe materials and metal accessories. Phase three has two large kirin statues outside the main doors. The top floors, (seven and six) are mainly offices and showrooms. Of these around fifty percent are currently vacant or closed down. The fifth and fourth floors are mainly accessory shops, with huge selections of clasps, buckles and other related items. The third, second and first floors are leather hides. From here it is also possible to walk straight into Kids Shoes World (万国童鞋世界) which takes up the lower few floors on the right hand side of the building.

Address: 26, Zhanxi Road 站西路26号

Contact: 020 8650-3333

http://en.shoesworld.net/

Guangzhou   Jinma   Shoes   City   Wholesale   Market 金马鞋业城

Located on the first and second floor of Jin Feng Building, this is one of the mid-sized wholesale shoe markets in the area. Vendors carry both men's and ladies' styles, mostly mid range.

Address: 39, Zhanxi Road 站西路39号

New Continent Footwear Plaza 新大陆鞋业广场

First opened in 2002, this is one of the most well established wholesale shoe markets, although it is now rather showing its age. Just a few floors of vendors, many of which featured curtained-off showrooms with thick heavy drapes. Quite clearly competition is intense, and like many other markets, margins are now so tight that cannibalising the ideas of other manufacturers has become quite common practice.

Address: 12,   Zhanxi   Road 广州市站西路12号新大陆鞋城

Guangzhou Jiulong Shoes City 广州九龙鞋城

Guangzhou Jiulong Shoes City is one of the most impressive in Asia's largest international wholesale footwear market, mainly for European and American markets, as well as Japan, South Korea, South-east Asia, and the domestic wholesale market.

Address: Zhanxi Road 站西路

Guangzhou Jinglongpan International Shoes Plaza 广州金龙盘国际鞋业广场

Also known as the Golden Dragon International Shoes and Leather Trading Plaza (金龙盘国际鞋业皮具贸易), this is mainly sports shoes and casual shoes, mostly for men rather than women.

Address: 235, Guangyuan Xi Road 广州市广园西路235号

Euro Commercial Plaza Shoes City 广州欧陆商业广场鞋业城

Four floors of wholesale shops with generally quite good quality. At present the third floor is ninety-percent dead and the second floor fifty-percent empty. Most of the first floor is high-end men's shoes, mainly rip-offs and replicas of designer styles.

Address: 24, Zhanxi Road, Hongji Building 广州市站西路24号宏基大厦

Metro line 2 or line 5 to Guangzhou railway station, Exit F.

Tien He Shoes Market 天和鞋城

One of the newest markets in the area, advertised as the 'The Land of Man Shoes.' The fourth floor is devoted to offices while the first three floors are devoted to men's shoes showrooms.

Address: 20-22, Zhanxi Road 站西路20-22号

Jianglong International Shoes Plaza 广州江龙国际鞋业广场

Yet another shoes market, this time in one of the

older buildings in the district.
Address: Huiying Business Building, Wangshengtang Hou Street, Guangyuan Xi Road
广州市白云区广园西路王圣堂后街汇盈商厦

Xindalu Shoe Market 广州新大陆鞋业广场

Guangzhou Xindalu Shoe Market is located in Zhanxi road's south side, is an area of over 3,000 square meters of an eight storey commercial building. The first to third floors are more than 200 independent shoe shops. The fourth to the seventh floors are professional shoes materials and shoes department trading office. The eighth floor is product display show rooms and the Executive Business Centre.
Address: 12, Zhanxi Road 广州市站西路12号

Metropolis Shoes City 解放南鞋城.

Just to the east of Onelink Plaza on the other side of Jiefang Nan Lu is the Guangzhou Metropolis Shoes City also known as the Jiefangnan Shoes City. The entire block, bounded by Daxindong Road (大新东路) to the North and Qiyi Lu (起义路) to the east is filled with small wholesalers specialising in lower end, cheaper quality footwear of all different kinds. Inside, a number of individual markets have been swallowed up, including the Dadi Footwear Market (大都市鞋城) and the Gaodi West Shoe Market (高第西鞋街). There is a section of street vendors that spread tarps out on the pavement up on Daxi Lu near the junction with Jiefang Lu, on the opposite corner to the PSB immigration offices that always have the very latest ladies fashions. I usually pick up half a dozen or so pairs of the most interesting designs for around 20 or 30 RMB a piece as gifts for lady friends whenever I am passing through Guangzhou.
Address: 88, Jiefang Bei Lu 解放北路88号
Guangzhou Metro: Line 2 to Haizhu Square Station, walk

north on Qiyi Lu to the junction with Daxin Lu
大新鞋业专业街

Huanan Shoes Wholesale Trade City
华南影都星美国际影城

Also known as South China Shoes City (海珠区华南鞋业城) there are another 700 wholesalers here with separate sections for children's shoes, sandals, sneakers, house slippers etc.

Address: 1629, Guangzhou Da Dao Nan, Haizhu District
广州市广州大道南1629号
Contact: 020 3413-8981

Guangzhou Guangda Foreign Trade Shoes City
广州广大外贸鞋业商贸城

Beyond the motorcycle accessory and foodstuff markets of Zengcha Lu, this large shoe market lies at the turn off for Guangda Clothes Market. Spread out on two vast floors and combined with Shijing Guangda Shoes Wholesale Markets (石井广大鞋业批发市场) prices are considerably cheaper that the high-end markets of Zhanxi Road but quality is also that much lower.

Address: Opposite the Meijing Hotel at the interchange of Zengcha Road and Shitan West Road
广州市石井凰岗路口

Fortune World International Shoes Plaza
财富天地国际鞋业广场

Five floors of as yet very sparsely populated, newly constructed mega mall. I am not sure why these huge modern complexes are continuing to be built, especially as the Chinese economy has been on the slide now for at least five years, but it seems that the property tycoons really do not know what to do with all their billions except further inflate the real estate bubble. This vast new indoor market seems to have more property management sales staff that actual shoe stores at the moment.

Address: 150, Xiwan Lu 广州市荔湾区西湾路150号
Located just across the railway tracks at the end of Zhanxi
Road Shoe Materials Market.

Tongdexi Shoes Wholesale Market 同德西鞋业批发市场

These days it is hardly worth venturing out past the
'Pipe Factory' (I just love these deadpan bus stop names)
to Tongdexi. In 2015, I found that most of the buildings
are now shuttered and 99% of the business have relocated
elsewhere. I only managed to find one outlet still open in
the Yifa Shoes Plaza(易发鞋业), but that was one more
that the surrounding buildings which seem to now be
slowly being taken over by delivery companies.

Address: Xicha Lu, Tongdexi 同德西

25 SPORTING EQUIPMENT

Hua Nan International Trade Centre of Stationery, Sports and Quality Goods 华南国际文体用品交易市场 Not to be confused with Guangzhou Huanan Shoes Market, here we find vast amounts of sports equipment and stationery, although the quality remains questionable at times. Most of the market is located between Nan'an Road and Butouji Street but it also extends out into the Nan'ao Stationery and Sport Goods Integrated Wholesale Market on Heliu Street and the Xingzhiguang Culture and Sports Wholesale Market (星之光文体用品市场).

Bear in mind that despite the nation as a whole being able to dominate the Olympics, the average Chinese is not very active when it comes to sports. The sports in which they excel are very well represented here such as badminton and table tennis, while other pastimes might only have a small selection of generic items. Some exceptions that impressed me were the 广州市乔飞台球商行 snooker shop at 南岸路44号 where foosball tables could be purchased for just over 100 RMB. I also spent an interesting half an hour with Ting Ting in one of the many well well stocked golf shops, discussing the pros and cons of big brand clubs and drivers.   (广州嘉朗高尔夫用品有限公司).

Most of the shops here are located on the ground floor. The first floor has only about twenty or thirty stores, some of which look as though they have been empty ever since the place first opened in 1992. Stand outs include an interesting cycle clothing store at 208 and a promising looking underwater wear shop at 203 with a good selection of wetsuits, goggles and flippers, although do not expect to find any Cetatek Aquabionic Warp 1s here.

Address: 44,   Nan'an   Lu,   Liwan   District
荔湾区南岸路44号
Contact: 020 8193-2688
http://hnwtsc.com/

Jinhuadi   Fishing   Tackle   Wholesale   Market
金花地渔具市场

Truly an angler's paradise, there are about 150 individual vendors here, stocking just about everything that a fisherman might need. This ranges from full sized inflatables, outboards and life jackets all the way down down to the smallest lures and weights. In between there are cases, nets, rods and reels as well as cases and clothing. There is even scuba gear and fish feed for those who want to farm their quarry. All of this is crammed into one small market. There is a small second floor but only a small handful of tackle shops exist up at that level.

Address: 3, Huadi Dadao Zhong 花地大道中3号
Contact: 020 8172-5687/8195-5083/8120-5252
From Kengkou subway station on Line One, take exit B and cross the foot bridge across Huadi Da Dao towards Fangcun Passenger Bus Station. Jinhuadi is just to the left as you exit from the footbridge.

26 STATIONERY

In 1994, large numbers of stationery dealers moved from Yide Road to newly constructed buildings just to the north of Huangsha Subway Station. (Actually the subway did not open until 1997, when Huangsha to Fangcun was the very first section to be open to the public. If you look carefully, you can see that these two stations are much older in terms of design than all the others). There are still plenty of wholesalers on Yide Lu but the area around Yiyuan is a one stop for this kind of product.

Huang Sha Yi Yuan Stationary Market
黄沙宜园文具批发市场
Since its relocation, the Yiyuan Stationery Distribution Centre has spread considerably. Dealers have spilled over into what was originally known as the B Building and has now been renamed the H & H Stationery Trading Centre (Zhi Guang) which itself has grown out onto the opposite side of the road.
The Yiyuan building is a typically-Chinese white-tile monstrosity, yet contains hundreds of shops trading in stationery and sporting goods. The first floor is filled with general office consumables and student supplies, all kinds

of pens, notebooks, calculators and ink stamps. Lots of small shop display equipment (much of it in Chinese) as well as flags, festival supplies and educational toys ranging from Play Doh to Lego (locally branded of course).

The second floor is more geared towards art supplies with vast amounts of easels, palettes, brushes and paints of all different qualities. I particular like the large shop in the back corner which has a vast selection of materials and where the easily excitable Cantonese owner sounds just like Zippy from that classic kids TV show, Rainbow. While around fifty percent of the shops here are devoted to traditionally western art forms, the other half is devoted to Chinese calligraphy. Despite the fact that few government officials or older businessmen have any formal education (due to the disruptive Cultural Revolution period when universities were closed for many years), one skill that is prerequisite is being able to write artistic Chinese characters. To western eyes, these often look like illegible squiggles or the output of an elephant sanctuary, but in China this is taken very seriously. Therefore many companies will invest heavily expensive brushes, antique ink stones and pricey parchment, so that the official that accepts all their bribes can bang out a few couplets of wisdom, that can be displayed in the boardroom. On a larger scale this can be seen at major tourist sites all over the country, where the hastily scribbled words of Mao, Deng and Jiang decorate popular locations. Needless to say every kind of Xuan, Pi Ma and even Dragon Cloud paper is available here. This is also a good place to buy chops, (what we would term seals) essential if doing business in China.

I remember a pair of very entrepreneurial French art students who were studying at Hangzhou University. They took the bus down to Yiwu and bought masses of cheap Chinese calligraphy brushes which they sold during their vacation back in Paris at huge mark ups. It was said that they paid for their entire education bill including tuition and accommodation fees with this clever little number.

The third floor reverts mainly back to office supplies, with much more larger equipment than the first floor. This is the place to find binders, punchers, staplers, shredders and currency counters of all sizes. Exceptions include a large Maries' paints outlet and a number of stores that specialise in string and tape.

The fourth floor is like something out of the surreal movie Brazil. The entire floor is used as warehousing space for all the vendors below, but each of the pallet locations is fronted by a padlocked cage, giving it the look of some gladiatorial holding area, where Christians and wild animals are held before being released into the amphitheatre above. Address: 28-30, Huangshadadao (Hall A), Liwan District
广州市黄沙大道28-30号
Contact: 020 8194-9499
From Huangsha Station, (Line 1) Exit B leads up out onto the Huangsha Bus Station. Look for the two large overpasses to your left that carry traffic on to the ring road. Walk towards these and then turn right before crossing the road. Yiyuan is about 100 metres straight ahead. If you find yourself outside Mopark Plaza, then you have walked too far to your right, and if you find yourself at Heping Road then you are walking in the wrong direction completely.

Xingzhiguang Culture and Sports Wholesale Market
星之光文体用品市场

Also known as the H & H Stationery Trading Centre. Next door to Yiyuan, this bright orange building consists of just two floors, dedicated to more of the same products that can be found in Yiyuan. This ranges from novelty stickers that are popular with schoolchildren, all the way up to quite sophisticated Point Of Sale equipment and automated clocking-in machines. I was actually first introduced to the place by some locally based English teachers who came here for classroom supplies, everything from chalk, all the way up to digital whiteboards. Directly across from Yiyuan, H & H continues to expand into yet another building, although this time both the first and second floor remain half empty.

Address: 25-27, Huangshahoudao (Hall B) 黄沙后道25-27号

Contact: 020 6286-8888

Guangzhou Tiancheng Road Printing Materials Market 广州市天成路印刷机械印刷材料市场

Just around the corner from the International Toys Market (国际玩具批发中心), Tiancheng Lu leads north from Yide Lu, up towards Zhuangyuanfang shopping street. The stores here offer all kinds of custom printing, from metal lapel badges to custom wedding stationery. For large scale printing on just about any kinds of material, this is the place to start looking. All kinds of paper, printing ink, printing accessories, related machinery and even packaging. PVC, UV printing, silk printing, all kinds of packages, stickers, even holographic security labels can be ordered here. Expect large minimum order requirements, 10,000 pieces for smaller items such as stickers, 1,000 for larger items.

Raw materials for these products, in terms of plastics and speciality papers can be found south of the river in Haizhu Industrial Zone, on Xingye Road off Gong Ye Dao Dao

Address: Tiancheng Lu 广州市天成路

Hua Nan International Stationery Trade Centre 华南国际文体用品交易市场

Also known as Na'nan Stationery and Sport Goods Wholesale Market, Na'nan Stationery and Sport Goods Wholesale Market is located between Nanan Road and Butouji Street in Liwan District. The anchor store is

Nan'ao Stationery and Sport Goods Integrated Wholesale Market located at 1, Heliu Street, Liwan. A massive selection of pens, school bags, printer cartridges and other stationery, mainly aimed at the domestic market.

Address: 44, Nan'an Lu, Liwan District
荔湾区南岸路44号
Contact: 020 8193-2688
http://hnwtsc.com/

Gao Ya Calendar Market 高雅 月历礼品文化精品城

While I have not yet used this market for export purposes, I have conducted large amounts of business here for the domestic tourist market, and it does show some promise for international buyers, willing to invest a little time and expertise.

There are well over a hundred outlets here for large scale printers that specialise in calendars, filofax type notebooks and other forms of printed stationery. Squeezed in between the Kota underwear Plaza to the North and the San Yuan Li Auto Accessories Markets to the south, this market is obviously most busy from September to Chinese new year.

While many of these manufacturers have fantastic printing abilities, they are seriously let down by their lack of understanding of western tastes and complete absence of English. These should be problems that are easily overcome by a savvy western buyer and yet the most serious hurdle here is the fact that the minimum order quantity for a custom order is stuck at ten thousand pieces.

The majority of calendar stock here utilises traditional Chinese designs. In the summer of 2008, I was able to leverage this quite successfully by supplying a small selection of very nice designs to four and five-star hotels in the popular tourist cities of Guilin and Yangshuo. By carefully selecting one or two high quality designs that focussed on the traditional Chinese painting that represents these stunning karst areas, I was able to hire a local with admirable sales skills to provide a very popular souvenir item for free spending overseas tourists, who have precious little else to spend their money on. One particularly beautiful example, printed on high quality paper and presented in a stunning cylindrical case proved to be extremely popular that season, and was at one stage selling hundreds per day over a selection of hotels with whom we had made previous agreements. This may not sound like much until I tell you that calendars we were purchasing at just under 6 RMB each were regularly selling for in excess of 200 RMB at the more upmarket hotel lobbies. This worked really well for one season but the following year, I simply could not find the same designs, or even anything matching up to a similar level of quality, and so due to a lack of stock, a very promising little sideline quickly dried up.

Even so, I still rate this area as very promising, with a great deal of potential for a creative and imaginative buyer. With the right customer, such as a large overseas tourist bureau, there are some very high margins to be had here. If I could organise a contact with the Aspara Management Company at Angkor Wat in Cambodia for example, I could easily meet the ten thousand MOQ and probably sell a hell of a lot more at the same time.

Address: 61, Jichang Lu 机场路61号

Yide Road 一德路

Yide Road remains a place packed with a lot of wholesale stores for stationery even after Yi Yuan's move. International Plaza, Yi Jing Yuan Plaza, Jin Jin Plaza and Hai Zhu Plaza all specialize in selling toys, stationery and decorations. However, the wholesale stores here are not as concentrated as before. They mainly lie on the first floor or inconspicuous places and give priority to selling middle-grade stationery for students.

Christian D. Taulkinghorn

27 TEA

The average tea consumption per capita in China is about 0.3 kg per year, yet in Guangdong Province it is almost 1.66 kg. Here tea-drinking is a way for people to escape the rush of urban life and to spend some quiet time with good friends. It is therefore no surprise that Guangzhou has the largest tea markets in Asia. Tea has long played an important role in Guangzhou's overseas trade. In 1640 a Dutch businessman became the first person to export tea from Guangzhou to Europe. In the 18th century book 'Oriental Commerce' by William Wilburn, a detailed table containing 17 years' of operations of the East India Company shows that tea accounted for 95 percent of all the goods exported from Guangzhou to London. After the American War of Independence, some of the first imports from China to America were tea. During the first half of the 19th century, over 50 percent of China's tea export was from Guangzhou. Today, tea exported from Guangzhou still amounts to billions of US dollars. Since 2000, Guangzhou has held annual tea culture festivals, tea trade fairs and the China Tea Expo in Guangzhou. Cantonese especially enjoy the ceremony of Gongfu tea that embodies Chinese tea culture, which is why there is such a huge range of specialised tea making implements available. They also enjoy 'cooling teas.' Take a stroll around the city, you will notice many cooling tea shops. Cooling tea, a Cantonese "invention," helps the locals fight the humidity and heat.

Fangcun Tea Wholesale Market 芳村茶叶批发市场

Although there are at least twenty tea markets in Guangzhou, this one is the largest, covering an entire neighbourhood and hosting more than 5000 merchants from all over the country, wholesaling an estimated sixty thousand tons of tea a year.

Different varieties of tea can be very similar visually. This will mean that each stop requires one to sit down and drink a variety of teas, making it an all-day endeavour just to penetrate a single block of this huge district. There is a stunning variety of every type of tea and the prices are outstanding, but the vast scale of the market makes it slightly intimidating to the novice enthusiast. Fortunately most dealers will be happy to sell you a kilo or half kilo (or more) and then package it into smaller, vacuum sealed bags.

Apart from the huge number of tea varieties, there is also a vast array of tea-related products for sale. These include packaging materials, processing machinery and even art that is related to tea culture. Of course, there is also a huge range of other tea-related accoutrements, such as cups, boilers and wonderful, hand-crafted tea trays. Some come from Chaozhou, but most is from far away Jingdezhen and Yixing, and better off purchased from the source.

As yet, no foreign tea companies are operating in Fangcun market, with the exception of Lipton which has its own tea blending plant in Guangzhou. The huge market in mainland China remains uncharted waters to foreign tea businesses. This may have some relation to the tax policy of the Chinese government in protecting local tea farmers.

Address: Dongqishi Road, Fangcun Dadaozhong
芳村大道中 东七十路
Transport: Take Metro Line 1, and get off at Fangcun
Station

As there are so many tea wholesale markets in
Guangzhou, I have only included brief details for just a
handful them here as follows:

Wealthlink Tea Mall 芳村 万象茶叶商贸城

A brand new tea wholesale market that opened at the
beginning of 2014. Not only were the front desk staff
surprisingly gracious, the management actually sent an in-
house translator up to meet me as I explored the upper
floors. Even though though she was freshly graduated, and
knew quite a bit less about tea that I did (which is not
much), it was a lovely touch and something that I have
never experienced in any other wholesale market. At the
moment the third floor is still largely empty and the
second floor only has about twenty percent occupancy but
the ground floor is full. The vendors were friendly and
there seemed to be a particular focus on Da Hong Pao
from Wuyishan, but perhaps that was because this was one
of the only varieties that I recognised.
Directions: From Kengkou Subway Station take exit B and
use the pedestrian footbridge to cross over to the opposite
side of the main Fangcun Da Dao. If you can successfully
navigate the bicycle paths of spaghetti junction like
interchange just to the south, then look for the GFC
Tower, the Fangcun Financial Building and the Wealthlink
Tea Mall is just beyond that.

Ruibao Tea Market 瑞宝茶叶城

A selection of relatively quiet tea wholesalers,
interspersed with a good handful of alcohol vendors, with
perhaps just one hundred stores in total. Very few
foreigners make it this far out of town and those who do

visit find the shop owners to be especially friendly to international buyers.

Nanzhou Mingyuan (Ruibao Garden) Nanzhou Lu 南洲名苑（瑞宝花园）站

Guangdong Haiyin Tea Market 海印茶叶市场

One of the smaller and lesser visited markets, tucked away behind the main road.

Address: 31, Dongxiao Lu, just south of Haiyin Bridge, Haizhu District 海珠区东晓路海印桥南

Nanfang Tea Market 南方茶叶总汇

More than 300 individual shops, located not to far from the much larger Fangcun Tea Market.

Address: 8-10, Qishi Road, Fangcun District 广州市芳村区洞企石路8-10号

GZ New Tea City 广州振兴茶叶商贸城

One of the city's oldest tea wholesale markets.

Address: 64-66, Nanzhou Lu 南洲路64-66号

International Tea Expo 九洲国际茶博城

A dedicated tea market amongst an area of dedicated food and drinks wholesale markets.

Address: Zengcha Lu, Baiyun District 白云区增槎路

A Crash Course in Chinese tea

T ea is produced in over 20 Chinese provinces. Chinese tea bushes (Camellia sinensis) are cultivated in the mountain areas of tropical and subtropical regions or wherever there is proper climate, sufficient humidity, adequate sunshine and fertile soil.

Chinese tea is classified in many ways, e.g., quality, method of preparation or place of production. The main processing methods include fermentation (oxidation), heating, drying and addition of other ingredients like flowers, herbs or fruits. These help to develop the special flavour of the raw tea leaves.

Tea is just one species but it has many different cultivars, like apples. There are many production regions and each has favoured different characteristics over the ages. The drying leaves are traditionally fermented to specific degree based on the variety and the region.

Tea generally ranges from green to black, depending on the degree of its fermentation. At the light extreme of this scale is "white tea," which is totally unfermented. Black tea in Chinese culture is called red tea because of the colour it makes the water, and is only famous from a few growing regions in China. Most black tea in China is imported from South Asia, particularly India. By contrast, the native Chinese teas are generally processed into green and oolong varieties.

There are eight basic classes of Chinese tea. These are as follows:

Chinese Green tea

Freshly picked leaves only go through heating and drying processes, but do not undergo fermentation. This enables the leaves to keep their original green colour and retain most natural substances, such as the polyphenols and chlorophyll contained within the leaves. The green tea is the most natural within the Chinese teas. It is dried as soon as is picked from the field and then fried. This process blocks the activity of the leaf enzymes that otherwise would alter the composition and the properties of the tea leaves. It has been proven that regularly drinking green tea can prevent cardiovascular diseases, obesity, cancers and diabetes. This kind of tea is produced all over China and is the most popular category of tea. Representative varieties include Dragon Well (Long Jing) and Biluochun from Zhejiang and Jiangsu Provinces respectively.

Chinese Oolong tea

Oolong refers to a type of tea that is partially fermented, in this sense it is an intermediate category between green and black tea. The change on the leaves' colour is caused by the fact that this tea is fried, rolled and roasted. Its taste is more similar to green tea than black tea, but has less a "grassy" flavour than green tea. The three major oolong-tea producing areas are on the south-east coast of China e.g. Fujian, Guangdong and Taiwan. Taiwanese oolong tea is particularly famous, with the high mountain growing regions being preferred. Oolong tea is quite potent in breaking down protein and fat, aiding weight loss.

Chinese Black tea

Black tea is dried, fully fermented and then roasted, giving it a strong flavour and dark colour. It is more oxidized than white, green and oolong teas. It contains more caffeine than any other class of Chinese tea. While green tea loses its flavour within a year, the flavour of the black tea can last several years. This is the main reason for which it has been traded to Europe for centuries. This is most popular form of tea in south Asia and Europe.

Chinese Red tea

Red tea got its name from the copper tint of its leaves and is often mistaken for black tea in the West. Even if at the beginning the Chinese red tea was similar to the Western black tea, with time the flavour of the western black tea has changed. Even if this is the most popular tea in the world, in China red tea never reached a global consumption. As for black tea, the flavour of red tea can also last a long time. Red tea that has undergone the full fermentation process has lost 90% of its polyphenols but retains its high caffeine content.

Chinese White tea

White Chinese tea undergoes a similar process to green tea. Since it retains its anti-oxidation properties it is considered one of the healthiest varieties of tea. The white colour comes from the hairs on the unopened buds of the tea plant. Even if the tradition of white tea production is very old this variety is quite rare and in the past only the emperor and is court could enjoy it.

Chinese Yellow tea

The process to obtain yellow tea is similar to that used for the green and the white tea. The difference lies on the fact that the tea leaves are left drying for a longer time so that they become yellow. According to Chinese Tea Culture's website, yellow tea may be more beneficial than green tea.

Chinese Flower Tea

Some teas are made entirely from fruit or from flowers. Flower teas involve dried flowers such as chrysanthemum, hibiscus, jasmine, lily, globe amaranth, gardenia, magnolia, grapefruit flower, sweet-scented osmanthus and rose. Scented tea consists of a bundle of tea leaves wrapped around one or more dried flowers. Jasmine tea is made by drying tea and jasmine flower petals together. These can also be various mixtures of flowers with green tea, black tea or oolong tea. There are strict rules about the proportion of flowers to tea.

To make things even more complicated there are many famous varieties of Chinese tea. Here is a list of some of the most famous.

Long Jing (龙井, Dragon Well) is a variety of pan-fried green tea from the Xi Hu (West Lake) district of Hangzhou, in Zhejiang Province.

Bi Luo Chun (碧螺春, Spring Snail) is also a green tea and comes from Tai Hu, in Jiangsu Province.

Tie Guan Yin (铁观音, Iron Goddess) is a oolong tea from Anxi, in Fujian Province.

Mao Feng (毛峰, Fur Peak) is a green tea from Huang Shan, the Yellow Mountain in Anhui Province.

Yin Zhen (银针, Silver Needle) is a yellow tea from Jun Mountain, in Fujian Province.

Qi Men Hong Cha (祁门红茶, Qimen Red Tea) is a red tea from Qimen County, in Anhui Province.

Da Hong Pao (大紅袍, Big Red Robe) is an oolong tea from Wuyi Mountain, at the border between Fujian and Jiangxi Province. For a stronger taste look for 3x fired Da Hong Pao.

Gua Pian (瓜片, Gua Pian) is a green tea from Lu'An, in Anhui Province.

Bai Hao Yin Zhen (白毫银针, White Fur Silver Needle) is a white tea from Fu Ding, in Fujian Province.

Da Long Qiu (大龙秋, Big Dragon Harvest) another delicate white tea, this time from the mountains of Yandangshan near Wenzhou in Fujian Province.

Ku Qiao Cha (苦荞茶) buckwheat tea is sometimes described as tasting like gingerbread cookies

Pu-erh (普洱, Puer Tea) is a deeply fermented tea made from wild tea trees in China's south-western Yunnan province, especially Simao County. It makes a strong, slightly musty red tea with a unique earthy flavour. The classic tea to accompany a meal of dim sum is ju pu, made with puer tea and ju ha (chrysanthemum). This is particularly good because dim sum is oily, and puer is thought to have pronounced efficacy in helping to digest heavy and oily foods. Modern research has shown that puer has the ability to reduce cholesterol. This variety of tea is usually compressed into different shapes like bricks, discs and bowls and should be stored in contact with the air so that the fermentation process can continue. As with quality wine, the value of puer tea goes up with time.

28 TOOLS AND HARDWARE

Huifu Xi Lu Tools and Hardware Wholesale Market
惠福西路五金批发市场

Huifu Xi Lu has hundreds of wholesalers selling power tools and accessories, everything from huge site equipment such as gantry cranes, all the way down to tiny scientific tools such as thermometers and refractometers. This is not a single large modern wholesale market, but instead, a street is full of small wholesalers and retailers offering these tools in small and large quantities. Major brands such as Bosch and Makita are widely available, as well as other less known, or unbranded items. This is the location to find power tools, nuts, screws and bolts, saws, hammers, and crowbars. One line that is relatively difficult to find here is that of non-power hand-tools. I had a few problems locating a bit-and-brace hand-drill for example, although there are a few smaller shops that specialise in these older tools just to the other side of the Jiefang Lu junction.

There are a number of smaller markets located along this road such as the Jianhui Market (广州市越秀今旭电子) just off Huifu around the corner

192 Haizhu South Road. The road is also interspersed with shops selling a wide range of small electronic parts. Near the junction of Haizhu Lu, there is a local second hand market which is detailed separately in another chapter.

Address: Huifu Xi Lu 惠福西路

Yuejing Hardware City 粤景五金交电批发市场

Located directly in front of the Nantian International Hotel Supplies Wholesale Market near Luoxi Bridge, this is an important shopping stop for local entrepreneurs planning to open their own restaurants and hotels. The market is divided into approximately two halves that are situated each side of the main entrance road. On the left are all kinds of fittings, from power boxes to light fittings. In between there are all kinds of cables, LEDs and fans. On the left side, the selection is more geared to tools. From the usual power tools all the way up to pallet trucks and construction site equipment. From heavy duty hardware to delicate surveying equipment.

Address: Guangzhou Road South and the north-west corner of Luo Xi Bridge 广州大道南

By Bus: The Guangxuan Hotel terminus of bus number 188 is located right next to the main entrance.

By metro: Take line 3 to Lijiao. Motorbikes cluster around exit C2 and will ferry you the five minutes across the river for around 10 RMB.

Xingda Wujing Electronics Plaza 新达五金电器商场

Despite the name, up on the second floor is a large used tool market where second hand tools (as well as those that have probably fallen off the back of a lorry) are laid out on the floors for all to inspect.

Address: Ruinan Lu 瑞南路

Directions: Subway line 1 to Gongyuanqian.Take the North West exit on Zhongshan Road and then cross over Jiefang Lu at the major intersection.Pass the Construction

Bank on the opposite side of the road and look for the first right which is Ruinan Lu. The market is about 500 metres up on the right.

Huan Cui Yuan Hardware Wholesale Market
广州市环翠园五金批发市场

Squeezed in between the stationary markets and the home decoration centres is a large hardware market that supplies tools for all kinds of building work, construction, repairs.

Address: 23, Heliu Street, Nanan Road
广州荔湾区南岸路河柳街23号

Metro: Take metro line 5 to at Xichang Station. From exit A the market is 1,000-1,200m south along Nanan Road.

Guangdong Metal Hardware Wholesale Market
广东五金城

If you cannot find the hardware that you are looking for at Huifu Road or Yuejing Market then you will probably need to head out to the Huangqi section of Guangfo Highway in order to visit the largest metal hardware market in China. There are over thousand wholesale and retail merchants in this area trading all kinds of hardware, as well as a number of sub markets including the Guangfo Electrochemical Iron Monger City (广佛机电五金城) and the Guangfo International Machinery Market (广佛国际机电五金城).

Christian D. Taulkinghorn

29 TOYS

Yide Lu 一德路

The stretch of Yide Lu between Haizhu Lu and Tiancheng Lu boasts a very high concentration of toy wholesalers. Almost everything that you can think of can be found here from the tackiest plastic soldiers to high-end action figures and remote controlled helicopters.

Take metro line 2 to Haizhu Square, take exit B2, turn right on Yide Lu, walk beyond One Link Plaza for another 400 meters and then you'll see it. On your way you will pass a decorations markets, fish and fruit markets and a catholic church. Alternatively, the new Yide Lu subway station has just opened at the beginning of 2015 which takes commuters directly into the heart of the main concentration of toy markets.

Address: Yide Road, Yuexiu District
广州市越秀区一德路

Onelink International Toy and Gifts Centre 万菱广场

Located at the very entrance the Yide Lu, One Link is one of the most popular wholesale markets in the whole city. Vendors here sell a lot more than just toys but it is

362

worth an explore as there are plenty of toy specialists tucked away on the various floors. The basement is well stocked with cuddly toys and children's gift items. The first three floors have a little bit of everything including jewellery, clothes and accessories and toys while beyond the fourth floor the focus moves towards furnishings and artsy home decorations.

Address: 39,   Jiefang   Nan   Lu
广州市越秀区解放南路39号
Contact: 020 8328-0088
Metro: Take line 2 to Haizhu square. Exit B2, then walk straight ahead for about 300 metres. One Link Plaza is the large building directly across the road at the first main junction.
http://www.onelinkplaza.com/en/main.php

Zhonggang   Boutique   Toys   Wholesale   Market
中港玩具精品批发城

Founded in 1994, this building on the south side of the road is three floors, devoted entirely to toys and games of all varieties. Much of it was refurbished in early 2015 and a number of the dealers have moved locations so be sure to update your business cards. There are dozens of shops selling collectors cards, water pistols and similarly massed produced junk. The shops that display action figures from the latest Hollywood blockbusters and TV hits will often refuse to sell individual pieces, only taking orders for large scale production runs. The outlets for action man/GI Joe type action figure brands such as Sideshow, Dragon, In Flames and Soldier Story require large minimum orders of at least 5000 pieces for new models. My own personal favourite stores are up in the rear corner of the third floor. Up here, you will find an outlet for high-end scale model racing cars, some of which, such as the Savage X Super Truck or the HPI Baja 5T regularly sell for thousands of dollars. There are some important brand names to look for in this arena as always, and these include names like Kyosho, Traxxas and Losi. Individual items range from entire engines and chassis all the way down through parts such as as wheels, fins and bumpers. There are especially good deals here on decals, especially limited edited editions that are often difficult to find outside of Japan. Just next door is a a cavernous den filled with DIY model kits from every historical era and most current manufacturers. If you were ever a fan of Airfix, then this will bring back some wonderful memories. There are a great deal of model shops on this floor as the hobby is growing very rapidly in China at the moment. These days the focus is more on Gundam Transformers than classic Spitfires, but the tools and paints that go with them are still in big demand. Towards the front of this floor is a specialist model train shop stocking quality brands such as Bachmann, Lilliput, Piko, Brawa, nearly all of which are now produced in Dongguan.

This whole stretch of road is devoted to toy dealers of different kinds although most of it is generic rather than big brand names. For example, there are plenty of Lego knock-offs here, but the official distributor is located in an anonymous office building up near Ximenkou.

Address: 399, Yide Xi Road, Yuexiu District
广州市越秀区一德西路399号
Contact: 020 8106-0319
Directions: Exit Yide Lu subway station on line six. The Zhonggang Market is located to the south west of the subway plaza.

International Toys Market 国际玩具批发中心

Directly across the road from the Zhonggang Toy Market, a high rise of more than 30 stories, with the first four floors filled with all kinds of toys and gifts. The top floor is taken up just a dozen large shops, featuring vast selections of unbranded discount toys. This is the place to look for larger items such as pedal-cars, mini-bikes and inflatable play-sets. The lower floors are filled with hundreds of small dealers selling every kind of cheap plastic tack that you could possibly imagine. My personal favourite is a board game manufacturer on the left hand side of the third floor that produces a vast range for western games companies. Many buyers are struck by the remote controlled blimps in the shape of killer sharks that float around menacingly at the top of the first set of escalators. There are far too many dealers here to list them all individually but a few highlights do stand out. On the second floor over in the far left corner is a great shop that sells all kinds of practical jokes and Halloween novelties. The girls in this shop as as fun loving as their products and I always come away with a good selection. Back at the front of the building is a far more unsavoury store that sells all kinds of specialist tactical gear including a large range of reproduction Nazi SS insignia. Illegal in many European countries, these are displayed here in plain view along side morale patches and other accessories that are produced especially for private mercenary forces such as Armor and Blackwater (recently renamed XE). At the rear of the second floor on the right hand side are a large number of consolidators that sell off grab bags of surplus toys, usually less successful releases, but bargains all the same.

Address: 390, Yide Xi Road, Yuexiu District
广州市越秀区一德西路390号
Contact: 020 8106-0319
Directions: Take line 6 to Yide Lu and the International Toys Market is directly to the west of the subway plaza.

The Toys, Models and Comics Wholesale Centre
海珠玩具模型动漫批发市场

On the east side of Haizhu Road the just facing the International Toys Market building is another small toy market that is usually overlooked by most buyers. The first floor has an interesting selection while the second floor

365

remains a wet market for the locals. There are a number of quality modelling stores here and a few recommended suppliers of Bandai type Japanese orientated models. There is also a large cosplay suppliers here, another market that is literally exploding in China at the moment. Sideshow Collectibles have their own shop here with some stunning display pieces, but almost everything that any knowledgeable collector will be looking for will be pre-order only. So, if you are a collector looking for bargain deals on the Clint Eastwood Blondie, Emmett Brown or the Stallone Dredd (each of which often push the thousand dollar boundary), I am afraid that you will be sorely disappointed. Plus the staff are surly and unhelpful, with a long standing reputation for being rude to collectors.

Address: 126, Haizhu Nan Lu 海珠南路126号

Contact: 020 8106-3420

Directions: Head north along Haizhu Lu from the Yide Lu Subway plaza and the Toys, Models and Comics Wholesale Centre is the first building on the right.

The Guangzhou International Toys and Gifts Centre (GITGC) 广州国际玩具礼品城

Designed to be the world's largest permanent "toys and gifts exchange' and instead has become just another Chinese white elephant, one of many ghost towns and shopping malls. Spanning a total area of 400,000 square metres and costing an enormous total investment of RMB1.5 billion, GITGC is a depressing sight indeed. Only a handful of tenants remain, while all the other shops have simply been locked up and abandoned. Outdated stock gathers dust on shelves while final demands pile up behind glass doors. Equipped with a grand exhibition and trade centre, a research and development centre, a business centre, and a theme park, GITGC seriously over extended itself. Businesses were mainly outlets for cheap plastic tack factories from Zhejiang and Jiangxi provinces, and these were some of the first casualties in the global recession. Compare this to some of the thriving enterprises on Yide Road were quality and collectibilty are paramount and it is easy to so why a monolith like this failed. Even the location is poorly thought out, nearly as bad as the notorious South China Mall in Dongguan. GITGC is stuck way out of the down town area. From Wenchong, the last station on subway line five, it is another ten stops on the bus to make it all the way out to GITGC. Unfortunately GITGCs situation is repeated all over Guangdong where similar empty wholesale markets blot the landscape, their corrupt owners wasting precious financial resources that could have been put to much better use if their had been improved transparency rather than the cursed guanxi system that permeates modern China.

Address: 3889, Huangpu East Road, Huangpu District
黄埔区黄埔东路3889号

Contact: 020 2264-9988

How to get there: Metro Line 5, Wenchong Station (then take a taxi or a bus).

30 TRADITIONAL CHINESE MEDICINE

Qing   Ping   Herbs   and   Medicine   Market
清平中药材专业市场

Set in Guangzhou's oldest district, this market is made up of some of the last colonial-era buildings in the city. The aged apartments are several stories high, and the bottom floors are reserved for market stalls. Blankets spread on the dirt road, covered in drying seahorses, legs of unidentifiable creatures, and mushrooms the size of small children are all common sights at Qingping.

The herb markets at Qingping are now separated into two main buildings. The smaller of the two is right outside the TCM (Traditional Chinese Medicine) Hospital rear entrance. Look for the TCM bus stop located on Liuersan Lu. The first part of the market has four floors but the top floor is more than half empty. On the third floor, look for birds nest in cold storage and expensive examples of ginseng is special display cases. The first and second floors are packed with jute sacks filled with dried seahorses and deer ligaments.

At the rear of this smaller market, with its main entrance of the junction of Qingping Lu and Tiyun Dong Lu, is the larger main Qing Ping Building, also known as the Qingping Dong Drug Market (清平东中药材市场). The fifth floor houses a branch of the Agricultural Bank and some very large scale wholesalers. The third and fourth floors are devoted mainly to well established local dealers with large well stocked stores. Each floor radiates off a main atrium area with a pair of transparent elevators. The aisles are well signposted ABCD and E, making shops easy to find.

The first and second floors sell a great deal of associated products as well as actual herbs. There are many shops here that focus on specialised packaging. Especially attractive is the range of apothecary glassware available, the kinds of vessels that would look more at home in a bizarre anatomical museum in the West.

Street side shops abound in all the alleyways, but the large buildings host hundreds of individual shops, each carrying a range of high-end stuff like cordyceps and dendrobium, which is a yin tonic that is derived from cultivated orchids and ginseng. Look out for unusual things: huge sacks of scorpions, centipedes, ganoderma, and seahorses stand out visually.

Chinese-grown American ginseng is common and is far less expensive than the North American grown product, but it is often slightly more yellow at its cross section and is generally inferior in flavour. Cultivated cordyceps is a new medicinal in the sense that it is different from the traditional product, which is a fungus that infects a caterpillar in the high mountains of Tibet, Nepal, Sichuan, and Gansu. Cultivated cordyceps is grown in a lab in glass jars, with a base of rice or soy beans and milk. It is the isolated fungus so no insect is involved, and it has a dramatically different appearance than the natural product. Natural cordyceps is shaped like the caterpillar that is overtaken by the fungus, with the fruiting body growing out from the head of the deceased caterpillar. Cultivated cordyceps has no caterpillar and is divided into its mycelium and fruiting body; the mycelium grows under the substrate and the fruiting body grows out above the substrate. The fruiting body gets long and is graded based upon its fragrance, colour, and shape. Good quality product has a rich, creamy, yellowish orange colour reminiscent of chanterelle mushrooms. The mycelium or "below ground" portion is larger and bulbous, with a similar fragrance and colour, but is much cheaper. Cultivated cordyceps is rich in polysaccharides and sometimes even surpasses the natural product in terms of its chemical profile. Nonetheless, it is generally regarded as inferior to the natural product because of the difference in their growing environments. It is essentially a new medicinal that has not been on the market for long, so there is not yet a clear consensus about whether the lab-grown and natural products can be regarded as interchangeable. However, it is hundreds of times less expensive than the threatened wild product, so it is increasing in popularity.

Many herbs are experiencing dramatic fluctuations in prices at the moment, with many Chinese fearing a bubble in the Chinese housing market and instability in the stock market. Many investors are flocking towards commodities as a safe haven. Food items like mung-beans and apples have doubled or tripled in price, and Chinese herbs have been experiencing huge fluctuations as well.

Wholesalers are waiting it out, running out of stock and waiting for the prices to drop. Retail and small-scale wholesale vendors are practically selling at cost so they don't lose their customers. Rare items like wild astragalus have increased ten fold in price over the past few years alone. Cordyceps is now fetching well over $15,000/kg after going up from $5000/kg just a couple years ago.

Qingping was the first private market to be permitted by the communist government in 1979 and it was considered a radical experiment, where an open market could co-exist within the communist framework. Ironically named Qingping, meaning peaceful, this market was more of a menagerie than a regular market. In those days almost everything was on the menu: sparrows, bunny rabbits, kittens, sleepy puppies, goats heads, leopards, monkeys, snake, seahorses, centipedes, ants, starfish, turtles, shellfish, and freshwater fish. With a huge array of rare and endangered birds on offer it quickly became a well known haven for illicit animal trafficking.

I first visited the Qingping Market in 1993 but it was cleaned up significantly just before the Olympic Games. In the bad old days, tourists flocked here to be appalled and disgusted as vendors beat cats and dogs to death and even skinned them while they were still alive. Before the SARS outbreak, this was a world famous market for all kinds of rare and endangered wild species. In those days it was easy to find all kinds of turtles, salamanders, snakes, dogs, monkeys, tortoises, foxes, wild boars, owls, martens, night cranes, sparrows, turtle-doves, ostriches, rats, civets, badgers, raccoons, bats, pangolins, peacocks ostriches and giant toads. Kidnapped house cats were crammed en-masse into inhuman little cages (25 at a time inside cages measuring 2ft by 3ft) and local restaurants did a roaring trade in rat, dog and snake. The only animals to found here now are small dogs and cats and birds being sold for the pet trade. Under pressure from animal rights activists, the cat meat market for example was been relocated out to Xinyuan in Baiyun District, where it is out of sight of tourists and therefore out of mind.

Xinyuan Market quickly became one of the biggest trade centres for snake, fowl and other animals. Opened 1996, it was located about 20 kilometres northwest of the centre of Guangzhou. There are a few other smaller animal markets such as Chatou, Dongbao and Nanjin in the neighbourhood. The area boasts around 1,000 traders engaged in the business of providing an array of live animals to the local catering industry. The official Xinhua news agency reported at the time that the four wildlife trading markets in Guangzhou raked in more than a million yuan (S$210,000) in earnings daily. The exodus from Xinyuan began when scientists announced that they had found a possible link between civets and SARS. Business licences were collected by officials from the Industrial and Commercial Administration and law enforcement officers launched thorough inspections of markets, restaurants, train stations and ports to crack down on the trade of wildlife. Perhaps the most amazing statistic was the more than 10,000 wild animals that were seized in just two days at Baiyun Airport.

Qingping still offers all kind of herbal ingredients for the soup pot. Dried deer tendons, deer musk, dried sea cucumbers, dried sea horses and the rows are lined with jars full of starfish, centipedes and scorpions. Large jute and hemp sacks of loose herbs stand packed against each other from one end of the hall to the other, ranging from goji berries to epimedium (horny goat weed).

Chinese herbal medicines are largely composed of roots, bark, flowers, seeds, fruits, leaves, and branches. Here you can find barrels of dried human placentas (for fainting sickness), dried three-inch stag beetles (for increased metabolism), dried flying lizards (also for metabolism), cockroaches (a topical anaesthetic), pearls (for influenza), pencil-sized millipedes bundled up and bound together in clumps (for a host of sicknesses), snakes (for arthritis), and a dozen different kinds of ants (for pretty much whatever ails you). Around every corner, there are hemp sacks overflowing with scorpions, seahorses, turtle shells, antlers, and every kind of root and flower imaginable. Guangzhou is currently the largest medicinal market in China with over 3000 different types of plants, herbs and treatments available for sale.

Traditional Chinese medicine is facing unprecedented scrutiny these days. Animal parts from more than 1,500 species are used as ingredients in traditional Chinese medicine, and some of them, like tiger bones and rhino horns, have contributed to significant declines in species.

Traditional Chinese medicine is deeply flawed, but it is a practice that has been carried out for centuries, so it is not so easily broken. Many claim that Chinese lack the ability to look at this in an objective and scientific way rather than from and emotional standpoint. There are supposed remedies for almost any condition. Soups made from the foetuses of anteater-like pangolins are said to increase a man's virility. Ground turtle shells are prescribed for febrile diseases, to stop night sweats, or to nourish yin and subdue yang. Dried sea horses are used to treat problems like asthma, impotence and heart disease, while snake oil is rubbed onto achy joints. Many of these animals are already on the brink of extinction from over-hunting and habitat loss; the increasing demand by Chinese medicine for their body parts is making a bad situation worse. In China, rhinoceroses have already disappeared. The rhino products used for Chinese medicine are now all imported from other countries, while tiger populations are also dwindling, and endangered Tibetan wolves are hunted down for medicinal ingredients. Tiger penis is used to treat virility, or rhino horn to cool the blood and reduce fever.

As an example of this flawed mentality, the Chinese character for maple bark is fong, and similarly, arthritis pain is tong fong. This coincidence forms the basis of the belief that maple bark cures arthritis pain. If the word matches, many Chinese believe they have found a cure for the disease.

Buckets of severed bears paws used to be a common sight at Qingping. Housed in tiny wire cages throughout the duration of their 30-year lifespan, farmed bears are milked of their bile through a permanent hole cut into their body. This open sore exposes them to bacterial infection and often provokes massive cancerous growths. Thousands of kilos of bile are harvested from 10,000 to 20,000 farmed bears using this method every year, and this is considered humane by both Chinese government officials and bear farmers. About 180 manufacturers in

China produce the 123 different types of products containing bear bile, which is effectively used to break down gallstones and help with chronic liver complaints, though synthesized drugs produce far better results than bile. Even the active ingredient in bile, ursodeoxycholic acid, can now easily be synthesized in a lab. Age-old remedies of Chinese medicine drive trade in endangered species and promote animal suffering, despite far move efficacious alternatives being widely available but the senseless cruelty continues unabated.

While you might not see illegal tiger and leopard bones, rhino horns, deer musk, and bear bile on open display, it is easily available to customers at Qingping. In the meantime masses of dried grass and petals and twigs and leaves in open bags piled everywhere are waiting to be weighed and ground and steeped and made into poultices.

These markets cater to the unusual culinary tastes of Guangdong province residents, famed for a willingness to eat anything. Some even savour small, live rats in a delicacy called "san jiao," or "three screams." (The rat is said to scream once as it is hefted with chopsticks; a second time as it is dipped in vinegar; and a third time when it is bitten.) In terms of Chinese medicine, Guangzhou is famous for its integration of herbal medicine into daily life, as well as its markets and Chinese medical universities and hospitals. In addition to American ginseng and other herbal beverages in 7-11s, Guangzhou also is famous for it's small shops that sell turtle shell jelly and cooling teas. It could be argued that the Cantonese use more herbs and drink more tea than the people of most other regions in China, and they sell a comparatively large number of things like fresh bai mu er (tremella fungus) with lotus seeds in convenience stores and other shops.

After scares caused by SARS and other diseases, the government forced most of the live animal stalls to shut down and now only the most hygienic and professional wet market stalls remain in existence. Otherwise, you will now find stalls dedicated to the sale of knick knacks, traditional herbal medicines, and other plants and food items. Another important factor in the decreasing popularity of endangered species is the corruption crackdown. For a long time, businessmen and government officials would order exotic wild game cuisine to impress their guests.

The street markets continue outside along to Shibafu Nan Lu but then peter out towards the E exit of the Culture Park subway entrance.

Address: Qingping Drugs Market, 53, Qingping Lu, Liwan District 广州市荔湾区清平路清平医药中心

Metro: Take line 2 and get off at Huangsha.

Herb Markets Beyond Guangzhou

The three largest wholesale herbal markets in China are located at Anguo in the North, Bozhou in the East, and Guangzhou in the South. Anguo (安国), nicknamed "Medicine Capital" (药都) is 52 kilometres south of Baoding in central Hebei province and 180 kilometres from Beijing to the north. The medicine market's prosperity originated from the "Medicine King Temple," which was first built in the Eastern Han Dynasty (25-220). The temple offers sacrifices to Chinese medicine king Pi Tong, who was also a senior general of the Eastern Han.

Located at the juncture of two important railway lines in the north-western corner of Anhui province, the dusty and rusty city of Bozhou also competes for the title of capital of the Chinese medicinal herb industry. The city of approximately three million people is centred around a massive 85-acre market, where some 6,000 traders come from every corner of south-east Asia to ply the ingredients of traditional Chinese medicine.

Owing to its southern location, Guangzhou is the main place that serves the wholesale markets of Hong Kong, Taiwan, Singapore, Malaysia, and Indonesia. Herbal bosses from all over come to Guangzhou to purchase goods for shops in their home country, and the emphasis on export has made Guangzhou a major centre for premium products such as ginseng, velvet antler, and cultivated cordyceps. While Anguo is geographically much closer to the production region of ginseng and velvet antler, Guangzhou actually tends to have superior products because it has a more high-end focus.

31 WATCHES

The Zhannan Lu Watch Wholesale District also known as Guangzhou Horological Wholesale Market or even the Guangzhou West-Station Watch City (广州站西钟表城) is the largest of its kind in Asia. In fact, this is the epicentre of fake watches for the entire world. It is filled with large and small wholesale centres where more than 3000 suppliers offer all kinds of watches, watch accessories and watch fittings. If you have ever been approached on holiday by some shady looking character whispering the words 'Copy watch?" then there is a very good chance that it originated here. What is really ironic about this area of town are the large number of government posters and billboards warning about trade in fake items. Huge signs with Chinglish phrases such as "Realize the Harmfulness of Counterfeits and Firmly Reject Them" are posted directly above the largest fake Rolex markets on the planet. There are at least ten markets here that are located directly behind the Provincial Bus Station, the one that is listed on maps as the Guangdong Passenger Transport Terminal.

These markets are filled with replicas of almost every brand in existence from Blancpains and Breguets to Tag

Heuers and Tissots. From simple Swatches to the most ornate Audemars Piguet and Patek Philippes. Dealers will start off by asking for 200 or 300 RMB for the latest designs but can often be knocked down to 50 RMB with persistence and perseverance. All of the dealers have very similar branded catalogues. No-one keeps the good stuff there in their glass cases just in case there is a "raid." Mostly it is rejects or old models from the same factories. Instead they will offer to take you to visit their 'showroom.' All stand owners have an apartment nearby, where they have all their fakes on display.

I always end up buying lots of gifts here but I usually focus of fashion watches rather than designer replicas. Here I can find all kinds of unique and trendy designs for friends back at home and I rarely spend more than ten kuai per piece. In addition, there are always plenty of related items to choose from. These include pens, cuff links, key rings, money clips and jewellery. On the main street in between these markets, there are dealers that specialise in every kind of watch box, from single presentation cases to collectors display cases. Further north, towards Guangyuan Lu, the markets specialise in individual parts, buckles, straps, watches, watch tools, movements, dials, bezels, cases etc. Most of these are brandless but it is possible to find replica parts by digging around a bit. Other stores carry batteries and all of the necessary watch making tools. It is possible for example to pick up a strap-removing tool for only a few kuai.

Some of these markets also cater to replica collectors. Replicas sometimes come from genuine factories, sometimes they source some out of house assembly. On other occasions a number of replicas are made on limited production runs, by an enterprising collector who commissions and/or buys in market, all the parts for a small run of say a hundred watches. There is a huge cottage industry for watch assembly. When you walk around the markets you see many stall holders industriously assembling all sorts of watches, and there are undoubtedly thousands more sitting at kitchen tables with boxes of components. Replicas of all kinds often come from the same factory or a "sister" factory across the street run by the same people ordering the same raw materials and using the same patterns without the knowledge of the designer who is having his products made in the genuine factory. Many designer handbags for example are made in China with "Made in Paris" or "Made in Italy" labels just sewn in. It is said that the designer companies do this to maximize profits and lie to us about it. The same is true for watches.

Most collectors are very clear about how to buy the high grade replicas. Prices are generally higher but can be negotiated. They will ask for Swiss quality or Class-A replica watches: Stainless steel material, high rigidity mineral glass or sapphire crystal and imported movements. Often times they will find a suitable seller and ask for the watch they want. Whatever they produce, the collector will hand it straight back and say 'No, I want top quality'. The best replicas are never on display, but these guys all have their reliable sources. Few vendors stock up on the higher grade replicas as they are often too costly keep in stock when the majority of customers will not spend the cash required. Even so, they will be happy to find them for you even though it might take a couple of days, in some cases. If you want to purchase a high quality replica, make sure that you do your research beforehand about make and build. Chinese pronunciation for foreign brands can be quite intuitive so often times it is good to have pictures of the models you are looking for. Sometimes these replicas will have minor flaws such as a slightly misaligned bezel or a misaligned index on the clock dial, but can easily be sent to a local watch repairman to have it fixed.

Below is a list of the ten largest markets in this area.

Sanyi Timepieces Market 三一钟表城

Address: 61, Zhanxi Lu广州市站西路

Yazhi Market 雅致商场
Address: 2, Bei Jie, Kuangquan Zhanxi Lu 广州市站西路

Wang Jiao International Timepieces Market
旺角国际钟表城
Address: Zhanxi Lu 广州市站西路

Nanfang Timepieces Trading Centre 南方钟表交易中心
Address: Rear Tower, 145, Huanshi Xi Lu 广州市站西路

Southern Watch Trade Centre 南方钟表交易中心 also
know as the Southern Trade Centre of Horologie (sic)
南方钟表城
Address: Zhanxi Road 广州市站西路

Zhanxi Kowloon Watch Centre 站西九龙钟表城
Address: 5, Qunying Lu, Zhanxi Lu 广州市站西路

Zhanxi Timepieces Market 站西钟表城
Address: 1-2 Floor, 65, Zhanxi Road, Yuexiu
District广州市越秀区站西路65号首至二层

Oriental Timepieces Market 东方表城 sometimes known
as the Dongfeng Watch Market
Address: Zhanxi Lu 广州市站西路

New Kowloon Watch Centre 新九龙钟表城
Address: 3, Qunying Lu, Zhanxi Lu 广州市站西路

Directions: From line 2 of the metro, take exit H from
Guangzhou Railway Station. This emerges into the ticket
office of the Provincial Bus Station. At the top of the
escalator, turn 180 degrees and step out onto a small paved

square. Look for the Post Office on the opposite side of the road. Follow this road and you will see the various wholesale watch markets up ahead.

32 ZHUANG YUAN FANG 状元坊

Located deep in the heart of what was once the old city, this was at one time a small lane where shops specialised in Cantonese opera costumes and temple fair ornaments. Goods ranged from traditional outfits for entire acting companies including huge replica ancient weapons, all the way down to tiny pearl hairpins. All that remains of this is just a handful of stores on the main Renmin Lu which still stock these kinds of items. With their Peking Opera masks and Dragon Dance outfits these shops are still worth a look inside. The most notable of these survivors is the Fang Costume Workshop (状元坊戏服厂) at 170, Renmin Nan Road. The manager of the shop, Dong Huilan, is a veteran embroidery master whose works have won national prizes and even supplied famous films, dramas and TV series with costumes, including the wonderful 'Once Upon a Time in China and America' (黄飞鸿), starring Jet Li and Rosamund Kwan. For a unique tourist experience, the shop also houses a professional photo studio, where you can try on as many costumes as you like and have photos taken of you as you pose.

These days Zhuang Yuan Fang has become a tightly packed shopping street for the city's younger generation, featuring hundreds of tiny hole-in-the-wall types shops, selling the latest and most up to date in fashion kitsch and 'in style' trends. Most of the customers here are too young to be called hipsters or fashionistas, terms that would probably be difficult to apply to Chinese culture when it is so cut-off from outside trends. This is certainly not Kings Road or Harajuku but for the People's Republic's standards it is quite daring and rebellious. Stores here are filled to bursting with every kind of cute, colourful, fun non-necessities that are produced especially for teenagers to waste their money on. Here we can find every kind of cuddly toy from Snoopy and Hello Kitty to Pikachu and Doraemon. A vast range of necklaces, rings, bracelets and all other kinds of costume jewellery as well as K-pop inspired clothing of all colours and varieties. There are pet shops and fast food stalls galore. This is also the best place in town to find novelty cigarettes, with every possible flavour from orange and lemon to cherry and chocolate.

Just remember that all these shops are aimed at easily-influenced teenagers with money to burn rather than international buyers. Nearly everything stocked here can be found elsewhere in wholesale markets at a fraction of the price.

Zhuang Yuan Fang is just five minutes south of Shangxiajiu shopping Street. Look for the large Chinese gateway flanked with the statues of the zhuangyuan. A zhuangyuan (状元) is a student who attains the highest score in an exam. Historically it referred to the civil service exam but nowadays is used for the Gao Kao (College Entrance Examination). Zhuangyuans are still feted and paraded in modern China and it is not uncommon for them to be invited to appear on the TV and in newspapers, and even be asked to appear in advertisements.

Despite a veneer of cuteness and innocence, this area also reveals some deeper secrets about China's younger generation. Illegal drug use is growing fast in the Middle Kingdom, especially in the larger metropolitan areas. Just around the corner from Zhuang Yuan Fang, opposite the laboratory supply shops of Renmin Lu, there are a number of DIY drug-dealer stores, where the beginning trafficker can kit themselves out with everything they need, from micro-scales to high-powered electroshock weapons. Along with impressive selections of drug paraphernalia from bongs to aluminium foil, there are now large ranges of vaporisers, papers and filters. Some shops even carry selections of knives, knuckle dusters and compact, concealable stun guns, all essential equipment for anybody starting out in this dangerous business.

Christian D. Taulkinghorn

APPENDICES

I BOOKS AND VIDEOS ABOUT GUANGZHOU

Background Reading

Fiction

River of Smoke by Amitav Ghosh
   The second book in Ghosh's Ibis trilogy, and set a year before the First Opium War, this was a wonderful opportunity to explore the roots of early globalisation at a time when revolutions (market and industrial) were newly under way in the West. Unfortunately Ghosh instead chose to focus instead on obscure wordplay and richness of language. As an Oxford-trained anthropologist, it is probably not surprising that he decided to make this an overly prosaic soap opera rather than an in-depth exposition of what were undoubtedly some of the century's most important events. His characters find

themselves caught between East and West, providing a unique vantage point to the various conflicts brewing in Canton, and yet the book amounts to little more that a a selection of lengthy and meandering disquisitions on the opium trade, botany and art, stalled and clumsily stitched together. Fascinating for lexophiles, logophiles and other lovers of unusual and obscure vocabulary but a real let down for anybody who wants to go beyond a lengthy regurgitation of pre-existing propaganda.

Tai Pan by James Clavell

Tai-Pan is a 1966 novel written by James Clavell about European and American traders who move into Hong Kong in 1842 following the end of the First Opium War. It is the second book in Clavell's "Asian Saga". He spent nine months researching the novel in Hong Kong but it is doubtful that he ever went to Guangzhou, considering the political tumult that was engulfing China at the time. Tai Pan is a riveting read. This was after all the same man that created stories like The Fly and The Great Escape, but Tai Pan could only charitably be described as historical fiction. Clavell is certainly entertaining but highly dishonest as he has reinvented history to suit current tastes.

Flashman and the Dragon by George MacDonald Fraser

Presented within the frame of the supposedly discovered historical Flashman Papers, this book describes the bully Flashman from Tom Brown's School days. This the eighth book in the series, takes place shortly after Flashman's service in the United States. There is no explanation as to how he ends up in Hong Kong, but it is from here that he begins his adventures in China. Flashman meets both the leaders of the Taiping Rebellion and members of the Qing Dynasty who resisted the British march to Pekin in 1860 - part of the Second Opium War.

In Hong Kong, Flashman is convinced by Phoebe

Carpenter, a lovely minister's wife, to take a shipment of opium into Canton, with the promise of a later, more pleasant meeting. On the way he discovers that instead of opium he is carrying guns to the Taiping rebels. The river journey is perhaps the most exciting section of the story and the most relevant for visitors to the contemporary city. In Canton, Flashman manages to convince Harry Smith Parkes that he was trying to stop the shipment. However, instead of being able to head for home as he originally intended, he is put on the intelligence staff in Shanghai. From Shanghai he travels to Nanking and meets the leaders of the Taiping rebels, in order to convince them not to march on Shanghai. Flashman then proceeds to the mouth of the Peiho to join Lord Elgin's staff for his march to Pekin. After being captured by the Imperials, he meets Xianfeng Emperor and becomes the prisoner and lover of Yehonala, the imperial concubine. When the British army arrives at Pekin, he witnesses the destruction of the imperial Summer Palace. But after that event, while heading for home, he is drugged and apparently kidnapped while attempting to fulfil his promise with Pheobe Carpenter. Admittedly, only a short part of this novel takes place in Canton, but it is still a lively and entertaining read.

Mandarin Preferred - Darby Jones

For a much more contemporary take on Guangzhou, Mandarin Preferred is an adventure similar to Neil Strauss' best-selling novel, The Game. Two young travellers romp through a series of exotic romantic interludes, with Guangzhou as the colourful metropolitan background. The book is actually part of a series which begins in Bangkok, where the two lotharios ignore the local female population to party with the influx of female Chinese tourists. In this the second of the series, they display an entertaining knowledge of the local culture and end up visiting a massive cosplay convention, the wholesale sex toy market and a number of the hottest nightspots, before heading up to the popular tourist town of Yangshuo. A revealing look at the lifestyles of young expats who are looking for love in Lingnan, but with considerably more style and grace that the likes of Tucker Max and his drunken fratboy antics.

Non-Fiction

The Opium War by Julia Lovell

Julia Lovell's lucid account of the opium wars in China shows their impact and how attitudes acquired in the mid-19th century persist to this day. Opium had been consumed in China since the eighth century and several emperors had sung its praises. It began to be smoked with the introduction of tobacco in the late 16th century, turning its consumption from a medicinal to a social habit. By the 1830s, China was producing large quantities of opium domestically, though the imported drug was judged superior. When the indecisive and harassed Emperor Daoguang, himself a user when young, came to the crumbling Qing throne in 1820, he attempted to stamp out a habit that was all but universal. He was ostensibly moved by anxieties about a balance-of-payments deficit and a shortage of silver, both blamed on the opium trade, but Lovell argues that the trade also became the scapegoat for the many ills and rebellions that beset the empire.

A large cast of characters played their part in the tragicomedy that resulted: incompetent officials, merchant adventurers, unscrupulous politicians, drunken soldiers, muscular military imperialists and the bewildered and vacillating emperor. No less interesting than the events themselves is Lovell's account of the war's afterlife. For the British, the opium war defined the Chinese as decadent orientals, caricatured in popular fiction in the early 20th century. Their influence lingers in recurrent racist stereotypes as China's rise sets western nerves on edge.

In today's China, the opium war has been elevated to

a national cause. For more than a century, the ruins of the Yuan Ming Yuan lay neglected. Today they sit in one of many memorials to the "century of national humiliation" constructed after the crushing of the student protests in Tiananmen Square in 1989. In that moment of national crisis the communist party's right to rule was challenged and its ideology discredited. The party's solution was to try to persuade its people that a party that had just turned its guns on the students was the sole defence against a West that had long conspired to sabotage China.

Much was made of the 150th anniversary of the war the following year. Scarcely mentioned in school text books until that point, the war became a narrative of heroic resistance to western imperialist aggression that led inevitably to socialism and communist party leadership. The Patriotic Education Campaign that followed had three key arguments: that China, with its long and unique history, was unready for democracy; that foreigners caused all its sufferings; and that only the party could save the nation. History remains, as the party defines it, a "meaningful security issue".

Foreign Mud by Maurice Collis

First published in 1946 and long out of print, Foreign Mud is a marvellous historical reconstruction of the events surrounding the illegal trade of opium in Canton during the 1830s and the Opium Wars between Britain and China that followed. Based largely on voluminous documents written by British doctors, missionaries, merchants, and government officials, Collis's tale, far from being a dry assemblage of dates and facts, is a fascinating example of twentieth-century Orientalist literature: "...you must picture the broad river puckered with little waves, the green sweep of the rice, on the horizon blue hills; you must conjure the many sorts of passing craft, the Mandarin house-boats, dainty and lacquered, the streamers and lanterns of passenger boats, the high tilted junks with demon-painted sterns; and you must plunge these images into a light more intense than we know in these countries, into a warmer wind and an air, purer and more scented than we can sniff except in dreams." Collis describes, in all its complexities, a moment in time when China is forced, after more than two thousand years of self-contained sufficiency, to open its doors to the culture, commerce, and evangelization of the West. The author has structured the work rather like a fantastic story in several acts. Interspersed with excellent maps, plans, and illustrations, Foreign Mud is a historical narrative the reader will find more entertaining than any Spielberg film.

Poorly Made in China - Paul Midler

A must read for anyone contemplating sourcing or otherwise doing business in China. It is a snappy, entertaining. and easy to read volume that very accurately depicts what you will be up against. Despite the warm eager welcomes you will receive from many companies, this book is a remarkably well-written account of the various (often-times nefarious) games played by Chinese manufacturers - especially when dealing with Western clients. This book is not a definitive guide to doing business in the region but for those giving it consideration, it at least will put them on their guard as to where the pitfalls and frustrations might lie.

Paul Midler narrates his various adventures as an intermediary between Chinese bosses or factory owners and Western CEOs or managers who are hoping to benefit from the "low cost" Chinese production environment. He shows with clarity as well as humour how local factory owners and managers engage in various shenanigans. In the old days it was certainly easy to make money trading and sourcing but those times are over and the average Chinese manufacturer these days will eat most foreign buyers alive (then belch a few times and light up a cigarette). What is most shocking about the author's experiences is, I think, quite how common and across the board the tricks, cons and outright illegal practices he witnesses seem to be. A great (although occasionally paranoia inducing) read. The current edge this country has is a mainly uneducated, disorganised, low expectation labour force enabling manufacturers to have very low labour costs, in a constantly evolving and largely unregulated manufacturing cauldron. In this sense Poorly Made in China is a thoroughly worrying and extremely 'off-putting ' tale.

Background Viewing

Addicted to Pleasure

A BBC documentary series from 2012, revealing the rich and controversial past of sugar, alcohol, tobacco and opium, hosted by Hollywood actor Brian Cox. The first episode looks at the world's growing sugar addiction and the growing diabetes and obesity epidemics. The second episode on opium turned out to be very disappointing. Filled with the standard Chinese propaganda, and Brian Cox spouting poetry as if he was high himself, the show was full of inaccuracies, misrepresentation and downright lies. Obviously they paid so much money to the presenter that they could not afford any decent researchers. Apart from a few street scenes in the Qingping market district, the entire series including the third and fourth episodes dealing with whiskey and tobacco are probably worth avoiding.

Bizarre Food - Guangzhou

For a much more entertaining look at Guangzhou, Andrew Zimmerman does his usual thirty minutes of sampling the most exotic food available. Produced back in 2008 during the second series (they are now on series fifteen), the show is a little dated, but still provides a fascinating introduction to Cantonese cuisine. The host hits a number of the most famous eateries in the city such as the famous Guangzhou Restaurant on Wenchang Nan Lu in Shangxiajiu. He begins with a veritable emperor's banquet of local delicacies including stuffed duck's feet, stir-fried milk with shrimp, turtle soup, pigeon, scorpion and suckling pig. At other locations he samples jellyfish salad, worm and hairy crab roe omelet and wood ear mushroom. Apart from a few pronunciation slip ups, this is really great show and almost as good as the Hong Kong episode. The local pollution looks rather depressing but the selection of foods is amazing. All in all a highly recommended show.

Paul Merton's China

I worked as a location scout in Guangxi province for this show, but not in Guangdong where I would have been ashamed to have any involvement whatsoever. The scenes filmed with the Guangzhou Hash was a real 'expats behaving badly' and an embarrassment to the rest of us. Even so, it gives a good picture of what ghetto expats are like the world over. Generally speaking, Paul hated his time in China, and this comes through quite clearly in the documentary. After the trials and tribulations of the Chinese countryside, Paul is rather taken by Guangzhou, especially the waterfront at night, where brilliantly lit "camp boats" pass in front of a skyline reminiscent of a "cleaned-up version of Blade Runner". During his visit he attends 'underground' church service where 82-year-old Samuel Lamb (who spent over 20 years in prison for his insistence on preaching "everything in the Bible" and passed away recently) preaches to a huge congregation in his house, so large that the service is played on TV screens in different rooms. He also meets westerners who are adopting unwanted Chinese babies, and talks to the mothers-to-be to find out more. Unfortunately this is one of the poorer episodes, especially when compared to his visits to a robot inventor in Beijing and attempts to film at a local landfill, which almost gets him and his crew arrested.

Brits Get Rich in China (2007)

While the set up is not as honest as it could be, the basic premise of this documentary is that it follows three entrepreneurs to find gold at the end of the Great Wall. Tony Caldeira's once-thriving Merseyside cushion business has been ruined by cheap Chinese imports. In a desperate bid to save his company, he has borrowed two million pounds and flown out to China in an attempt to build a cushion factory in a paddy field. Ex-colonel Peter Williams has spent his life savings on an energy-saving device that he thinks he can sell throughout China. And controversial kitchen retailer Vance Miller, has built a huge business buying cheap products in China. A year before the Olympics, he criss-crossed China in a coach with "Olympic Inspection Committee" painted on it, which, he found, smoothed his way remarkably. But along the way, he says he has suffered a deluge of scams at the hands of his equally ruthless Chinese suppliers. He is building a new factory on the North Korean border and arrived to find, in a fusillade of fucks, that only the wall was built. "It's more expensive than the fucking Great Wall of fucking China." He has also served time for kidnapping, been shot when he became caught up in a coup in Sierra Leone, where he was part-owner of a gold mine, and seen his factory and two houses become arson targets. Despite the reticence about his money, there's no doubt that Vance Miller's greatest talents are the abilities to spot a bargain and do a good deal. Romantics would describe him as a sort of Del Boy; disgruntled customers would opt for something stronger. On one trip to China he bought 1,100 quad bikes which he planned to sell in the UK, only to be told they did not meet safety standards. "They're still in the bleeding warehouse," he moans, along with 144,000 pairs of £1 Chinese shoes and 10,000 £6.50 suits. Despite his wide-boy personality his openness is refreshing and his passion contagious.

All three are in different product categories, (cushions, energy efficiency and plumbing) all have different strategies (China based manufacturing, HK based JV distribution and manufacture direct sourcing) and each has different levels of China experience (market killed by the Chinese, not sure where it is on a map and very experienced) and for added pleasure none of them speak a word of Chinese. All three are acclaimed successes in the series since they have huge orders. Orders are not sales, sales are not revenue. All three make the fundamental mistake of trying to control matters in China. They have neither the skill, nor the direct intervention necessary to achieve the goals they seek. The Chinese counterparts in this series are stereotypical of Chinese, but not typical of Chinese. I recognize the kind of biz partner each has acquired, and they are the kind I would run from. It is almost as though the producers winnowed through enough stories to get to the kind of Chinese partners prejudiced people might expect. "Chinese lie, cheat, and steal as part of business and it's not easy to succeed there." That's business in general. In the U.S. you will find many cheaters and stealers alike. Unless you know of a certain utopia where everyone succeeds with ease, then I would not exclusively call China out on this.

A final point, these are not examples of Brits doing biz in China, these are examples of Brits being filmed doing biz in China. If the cameras were not rolling, the outcomes may have been very different. Although it it makes for good TV, that is all it is. If you want to understand China, Chinese business culture, and what it is like to be a foreigner in China, I think this documentary will be an entertaining means for you to have all those answers questioned. To go to China and take a bubble of your own world with you to live in is disastrous.

Foreign businesses, unlike their domestic

counterparts, were largely reared in environments that had rules and laws that were not by-passable with a dinner and some KTV girls. But after listening to the problems one runs into by doing business in China, you are floored by the amount of shit that can go wrong, how stupid many, many of the people you will deal with are, and things that just blow your mind until you accept the "this is China, anything and everything can go wrong, and don't expect anything" kind of mentality.

I used to think this was contained to smaller manufacturers or shops – thinking the bigger companies that dealt with multi-nationals would be far superior. Now, I know better – the quality of Chinese workers in multi-nationals is quite high, but the quality of Chinese workers at their suppliers is not necessarily so. That does not mean there are not plenty of good suppliers in China – it means there is plenty of sub-standard suppliers to sort through before getting to the best of what China has to offer. There are 193 countries in the world, plus China. China IS different. And there is no way anyone can ever even begin to understand the how's and why's of it until after they have lived here, done business here, been screwed over repeatedly here, for quite some time.

Disorder (2009) (现实是过去的未来).

This movie shows about twenty different actual events without intervention, exposing absurdity and outrage. A madman dancing in the middle of the road without his shirt, pigs blocking people on the roadside, citizens hanging their laundry on city electricity wires, labourers attempting to continue construction even after finding cultural assets in the grounds, policemen beating people and locking them up in squad cars in broad daylight. There is no order that matters. As the title says it, it's complete chaos and disorder. Sums up GZ perfectly. Directors, Ou Ning and Cao Fei, worked with a team of twelve artists documenting a day in the life of Guangzhou.

The highly stylized Koyaanisqatsi-type video reveals the paradox of economic growth and marginalization that is so much a part of this modern mega-city.

Much of it takes place in the old quarters of San Yuan Li District. What was once a tiny countryside hamlet has dissolved into obscurity, swallowed up by the megalopolis, caught up in the rush for economic development. The rear has long been known as a den of sleaze, a centre of murder, prostitution, and drug dealing. Only a few years before this documentary was made the narrow back-lanes and tight passages of the village were a vast red light rabbit warren, which has since been moved to the outskirts of Panyu. What remains is a maze of winding lanes, alleyways, and blind passages, creating the crinkles in a larger tapestry that we call the City. Its dank, seamy side-walks and dark back-lanes are home to a great many migrant workers from the provinces. The latecomers' resentment and envy towards the well-established native villagers, who charge exorbitant prices and ostentatiously display their wealth is clear. Every inch of space is covered with advertising, a seething mass of other posters and bills peddling anything from STD treatment to electrical appliance repair, private detective, noodle chef training class, and go-go girl service. These contrasting graffiti art exhibits a pageantry of anarchic, free-wheeling urban commerce. Under a bleak and cloudy sky, the damp air becomes unbearably stifling in the already poor air quality of the village. A stinking odour from piles of garbage permeates the passageways. Totally oblivious to people's presence are packs of well-fed rats merrily scurrying back and forth along the gutters and between their various hideouts.

Other parts of the film focus on random, anonymous city locations, but often the activities are more important than the place. The incompetence and utter lack of professionalism of the authorities such as the police, emergency services and civil servants is shocking for viewers but common place for the long suffering residents.

Despite being in black and white, this is a rare and valuable fly on the wall type record of the real Guangzhou. Away from the five star hotels and glitzy shopping districts, this is Guangzhou's true personality. It is amazing that the whole city does not implode on a daily basis.

All In This Tea (2007)

This is more than just a well-crafted, information-filled documentary about tea. It dips effortlessly into a half-dozen modes - travelogue, biography, nature film, business story, historical summary and environmental wake up call, offering keen insights into the flaws of the modern Chinese economy through one man's quest to encourage organic, fair trade, and honest farming practices. It is especially interesting if you are thinking of exporting agricultural products such as tea. It does not feature Guangzhou, but for anybody just starting in import and export it is a fascinating introduction.

Tea importer, David Lee Hoffman (the founder of Silk Road Teas) originally spent more than a decade travelling around Asia during his twenties and developed a life long love of good tea. In India and Nepal he hung out with Tibetan monks in exile, and befriended a young Dalai Lama. The now sixty-something eccentric has become a merchant connoisseur, struggling with language barriers and Byzantine business codes to introduce cutting-edge permaculture practices that are still considered avant-garde in the West.

I personally found the film very easy to relate to, as it mirrored so many of my own experiences in China. It begins in the big cities like Hangzhou, overwhelmed by bureaucracy and officialdom. One can only admire David Hoffman's level of tolerance as he faces a seemingly endless succession of ignorant officials and profit obsessed businessmen. The coastal cities are filled to the brim with buyers from huge Western conglomerates, all quite happy to purchase endless containerfuls of cheap plastic tack, enriching only factory owners and corrupt party members in the process, but David's experience is much more similar to my own. Without the benefit of deep corporate pockets, we both had to look for high margin quality items, rather than buying hundreds of thousands of identical items in order to make a few tenths of a cent on each one. Rather than buying from the highly exploitative sweatshops that are quickly turning China into the most polluted country on the planet, he believes that 'everyone should be able to make a good profit', a sentiment that strongly influences my own business dealings in the PRC. David chose artisanal teas, while my own experience was with rare and unusual collectibles, but we still followed a very similar path. All the time we were swimming against the tide of the modern industrial economies, and so I have the utmost respect for the tenacity of a person like this, who can remain calm and retain a sense of humour while banging his head against a brick wall of Chinese protectionism, and their reluctance to change.

As he wound his way through China's insufferable tea bureaucracy, he found that the companies do not want to deal directly with the farmers, including those craftsmen who produce the finest teas. His battles against bureaucracy and government pig-headedness demonstrate very clearly the disdain that business people in China have for the rural peasantry. David travelled extensively through the country in order to find the quality teas he prefers and succeeded on his mission of encouraging more organic tea farming, by buying directly from farmers. It was inspiring to see how much change could be brought about by one determined man, as he dragged the reluctant factory managers up lush, terraced mountainsides to bring them face to face with the "dirty" farmers. It is extremely ironic that he is simply reintroducing them to their country's oldest traditions. During the Cultural Revolution the old ways were vilified and demonised by Mao at the cost of many millions of peasant lives. Instead, industrialisation and modernism was glorified leading to biblical famines and decades of hardship.

On the way, we gain valuable insights into the real China of the 21st century. We see how the vast majority of the population still live in harsh rural impoverishment, having very little in common with their urban counterparts. Some Western reviewers have heaped criticism upon the protagonist, describing his attitude as patronizing, bordering on pompous, talking down to the managers he meets as if they are the foreigners on his turf. What they do not realise is that few of these people have any formal education. All of the universities were all shuttered during their youth, and instead they received only the constant indoctrination of Mao's Little Red Book. Westerners that have never visited China criticise his lack of fluency in Mandarin, but as he explains, once you reach these areas of the countryside, almost every mountain has its own linguistic dialect. Despite the relentless party propaganda, more than half of the population of China still do not speak Chinese.

The documentary was filmed over a ten year period by Les Blank (who later went on to make films about garlic, polka music, and women with gap teeth) and clearly captures the frustration of Hoffman as he pushes for a different sensibility in the buying process, as well as a return to organic sustainability. Techniques that bought about some of the most successful and long lasting civilisations in history were recorded by American Agronomist F. H. King in his classic 1909 treatise Farmers for Forty Centuries, but all of that was lost once the Cultural Revolution arrived, as the farmers started growing for quantity over quality. As is happening in the West, after the initial boost provided by chemical fertilizers, crop production lessens, and soil quality depletes.

It comes as no surprise that this film is used in a wide variety of university courses including human geography, anthropology, environmental science, food studies and business subjects. Professors report that when students begin to despair at the unevenness of development in the world today, and the unfairness of big business and corruption, David Hoffman provides an intriguing antidote, advocating the development of fair trade as a solution to the rising inequalities globalization and modernization.

In addition, the film is steeped in historical footnotes that only enhance the viewing experience. It brims with fascinating information about the history of Chinese and Indian teas. Did you know for example that for five thousand years tea was essentially unknown to the outside world, or that Darjeeling tea is actually all descended from a single line of Chinese tea plants that were smuggled out of China by a Scotsman working as a spy for the East India Company in the 1840s?

Just as a travel documentary about France would deal extensively with the wine producing regions of Bordeaux, Burgundy and Champagne, this film is voyage of discovery in more ways than one. The end result is fascinating look not just at tea, but also at the culture that spawned it. Seeing the beautiful countryside where tea is grown, and how the different teas are made and tasted is a fantastic advertisement for Chinese culture. If the Chinese tourism bureau were to sell this DVD with a small collection of taster sachets of the different teas mentioned, I am sure that they would see an immediate rise in tourist arrivals.

For me it was the glimpses of the countryside that made this documentary so special, the ancient routes that were covered by Robert Fortune, the original tea thief of the eighteenth century. From Ningbo to Wuyishan, I have explored these trails often made up of seemingly endless disc-like stone slabs, rising up into the mist shrouded terraces or clinging tightly to the banks or remote winding rivers. In places like these, it is still possible to smell the 500 year old tea bushes atop foggy mountain slopes, even though they have been relentlessly pummelled by progress.

This California entrepreneur is more than a little obsessed with the savoury ancient brew, especially the fermented pu'er variety. Back in the US, he hosts regular Himalayan Fairs at his home in Berkeley and customers report that teas from the Hoffman estate are exquisite.

'All in This Tea' is a delicious documentary, packed as tightly as a black brick of aged pu'er. It is a valuable addition to the growing canon of slow-food films for our fast-food nation that is both delightful and informative at every turn, and packs in more information (not to mention pleasure) per celluloid foot than most other documentaries on China combined. It is a behind-the-scenes tour that brims with fascinating information about the process of camellia horticulture, where the tea becomes a lens for us to consider the fragility of our environment. The soundtrack of mostly traditional Chinese instrumentals adds yet more character and there is even a cameo appearance by the documentary director Werner Herzog. One scene that did not make it into the final cut was where David took a box of regular teabag tea, like Lipton, and he opened one of the teabags to let all the dust fly out. He went on to explain that this dust is the junk they sweep off the floor when they are making the good stuff.

Inside Guangzhou

InsiderTV has put together a number of short introductory documentaries on the city but the presenters are plastic and annoying, and the content is mostly advertorial. These shows are produced for five-star hotel channels (although they are widely available on Youtube) and so the content reflects that particular demographic. Stories are generally for the most expensive places in town, with little attention being paid to the real culture of the city. Tolerable for first timers to China but cringe-worthy for anybody familiar with the PRC.

II GUIDES AND INTERPRETERS

Despite the claims of some guidebooks, a good guide is worth their weight in gold. Of course, finding a good guide can be almost as difficult as prospecting for the elusive precious metal. It is quite difficult for the average tourist to find a great deal of the best bargain priced items because of their time constraints and unfamiliarity with the country. Best of all is to get a personal recommendation, but even then it takes a certain chemistry to find someone with whom you can get along easily all day and everyday. It is sad to say that few know less about China than the Chinese themselves (although this is obviously not their fault.) Almost none are capable of seeing it through Western eyes. A better strategy might be to find an old China hand who knows the specific location to which you are heading, and ask them to be your guide. If you choose carefully, that kind of person should pay for themselves quite easily. The Linked-in website can be useful for making local connections.

Potential problems

The over-developed sense of patriotism in China can often express itself as jingoism and xenophobia. This can sometimes be seen in collusion between guides and vendors. Sales people will immediately assume that a foreign visitor's guide is also their translator and try on tricks that they could not possibly get away with if a language barrier did not exist. If I do use the services of a guide, I personally prefer to do so to make use of their local knowledge rather than their language ability. Fortunately my own Chinese is good enough not to need an interpreter but other businessmen are not so lucky. I have often heard business owners trying to cajole guides into helping them exploit clueless foreigners. Often the conversation will be along the lines of "Come on, we are both Chinese. Why are you helping this white devil? You should be helping your fellow countrymen to make money, not some rich foreigner." Other times, the guide will not need any prompting to make a little extra on the side. Numerous times, I have heard the boss of shop quote a price to the guide of say 100 RMB who will then turn to the customer and immediately inflate it to 250 to ensure that they obtain a good kickback.

ABOUT THE AUTHOR

About The Author

I have spent countless hours foot-slogging up and down seemingly unending acres of wholesale markets that are spread all across the city. If a market is included here, I think that it is only fair to the reader that I walk at least one full circuit of the building to check out what is on each level and that it is indeed worth a visit. During the nineties, I lived and worked in Guangzhou for nearly ten years, and ever since then I have been returning at least two or three times to further explore this amazing megalopolis. I was lucky enough to ride the subway on the very first day of its operation, when only three stations had opened out in an obscure suburb, south of the river. These days I am proud to hold the world record for the fastest coverage of every single one of the 144 stations and 236 km of tracks stations on the entire network. It is in my nature to be exploring constantly, which is why I have been so successful as a travel writer, and I soon earned the nickname Guangzhou Di Bao (广州地保 Guangzhou Expert) among my local friends. Every time I return, I am always on the look out for new places to explore and new bargains to be identified. I will be the first to admit, that not every single product of the 21st century economy can be found in Guangzhou, but if you do your homework, it is very difficult to be disappointed. I occasionally work as a buying guide and investment advisor but these days spend most of the time as mountain trekking guide up in the Tibetan foothills of Yunnan Province.
Please feel free to contact me at:
chris@guerrillainchina.com

Also by Christian D. Taulkinghorn:

A Guerrilla Guide to Doing Business in China

Lijiang - The Holiday Romance Capital of China

Is Nothing Sacred? Making Money as a Wedding Priest in China

Made in the USA
Lexington, KY
10 June 2017